ALWAYS *the* SOUND *of the* SEA

THE DAILY LIVES OF NEW ZEALAND'S LIGHTHOUSE KEEPERS

HELEN BEAGLEHOLE

craig potton publishing

To Tim and my grandchildren

First published in 2009 by Craig Potton Publishing
98 Vickerman Street, PO Box 555, Nelson, New Zealand
www.craigpotton.co.nz

© Text: Helen Beaglehole
Diary extracts reproduced with permission of
Alexander Turnbull Library and Elizabeth Benjamin
© Photographs: reproduced with kind permission of those credited

ISBN 978 1 877333 99 6

Printed in China by 1010 Printing International Ltd

Photographs:
FRONT COVER The second Farewell Spit tower. ATL: TYREE COLLECTION 993
BACK COVER TOP LEFT The Langman family BARRY LANGMAN
BOTTOM LEFT The *Enterprise* at Stephens Island BARRY LANGMAN
RIGHT Alan Martin at Nugget Point ALAN AND SHIRLEY MARTIN

Contents

Acknowledgements

Books, certainly non-fiction, are rarely the product of one person, and in my case I am very indebted to a number of people who have helped me in all sorts of ways. Jonathan Beaglehole, Julie Lubber and Linda Tyler provided me with bed, lodgings and creature comforts while I trawled my way through the lighthouse letterbooks held in Auckland and in Dunedin. Scientists John Andrews, Conon Fraser, Ricardo Palma at Te Papa, Simon Powell at Canterbury University and Christopher Robertson answered the scientific enquiries that rose out of Charles Hepburn Orlando Robson's correspondence; Anne Rimmer generously forwarded me some of Anders Hansen's correspondence for my use. Staff at Archives New Zealand made sure I had the files I needed; at the National Library and the Alexander Turnbull Joan McCracken and John Sullivan helped me ensure I had seen all the relevant material.

But particular thanks should go to those individuals who gave so generously of their time, their memories and their photos of their lighthouse life – Jo and Les Broom, Jean and George Kroening, Barry Langman, Shirley and Alan Martin, Bill Megennis, Chris Staley who, sadly, died before the book was published, Alan Wright and Steve O'Neil. Their very generous assistance and interest, and their patience in answering the queries that inevitably arose while I was working with the material they had given me, enabled me to realise my idea for this book – as the reader will rapidly recognise, it could not have been written without their contributions. In a different way I am also indebted to that earlier generation of lighthouse keepers whose letters and reports I have used so extensively. Although compiled for a different purpose, that correspondence has given me a depth of acquaintance with lighthouse life on which I have drawn while compiling this book; the lengthy excerpts from much of it lets readers develop a picture of lighthouse life whose intimacy and detail is quite missing from published head office reports.

Others have also been generous with their photos and information or family material that has enriched this book. George Gibbs offered photos from his archive of The Brothers that capture aspects of the life there. Roger Hart provided photos and information on his grandfather Samuel; Betty Benjamin sent Alexander Parks' diary and letters as well as his wife Hannah's diary and has made available her assiduous research into her family history and on her great-grandfathers Alexander Parks and Andreas Sandager; Denise and John Sangster, getting wind of my project, offered a photo of Anders Hansen; and Eileen Tiller gave me free rein with what I wanted from her grandfather Anders Hansen's extensive collection and has filled me in on details of his life and lighthouse career.

I want also to acknowledge the help I had from Marita and Peter Taylor. Although I discovered their whereabouts too late to quote their recollections of their lighthouse days, they also offered photos from their very considerable collection, and their talk and interviews gave me invaluable bits of information that help anchor events, people and information in a reader's mind.

I am very grateful to my publishers Craig Potton Publishing who responded so immediately and positively to the manuscript and who brought their high production values to this book.

Finally, I want to thank family and friends who have listened to me talking about this book over the three or so years on which I have been working on it. Three I want particularly to acknowledge: my husband, Tim, willingly and usefully trawled through various drafts; Heather Roberts' critical eye was a considerable help in moving from the penultimate to the ultimate draft; and Simon Blakiston's continued warm interest and questions always helped validate my ideas for the book and bolstered my belief in it.

Helen Beaglehole, 2008

Introduction

I moved into the world of lighthouse keeping when researching my first book, Lighting the Coast: A history of New Zealand's coastal lighthouse system. *Its primary focus is on how that system was developed, maintained, equipped and finally demanned, not on the men and their families. All too often space constraints meant I had to summarise in a few words what keepers' letters and other records gave at greater and fascinating length.*

With that book finished, I turned again to lighthouse keepers, not this time to describe their lives but to use their words, and often their photographs, to illuminate their world, their experiences at different stations and, over time, to throw some light on the sort of people they were.

To do this I sought material that would bring readers as close to the keepers as possible: relatively lengthy excerpts from private letters and diaries (one of a keeper and one of a keeper's wife) and from the official station correspondence; and excerpts from interviews I conducted with six men and two women who served on the lighthouse stations from the late 1940s to 1990. The keepers' photographs, too, form another aspect of the narrative.

The interviews enabled me to explore areas that the written material does not cover. Moreover, while memory, time and retelling may have shaped these twentieth-century recollections, they carry the immediacy of the spoken word. Perhaps it is not unimportant, either, that the interviewees often, apparently unconsciously, lapsed into the present tense.

Of the written material, diaries compiled by Hannah Parks and, especially, Charles Hepburn Orlando Robson provide that apparent trivia so essential in building up an understanding of individuals' lives that forms our collective history; the private letters round out further our sense of who some keepers were. However, the official letterbooks are the primary source for all but 50 years of the lights' operation.

Each lighthouse station had outwards and inwards letterbooks into which all correspondence was supposed to be copied or pasted (and until the mid-twentieth century it mostly was). Outgoing letters were written by the principal keeper or the keeper-in-charge, though on disputes and matters of discipline individual keepers wrote their own.

Three fires destroyed many Marine Department records — letterbooks now exist for only 23 of the 33 (or 34 if one counts East Island) once-manned stations, and the extent of the record for each station varies hugely. The nineteenth-century books are large, hard-cover, folio-size volumes, sometimes running to over 300 pages; by the mid-twentieth century they became less lovely objects. At times the early records are in beautiful copperplate, at others in almost indecipherable scrawl. As the twentieth century progressed, elegant penmanship vanished, and by the 1950s phone or telegram largely replaced the letterbooks with their more fulsome written record.

The monthly reports, which made up much of the outwards correspondence, were written to the head of the Marine Department. Early letters and reports invariably began, 'Dear Sir, I have the honour . . .' and, until about the 1940s, typically ended with versions of the business letter's usual official ending, 'I remain, Sir, your most obedient servant'. In broad terms the reports acknowledged incoming official mail or circulars, described maintenance and other tasks that the keepers had been doing, indicated areas for future work, requisitioned necessary materials and detailed other events of note. These reports and letters, covering a considerable range of issues, indicate not only what was happening and the conditions under which the keepers lived but also keepers' aspirations and concerns. For all their official status they signal something of what it must have been like to be a lighthouse keeper.

Yet these reports have their limitations. Few letters (or reports) of any sort can be read as straightforward communications — most have their own agendas. In addition, and in terms of providing a historical narrative, the lighthouse monthly reports and letters have the shortcomings of any official reports. Even if keepers were inclined to reflect on and record the details of their lives or the reasons for being there, such material would have no place in these reports, which are concerned with official lighthouse business. The world they were recording was the male world of work.

The official perspective is not only limited to that of the male but mostly to that of the principal keeper, the man in charge; the women's voices are unheard. If their lives are only occasionally visible, it is through the men's eyes and perspectives (casting interesting light on gender attitudes of the time). Private lives or tragedies, except when they are in some way to do with the stations' operations or when officialdom has to be informed, are excluded; after-hours activities are not mentioned.

Moreover, while lighthouse keepers had to be able to read and write, literary ability was not one of the job specifications. As I worked though the letterbooks I could find myself flicking past page after page where quite formulaic monthly reports indicate little beyond that there was nothing of concern. (Given the highly centralised department, it now seems surprising that fuller accounts were not required.) As the service moved into the twentieth century, the discretion that the keepers had in recording that world was further limited by set headings delineating subject matter.

But despite such limitations, some of the people who helped compile this record emerge from the page. The very unliterary quality of some letters suggests a closer relationship of writer to letter than might be the case in more consciously crafted letters. The writers are urged into print by anything from natural events to station dramas; different styles and tones bring them vividly to life. A. V. Pearce was desperately concerned about a sick miner at Puysegur in 1917; by contrast, W. Smith reported quite factually a keeper's death there in 1934; Percy White wrote an excited and dramatic account of getting someone off Portland Island in 1928;

H. A. Wakefield struggled for the words that would enable head office to understand what was going on with the revolving apparatus at Cape Palliser in 1902. Occasional transitions into direct speech give a dramatic immediacy to writing unaffected by literary artifice, reinterpretation or memory. Our sympathies lie with keepers fed up with the state of their houses or desperate to get transferred so their children can continue an education they see as essential.

Bringing such material together for publication raises questions about the picture it portrays. The most interesting letters and reports, the material where drama resides, are about what was wrong. What was right was either not the stuff of official reports or was covered by that useful phrase 'routine duties'. The very content of the letterbooks, therefore, can give a somewhat distorted view of lighthouse life (and, to some extent, of the Marine Department. Whatever its incompetence in relation to existing stations, whatever its cavalier treatment of its far-flung employees, it did create, under not always easy circumstances, a system of navigational aids round the country).

The very process of selecting and editing the reports contained in the letterbooks creates a further distortion. Inevitably, I omitted much as I trod the fine line between retaining reader interest and verisimilitude. The lists of jobs completed or correspondence received, the repetition of the formulaic 'routine duties', which set up their own rhythms, are absent in this book. Those who have not turned page after page in volume after volume of letterbooks, all attesting to 'routine duties', may find it difficult to appreciate how often lighthouse life was as unremarkable as that on the mainland. We have to remember the even keel of Robson's diary, that days often succeeded each other with so little notable variation that the passing of US ships in formation warranted standing to attention and a letter to the secretary of the Marine Department.

On the other hand, the issues with which this volume does deal, the worrying over transfers, the frustrations with faulty equipment, sub-standard housing and domestic conditions, and the impacts of isolation, as well as irritation with head office, were sufficiently widespread across stations and time to suggest that the material reproduced here does represent aspects of a general experience. In the last 40 or so years of the Lighthouse Service (from the 1950s to 1990) technological changes and staff retention problems brought about improvements in conditions so that the lot of many later keepers and their families was qualitatively different from those of their forbears; the final rounds of demanning were something totally new.

If the life could be so frustrating and demanding, why did people stay on? Here the oral accounts are particularly valuable. They often deal with the quietly humorous, the unreported everyday events that make life memorable; I came away from the interviews with a sense of my respondents' enjoyment of a life that, in its living, was often anything but mundane. But these are mid- to late-twentieth century individuals' experiences. Were their views shared by their earlier counterparts? Did the unending routine of tough physical work carried out with few, if any, of the later amenities allow those earlier generations to look back on the job with comparable pleasure? We cannot be sure.

A brief word on structure. I have organised the text thematically, developing categories that arose naturally from the material. However, these categories do not reflect how particularly early keepers tended to move seamlessly from subject to subject. I have occasionally attempted, while balancing considerations of space and interest, to indicate that fluidity. Similarly, I have not always sought to regiment the oral material strictly to the subject in hand but retained the way my interviewees unfolded their narrative, keeping their voices and the way they developed their story; this seemed more important than fitting material into rigid categories. I have, too, edited those excerpts but not, I hope, to lose the individual voices and a sense of an oral, as opposed to a written, account.

There are things the book does not do. First, the loss of the historical material means not all the stations can be covered; nor have I attempted to provide equal coverage for the remaining stations. Rather, I have been guided by the interest of the material. However, except where the material is noted as exceptional, the official reports should be read as accounts of a more general experience. Second, although the book is about the keepers' experiences, and while children were frequently a part of that experience, this book does not attempt to explore lighthouse children's lives. To have attempted to broaden the scope of this narrative to include that would have resulted in a book that sprawled beyond manageable length.

A note on spelling and measurements. In all written excerpts, omissions are marked . . . Words I had to guess at are marked [?]; indecipherable words are indicated [indecipherable]. Spelling, punctuation and grammar have been transcribed as in the originals. While it is tempting to see these as indicating something of the composer, this is not always justified. Quite frequently the principal keeper's duty of transcribing the letters into the letterbooks was relegated to someone else. Finally, I have not converted imperial measurements into metric. For the post-imperial generation, roughly speaking there are three feet to a metre, a yard (36 inches) is a little under a metre (39 inches); and one mile is 1.6 kilometres. In relation to weight, a hundredweight (cwt) is 51 kilos, and one pound is .45 of a kilo. In relation to volume, a gallon is 4.5 litres.

Excerpts from Charles Hepburn Orlando Robson's diary

On 1 October 1872, 22-year-old Charles Hepburn Orlando Robson, the son of a lighthouse keeper, took up a position as assistant lighthouse keeper at Dog Island and began his diary.[1] That initial appointment to an island station was, and would continue to be, usual practice for testing a man's suitability for the Lighthouse Service. Keepers were moved from time to time, and Robson was later transferred, first to Taiaroa Head (23 June 1876 to 30 September 1877), to The Brothers (30 September 1877 to 18 June 1879) and thence, as first assistant keeper, to Ponui Passage (June 1879 to 15 April 1881). That same year, promoted to principal keeper, he was moved to the Cape Maria van Diemen station on the little island of Motuopao; he did a brief stint relieving at Pencarrow Head, returned to Cape Maria and from there was appointed to French Pass on 1 October 1884, where he arrived, aged 34, on 14 December 1884. At this point his diary entries, which until then had been pretty spasmodic, appear much more regularly, although most entries are little more than a line and there are still quite a number of chunks of time over which he wrote nothing. He was transferred from French Pass to Farewell Spit in July 1885, then, seven years later, to Portland Island. At this point we take up his narrative.

His diary, 36 transcribed, typed pages, is the longest unpublished piece of writing by a New Zealand lighthouse keeper within the public domain that I have found. It is a straightforward record of events and uses plain language. Robson rarely refers to his family, though he records his marriage, while at French Pass, to Rose and the birth of his children, Charlie, Amy, Flossie and Mabel; he describes his work only in the most general terms. Yet at times the entries' simplicity is their power; repeated entries of illness or accident can quickly accumulate into the record of an inexorable march towards death. Robson's sparse record, too, builds up a picture of the pattern of his days, the sorts of issues keepers faced, the communities in which he lived and his role within them. But the diary does more than provide a context for the records we shall meet later. As always, what writers choose to document and how they do so is revealing. The occasional mention of what he's feeling (the more telling because infrequent), the quiet amusement at Mrs McCartney's 'new

Portland Island and the lighthouse station in the 1950s. The features that ruled the keepers' lives — the great, flat, exposed top, the steep papa cliffs, the often stormy stretch of sea between the island and the mainland — were constants.

ANZ (WGTN): ABPL 8848 W5221 PHOTOS BOX 19

teeth and smile', his noting his techniques for avoiding conflict (even while using his diary to vent irritation) mean that by the time the diary ends, lighthouse keeper Charles Robson is not entirely unknown to the reader.

PORTLAND ISLAND

1892 ...

13th March Arrived at Portland Island 3 p.m. Glad to get ashore. Scopes and Family [the transferring keeper and family] went on board.

14th S.S. Hinemoa [one of the noted government steamers that served the lighthouses] landed luggage and stores, and sailed again.

15th All hands to Whares for picnic. Good Friday. Dickson and Mac went on board.

29th April Mc'Cartney found a baby whale on the beach near Whares.

3rd May Bull killed, by falling over the cliff.

4th All went picnic at Whares. Working at the Zig-Zag [the road down the top of the island to the landing].

13th June S.S. Hinemoa arrived here 7 p.m. yesterday, but not seen till 2 a.m., anchored close to east side of Island. Landed stores and Mac's organ. E. Wilson and family on board, bound for Cuvier Island.

15th Aug Visitors, Bentley and Maories.

16th Visitors left again.

23 Sept S.S. Hinemoa arrived with stores and kitchen ranges.

10th Nov Old Naipi brought pork for sale ...

26 Nov Komeni and Maories arrived with stores.

10th Dec Komene and Boy came to ship his wool.

Portland Island station, with the lighthouse in the background, c. 1890s. Our diarist and his father, as principal keepers, lived in the house on the left, the biggest — on many stations, the size of your house reflected where you came in station hierarchies. A rough fence encloses grazing for the cattle.

ATL: G20441 1/1

12th Komene left, his Taipo said, "Steamer not coming".

13th Splice new piece on end of lightening conductor.

19th Komene came again to ship his wool.

20th Komene left, no steamer called, as he expected …

1893 …

17 March News of Father's death, on 24th February last.

20th Portland Island Rifle Club formed. Painted boxes for Target.

21st Choosing site and erecting Target.

22nd First shooting match of Club

3 April Stopped S.S. Waihora, Wife, Nettie, Amy, Flossie, Mrs Dribery and Son left.

1st June All hands on station left 8 a.m. and boarded the Ketch Venus outside Bull Rock, Charlie and I went in her to Napier 8 p.m. still off station.

2nd Daylight, still in sight of Island. Arrived Napier 8.p.m.

3rd Left Napier by train for Wellington. Mabel born

5th Left Wellington for Nelson.

14th Left Nelson for Wellington, taking Mother, Charlie and Nettie. Obliged to leave wife to come to Portland Island by S.S. Hinemoa …

1894 …

1st April Heavy S.E. gale. 9 sheets of iron torn off my roof. Barquentine Gresian Bend lost with all hands, between here and Napier.

2nd S.E. gale continues, Lashing down iron on my roof with ropes, securing sheets of iron blown off last night. Mc'Cartney's fowl-house blown completely away.

18th June Heavy S.E. gale, Barque Alex Newton from Port Stephen New South Wales to Napier, lost on north point of Island at noon. Captain Harwood and two of the crew drowned. Mc'Cartney, Dickson, and I went to scene of wreck, to bring up those saved, (6), and to look for the bodies of those drowned, but did not find them.

19th Searched for dead bodies, but found none.

20th Stopped S.S. Poherna from Lyttelton to Auckland for the shipwrecked crew.

27th Young Walker came from Nuhaka to enquire about buying the wreck.

20th Aug Beautiful Aurora Australis from 7.30 p.m. Grand cauliflower supper.

25th Aug S.S. "HINEMOA" arrived with stores. Minnie Fletcher came to teach the children …

20th Oct Dickson turned Seventh Day Adventist.

1895 …

28th April Mrs Dickson has a supposed abcess forming very close to her throat, anxious for medical advice.

29th Stopped S.S. Southern Cross 7.30 p.m. to take Mrs Dickson to Napier for medical advice.

3rd May Send urgent wire for leave of absence for Dickson.

7th Dickson left for Main-land in old mail-boat.

10th S.S. Weka called with Hamopo and a sick Maori. Landed flour for the Maories. Lent my boat to take the sick man to the point near Taupata [Tawapata?] …

14th July S.S. Hinemoa arrived, with Mrs Mc'Cartney with new teeth and smile. Send shaft [down which the weights that powered the revolving light mechanism or 'machine' dropped] of machine to Napier to be straightened. Turning the apparatus by hand all night.

15th S.S. Hinemoa returned with the shaft late …

1896 …

1st Jan. New Years Day. Went on a picnic and to see the Maories shearing sheep. A Carrier Pigeon seen flying about the Island.

4th Caught the Pigeon, found a message tied to the leg for A Dewing, Gisborne.

5th Tried to start the Pigeon on his journey, but it would not leave the Island …

On 6 April 1896 Robson recorded 'Sciascia's Easter Grand Turkey Picnic' — can this have been it or was it merely one of the many picnics that keepers then and over later generations enjoyed? The cross identifies Keeper Sciascia, who was later gored by a bull and buried on the island. Anders Hansen, whom we shall meet later, is standing. HANSEN COLLECTION

11th March S.S. Hinemoa arrived with stores, landed timber for School, also carpenter J. Cleary from Napier to erect it ...

14th April School building finished.

24th S.S. Fanny from Napier called, landed Miss E. Hodgkinson (school-teacher) also furniture for school. Carpenter J. Cleary left.

27th Portland Island School opened for the first time ...

1897 ...

27th Jan On the look-out for S.S. Tutanekai, [another of the noted lighthouse steamers] with wife & children.

30th N.E. to E.S.E. Very heavy gale, with heavy rain, Glass 28/80 at 5 a.m. and falling fast. 9 a.m. 28/75. While at work in Lighthouse 10ft of sheet lead on platform round the lantern torn up. Cart-shed blown down, smashed to atoms.

5th Feb Erecting cow-shed out of wreck of cart-shed.

11th Mail arrived late, S.S. Tutanekai Overdue. Anxious about wife and children since heavy gale.

19th S.S. Tutanekai arrived 7 a.m. Wife and children on board for three weeks.

16th April Good Friday, S.E.S.E. gale, thick weather. Three masted scow Pirate wrecked, 7.30 a.m. East side of Island, she was coal laden from Newcastle, N.S.W. One of the crew, Carl Berner, was brought ashore dead. We buried him on the Island. Six were saved.

18th Helping crew of Pirate save stores etc from wreck.

19th Helping crew of Pirate save compasses, rope, etc, for the owners.

20th Signalled S.S. Anglican for crew of Pirate, she took the crew to
   Gisborne.
24th S.S. Weka called for ships papers, left on the Island by the Captain
   of Pirate.
28th Wife and I began to fence round grave of the Sailor.
2nd May S.S. Dingadee arrived with Mr Henderson, Insurance Inspector,
   to report on wreck.
12th S.S. Dingadee arrived with Mr Matthews and men, to dismantle
   Pirate.
2nd June Signalled S.S. Dingadee to take Mr Matthews and men away,
   they having dismantled wreck.
5th S.S. Hinemoa arrived with timber for new cart-shed and work-shop.
   Had on board Dickson for Kaipara, Dawson for Cuvier Island,
   Sinclair and Mc'Lean for Cape Maria.
27th S.S. Dingadee arrived for cargo of Pirate. Remained all day, taking
   in about 30 tons of cargo.
29th S.S. Tasmania lost off Table Cape [on the east side of the Mahia
   peninsula].
6th Aug Wife found a case of 16 gallons of castor oil, and some deck
   fittings washed ashore from wreck of S.S. Tasmania.
16th Received wire to be ready to remove to Taiaroa Head, in about
   three weeks.
30th S.S. Hinemoa arrived unexpectedly for A. Anderson, (who had resigned).
   He and I getting luggage down all day, could not get all on board.
31st Anderson and I left Portland Island for good, landed at Napier 1.p.m.
   from S.S. Hinemoa …
3rd Sept Arrived at Wellington, was offered The Brothers Lighthouse,
   instead of Taiaroa Head, I refused. Sailed 5 p.m …
5th Arrived Dunedin 10 a.m.

*Karl Berner's grave on Portland Island.
Many years later another keeper and his
wife would spend time restoring it
(see pp. 104–105).* HANSEN COLLECTION

*Taiaroa Head was initially an isolated station, but in 1897 the Robsons arrived to a com-
panionable little settlement of harbour board employees at the signal station, the pilot launch
captain and crew, prison officials (from the 1870s) and the Army contingent (which during
the Russian scare in the 1880s manned the gun installations). Good relations were enjoyed
with the Maori at the Kaik.*

TAIAROA HEAD
   7th Sept Left Dunedin in Launch Gordon for Taiaroa Head. Heavy
      S.W. gale snow and rain squalls. No landing at Heads landed at
      the Kaik with bedding and walked to the Station bedding carted.
      Launch took luggage back to Port Chalmers till more favourable

*Taiaroa Head, 1888, a decade or so before
the Robsons arrived.* ATL: 112178

weather. Sheltered and had tea with old Jack May (Carem).

8th Launch returned and landed luggage, weather fine, prisoners brought all luggage up to the house ...

27th Launch Gordon brought new Cannon for Battery on Hill. Helping Soldiers to land it. Cow I bought rushing at the children. Wife and I went to arrange for a quieter one ...

13th Oct Leighton [assistant keeper] and I started collecting money to purchase a school organ.

22nd People at Heads gave a social and dance in aid of organ funds ...

1st Nov J. Louden appointed to Pilot Crew, vice Burns resigned. Meeting of School Committee, I am elected a member.

5th S.S. Hinemoa came, landed coal and oil. Leighton and I dined on board with Captain Neale ...

3rd Dec Meeting of Otago Heads School Committee, K. Mc'Donald resigned the Chair, I am elected in his place, J. Louden elected member in place of T. Burns, (resigned) ...

6th Wife, Mr Hamilton, and I went to Port Chalmers in Launch Gordon, also a shooting party of Soldiers. Dined at Mr Hamiltons. Saw University and Museum at Dunedin, and left my Quail and other specimens to be set up ...

1898 ...

8th Jan Went to Kaik School Picnic, enjoyed it very much.

20th Went to funeral of Karetai's Infant at Kaik ...

7th Feb School opened, repairs nearly finished.

12th Port Chalmers Navals came for practice with Nordenfeldt Gun. Great scare, Flossie not to be found, she was hiding in the front room until dark.

1st March Received photographs of Captain Fairchild [Fairchild, and a later master, John Bollons, were the noted lighthouse captains and mariners of no mean repute], and the S.S. Tutanekai ...

15th S.S. Hinemoa called to land my boat from Portland Island.

25th Took the children to Dunedin, to see the Jubilee Exhibition.

7th April Artillery men came to repair for Easter Encampment. Leighton and Family returned. Captain Milne and Family entertained at Farewell Party, and were presented with a Clock, Nelly with album, on their leaving Otago Heads ...

15th Launch Gordon came with Artillerymen from Wellington to replace those ordered to Wellington from here.

26th April J. Dick making a great noise about school affairs, re election of new committee. I cannot agree with him, so resign the chair in consequence. J. Louden elected chairman, Corporal Richdale a member, vice J. Karetai …

28th Snow and hail, very cold, 38 degrees outside and 40 degrees in the house.

29th S.S.E. gale, S.S. Tutanekai unable to go South, returned and anchored off Lighthouse.

2nd June First of our Winter Socials, held in School-room.

24th Artillery gave a Ball in the School-room.

29th S.S. Hinemoa landed 1 ton of coal.

4th July Captain J. Fairchild killed by accident in Wellington …

13th S.S. Hinemoa called with coal and stores, I went on board to see Captain J. Bollons …

2nd Aug Leighton and I went up near Alice Karetais for turnips for cow-feed. Obliged to dig them out of the snow, it was 8 inches thick on the ground and very cold …

17th Nov Leighton and I interviewd Captain Morrison (Jelly B) re water for cattle, owing to being shut out of paddock, got no satisfaction …

9th I sent in my resignation as member of School Committee …

24th Dec All sent to Kaik School Picnic.

26th Boxing Day, went excurtion in S.S. Invercargill from Kaik outside Heads.

27th Went excurtion outside Heads in S.S. Invercargill.

28th Captain Morrison and Family came to Heads to stay for the Holidays.

31st Wife and I helping Annie Louden pack up her things before her marriage.

1899 …

10th Feb Wife and I went to visit the Clarks at Hooper's Inlet, spent a pleasant day.

13th 19 fishing boats caught off here in heavy S.W. gale. One blown to sea, but got back by evening. Tug Plucky went in search of her …

1st March Went to help stack hay at Quinns …

3rd April Easter Monday. Navals finished firing, struck camp in the evening. S.S. Hinemoa landed stores. Steamers Rimu and Invercargill came with excurtionists from Dunedin …

Anders Hansen, his wife and future daughter-in-law on an outing at Taiaroa Head 20 years after Robson's time. Hansen was born on 3 November 1853 on the island of Zealand, Denmark. Orphaned early, he lived with an uncle and aunt, and left for New Zealand in October 1874. He arrived in Wellington in January 1875 and for four years worked as a labourer, on surveys, reclaiming land, farm work, draining swamps and so on. In 1879 he joined the Lighthouse Service; Pencarrow (in 1880) was the first of the 11 light stations at which he served. He retired from Taiaroa Head in 1920 and died in Wellington in 1939.

HANSEN COLLECTION

5th May Mr Brown (Chief Mate) and 4 of crew of the S.S. Hinemoa were drowned, landing at East Cape ...

17th Aug Leighton strained his back badly, telephoned for Doctor. Engaged E. Fowler as Temporary Keeper.

22nd S.S. Hinemoa landed stores. Captain Bollons visit.

28th Leighton's back better, resumes duty. Fowler left.

30th Messes Gourlay and Conn visited and took photographs of Lighthouse ...

1900 ...

7th Jan News that S. Gourlay was killed by the Boers. Patriotic Concert at Kaik ...

27th Went out in Launch Gordon to anchor targets outside Heads, Dunedin Navals arrive for firing the Nordenfeldt ...

23rd Soldiers gave Dance to girls, catered on tick. Could not raise 3/9 ...

2nd Feb Went to visit Milnes at Caversham Rise ...

2nd March Went to Port Chalmers. News of the Relief of Ladysmith. S.A ...

3rd April S. S. Hinemoa arrived at Port Chalmers.

4th Captain Blackburn [another lighthouse steamer captain] inspected Station.

27th April Mr O. Harwood buried at Portobello by Leighton, he was 84
    years of age. Had arrived in Colony in 1835.

31st Pretoria captured by the British. Social, a clock was presented to
    R.H. Leighton and his Wife ...

11th June Leighton and his Family left here for East Island Lighthouse,
    A. Harwood as Temporary Keeper ...

3rd Aug Went to Dunedin, Wife not well, wait at Port Chalmers.

5th Heavy sea, S.S. Aotea took Pilot Mc'Donald on to Wellington.

8th Mrs Wainwright came to visit her father, Captain Louden. I went to
    my first meeting at the Masonic Lodge Portobello ...

1901 ...

9th Feb Turner arrived on S.S. Hinemoa to relieve Butler, who left for
    Centre Island. Port Chalmers Navals firing 7 inch and 64 pounder
    ...

17th May Went as one of the crew of the Pilot Boat to Port Chalmers
    to take J. Dick to Doctor, accident to his eye with a piece of wire.
    Concert in School.

18th S.W. heavy gale. Turners chimney falling ...

7th Aug Find that Turner and I cannot agree with the same garden, he
    is far too grasping. Fixed dividing fence ...

25th Aug Captain Louden off duty, ill.

28th Captain Louden no better. Went to Dunedin to consult Doctor.
    Walked to Launch Gordon at Harrington Point. Turner passed at
    Lodge ...

3rd Sept Captain Louden very ill in Dunedin.

5th We rode to Portobello, went to see Captain Louden at F. Taylor's,
    Captain very ill indeed ...

17th Captain Louden died, 7.30 a.m.

19th S.S. Plucky sent to take people to Captain Louden's funeral. Nearly
    everyone at the Heads attended. Masons wearing regalia ...

5th Oct Grant and I took Rose to Port Chalmers to get a splinter taken
    from under her thumb by Doctor. Went up in the dinghy, and returned
    by Portobello. Left wife at Mc'Donalds. Hurt my arm at wharf.

7th Turner blocked me from going to Port Chalmers for wife, through his
    wife pretending illness, he taking her instead. My arm very bad I wanted
    to see the Doctor about it. Rose returned in Launch Gordon.

23rd Nov Antarctic Ship Discovery arrived.

24th Antarctic Ship Discovery sailed for the South Pole. Turner goes out
    in her as one of the Pilot Crew, and was paid for the trip ...

27th Dec Went on leave of absence. Maggie Wilson in charge of house.

Puysegur Point station and garden in the early 1880s, now entirely overgrown. Without shops to fall back on, a continuous supply of fresh vegetables needed big gardens, considerable expertise in cultivating them and hard work. The road to the landing is on the left. HANSEN COLLECTION

Left Dunedin for Lyttelton and Wellington …

29th Arrived in Wellington, stayed on board S.S. Waihora.

30th Went to see Mr Allport [then Marine Department chief clerk. He would become secretary late 1903] at the Marine Dept Office. Visited Wainhouse in afternoon. Left for Nelson …

1903 …

16th Jan Went to Quinns, carting hay.

17th Obliged to turn hay out of shed through heating. Port Chalmers Navals here for drill at Harrington Point. Mrs Bailey and children came on a visit to us …

21st Went seining [fishing with a vertically hanging net] on Kaik beach with Jonty. Tommy and Nosey went to Port Chalmers with Reid and Florry. I beat old Archie Fullarton at cribbage 8 games out of 14.

28th … Tommy Turner abusing the children for standing on the fence.

29th Tommy and I have some words about the children. Carpenters finished our new room …

10th Feb S.S. Hinemoa's Launch came with coal and stores. Captain Bollons enquired into Tommy's grievance about children …

9th Received wire, Tommy Turner to go to Portland Island.

10th Sent letter re my removal to Manukau.

20th Received wire, Tommy Turner to leave for Wellington first boat …

23rd Tommy and Nosey Turner left for good. H. Kent relieving him …

21st April Light blown out 4.40 a.m. Strong S.W. gale. First snow on hills this year. Keeper Arthur's luggage landed.

29th Painting round the Balcony of Light-house …

5th June Took wife to Dunedin to see Winter Show, drove in Karetais
trap …

11th Aug Painting the Tower Balcony Rail. J. Harwood's daughter badly
burnt at Kaik.

24th J. Harwood's daughter died from burns in hospital. Received notice of
transfer to Manukau Head. Posted letter re my state of health …

10th Sept Examined by Dr Ogston and Dr Couthery, re state of health.

11th Went to a Tangi at Kaik, for Maaka's Daughter.

12th Sold piano to Pilot Mc'Dougall …

6th Oct Young Joe Karetai, shot with a pea-rifle accidentally by his
younger Brother …

12th Mrs Quinn very ill, they sent for [my] wife. Joe Karetai very bad.

14th Packing up linoleum. Mrs Lyell and daughter from Cape Saunders
visited us.

25th Mr Fawcett preached his last sermon here. Wesleyan Church gives
up the services at the Kaik and Heads.

28th Joe Karetai died about 9 a.m.

1st Nov Went to Joe Karetai's funeral at Kaik …

9th Steamers Invercargill and Rose Casey at Kaik with Excurtionists. 27
came to the Head to see the Lighthouse.

10th Surprise party visited us, headed by Pilot Mc'Dougall, with an Address and Presentation …

14th The Pilot Crew gave me a send off Spree at Kennys.

16th retired from the Light Service for good.

Family history narrates he had a heart condition; Marine Department records show he retired on compensation. His daughter, Amy Robson, then 16, recorded a trip on the Hinemoa *with Captain John Bollons, around the Snares and southern part of the South Island, which the Marine Department had arranged for her father and family on his retirement.*

Robson's diary represents the bones of one keeper's world. The issues it touches on — the keepers' socialisation, their involvement with local communities and with their Maori neighbours, transfers, weather, wrecks and education, all regularly punctuated by lighthouse steamers' arrivals — we now look at over time and within the wider perspective of the Service as a whole.

CHAPTER I

Joining the lighthouse service

The Lighthouse Service, as it would become, got off to a somewhat rocky start. Only four lighthouses were operating when, in 1865, the Postmaster-General, responsible for the Marine Board Department, the body then in charge of maritime issues, called for 'a stringent check ... on the consumption of stores,' on who was appointed and for 'a ceaseless vigilance with respect to their conduct, and the order in which the optical apparatus is kept.'[1] Things did not improve. In 1866–67 two keepers resigned, four were dismissed because of drinking, and one, ill, had to be removed — 'inconvenient' losses that were 'annoying and costly.'[2] Keepers were also quarrelling among themselves.

James Balfour, New Zealand's marine engineer and superintendent of lighthouses and nephew of the great Lighthouse Stevensons, the lighthouse and optical engineers of no small repute, resolved the problem with Scottish thoroughness. His five densely printed pages of instructions to keepers delineated their duties as a way of eliminating common sources of disagreement; his sections on maintaining the correct pressure for the lamps to burn effectively, or on how to clean the great array of lenses, are training manuals in themselves. He also set out what sort of people he wanted as keepers — literate, industrious, honest, sober, obliging and in good health (being married was not a prerequisite) — as well as the conditions under which they were to live.

What are striking now are the almost military hierarchies and the demand that senior officers be obeyed; the extent to which keepers were restricted to the stations; the pattern of unrelenting four-hourly night watches; and the provisions for swift dismissal for leaving the lightroom, falling asleep while watching, letting the light go out, taking leave without permission, or showing the 'urgent' signal without due cause. Yet these provisions established a blueprint for the Lighthouse Service that remained surprisingly unmodified for the 150 years of its existence.

So why did the Service attract recruits? The only extant letter of application in the letter-books is dated 1919; the writer, unhelpfully, wanted to join because he enjoyed the life. Yet for the nineteenth-century settlers and until at least the mid-twentieth century, lighthouse keeping meant assured employment and wages, and a house and some furniture came with the job. The isolation, the need for wide-ranging technical ingenuity and hard physical labour that might deter some later on were already a part of the colonists' world; perhaps too they experienced the somewhat authoritarian environment differently. Many clearly thought the job was important and responsible. The opportunities, too, that the twentieth-century keepers found may well have been valued by their nineteenth-century counterparts.

George Kroening was appointed to a position on Portland Island in November 1945, a time when the Lighthouse Service was facing recruitment and retention problems. I was in the merchant navy during the war and when that finished in 1945 I'd been courting Jean for about eighteen months and we wanted to get married. I wasn't going to go back to sea and be a married man at sea and only come home about once every month. I'd seen too many homes broken up. Speaking to the skipper of the last ship I was on – his wife was the daughter of a lighthouse keeper – that's what put a flea in my ear. I made a few inquiries, applied to the Marine Department in Wellington. At that time a lot of the older keepers who were kept on during the war years were leaving the service so it was a golden opportunity to join up. My application was only in for about four or five weeks and I got a letter back saying I'd been accepted and when could I start. Well I said, I'd hoped to get married before I started, so they said, 'Go ahead and let us know when you're ready.' So we got married, had a short honeymoon of about ten days, I notified Wellington and I was appointed to Portland Island, just like that!

I don't know how desperate they were for keepers but I imagine a lot of the older keepers who were up to 65, 68 years old wanted to get out. During the war, of course, you were manpowered into a job and you couldn't leave a job without the sanction of the Manpower.

I think there was the fascination of steaming round the New Zealand coast and going past all the lighthouses and seeing them on good days, bad days, thick weather, good weather and always fascinated by the life – service to shipping I imagine and probably the remoteness – it didn't worry me that I'd be virtually somewhere away from civilisation. It appealed to Jean, too. As you can imagine, everything newly married, everything in the world was our oyster, just go for it.

Barry Langman joined in 1954. I was married so young, had two children, state housing had a very long waiting list. It was obvious to keep my family together I'd have to find a job with a house attached. I contacted the Railways Department knowing they had settlements alongside the railway, and they offered me a position at the top of the Rimutakas called Summit. But this was not attractive, so I decided to approach the Marine Department. And they said, 'Yes, we have a position at Stephens Island and we will get you out there.' So I accepted. It was not for any romantic reasons. It was a case of the necessity of getting a house and a job.

George and Jean Kroening, newly arrived on Portland Island where George had been appointed second assistant keeper. They were there for two years before being transferred to Mokohinau (1947–1950). After two years he resigned, fed up with the conditions in which he was living and working.
GEORGE AND JEAN KROENING

Barry Langman in 1955, a year or so into the job, working on the newly painted Stephens Island DC generators. After a two-year stint on Stephens Island, Barry was transferred to Portland Island, relieved at East Cape and then resigned.

BARRY LANGMAN

Some eight years later, and in a different climate, Alan Martin and his Kiwi wife, Shirley, joined. Alan: I had spent a lot of time on the ornamental lake at Rhyl, learning to row a boat at 2/6 an hour! I bicycled for a long time, then I had a tandem and a girlfriend. I was quite keen on fishing and boating. The place I was working at was actually a tubular steel factory, I was an engineer there. One of the guys at that time had been a lighthouse keeper, he was a Pommie like myself and he'd been at Cape Brett and he was eulogising about this business — he actually got thrown out for being drunk. I just went home and said as a joke to Shirl, 'How would you like to live on a lighthouse station?'

Shirley: And I said, 'Oh, what do you mean?' 'Cause living in Auckland at the time we'd seen Tiri [Tiritiri Matangi] in the distance, and he thought, lighthouse keeping, go and live out there, it'd be fun. I picked up beachside holiday for the rest of your life!

My interviewees applied to the Lighthouse Service with fairly minimal information about what they were taking on. George: I didn't talk to anyone really, apart from the Marine

Department and the skipper of the last ship I was on, the *Gael*. He said it was a good life, his wife enjoyed it while she was there, so away we went. It was always in the back of our mind, we'd try it out anyway, get a chance to get organised.

Jean, who came from the small, close-knit mining community in Rununga, where she had led a very social life, knew no-one she could ask. I didn't know what to expect. Not having travelled very far round New Zealand I'd never given lighthouses a thought but when George said would we go and start our married life out there, we didn't have to worry about finding a house, finding employment ashore, away we went. I didn't even think about it. I just thought, well, we're getting married and we're going to live on the lighthouse, and that was it. At the interview I sat there and listened, and you're going to be a new bride – I was thinking more of my wedding than where I was going to go!

Alan: I didn't have any family here. The old man thought it was a good idea. My mother said he went round the building site telling everybody his youngest son was going to be a lighthouse keeper – quite proud.

Shirley: We went into the Marine Department and applied for a job – you did it as a couple. We had an interview and they put our name on the waiting list – there was a waiting list then – and they showed us a picture of Mokohinau and I thought, Oh, that looks a bit of all right. They explained we'd have to make our own bread, school the children and that, although ours were only three and a half and two and a half at the time. Within two months we set out to Mokohinau. I was a city girl, we'd always had seaside holidays. I had no idea what it would be like living out there in a place like that where the stores only came in once a fortnight and that was dependent on the weather. And being in such a small community and restricted to the station and there were no other children – I was the only one with a family – and the animals and things. I wasn't used to farm animals – I was used to hens – but didn't know anything about cows, and geese absolutely terrified me. But by the end of our service I'd got quite blasé about it all!

Selection processes differed. The Martins were interviewed, George was accepted on the basis of his application alone. You realise then I was only 23, I hadn't had much work experience apart from being at sea during the war. I think that appealed to them very much. I think character was a big thing. Of course you had to have a clean sheet, no convictions or anything like that. The way the Public Service was in those days, it was fairly straight-laced and if you stole a loaf of bread or something you wouldn't have got a job in the government.

Barry: I was working for the Union Company and I was able to go round to the Marine Department in Wellington and had the interview there. But unknown to me there had also been an investigation taking place in Picton

Alan and Shirley Martin and their two boys on Mokohinau in 1963. After two years there (1962–1964), they were transferred to Cape Reinga (1964–late 1966), then Dog Island (1966–early 1970), Baring Head (1970–1973) and Cuvier (1974–early 1982, just before it was demanned). Seven years at Nugget Point followed, and Alan was made redundant when that station was demanned in March 1989.

ALAN AND SHIRLEY MARTIN

because my mother later phoned me to say different people had referred questions from the Marine Department through from the headmaster of the school, the primary school, the local harbour master and one or two of the local businessmen as to character. Obviously the information must have been good because I was approved as a lighthouse keeper. Possibly the fact I had a seafaring background of working for a shipping company and also that I'd grown up in the Sounds towards the end of the war and I had a lot of boating experience I think may have been in my favour.

Ex-navy Chris Staley became an assistant keeper on The Brothers in the early 1960s. Staffing problems there (at one stage the station complement of four — three on, one off — was down to two) saw him promoted to charge keeper, then, at his insistence, principal keeper. I'd always been a seaman, interested in marine matters. The Marine Department just said, 'Come down and see us.' I did, for the usual job interview. It was obvious to me that they needed someone desperately because they said when could I go and I said, 'Right now, if you like.' In those days on The Brothers we used to do three months on and one month off. On there they want rather jack-of-all-trades type of people and I fitted the bill. I think it's very similar on the other stations. They don't want specialised people. They would prefer someone with a broad general experience — experience with machinery, because you have to do a wide variety of jobs on a place like that, from attending to machinery, radio work, painting, cleaning, maintenance of buildings etc., etc. I was willing to have a go at anything in those days. I must have been in my thirties, I guess. We agreed on the spot.

New recruits, generally on a year's probation, then common in the Public Service of which lightkeepers were part, were generally first posted to an island. Alan: If you could stick it for a year they reckoned they'd got somebody that could be a lighthouse keeper and could stand the isolation. Quite a few of them didn't make it.

Jo and Les Broom joined the Service in 1949 and were posted to Centre Island. In 1954 they were transferred to Puysegur Point, to Cape Reinga in 1957 and to Moeraki in 1959, from where Les resigned. Jo, a lighthouse child herself, knew what to take: All the furniture, all the linoleum was in the houses, and your beds, all your dressers, drawers, everything like that was always there, so you didn't have to cart those round. You took your blankets, your crockery, your cutlery, your pots and pans, your mattresses. In those days they were kapok mattresses that had to be rolled up and put into the great big long sacks so they'd fit into the surf boats — ordinary sacks in those days. You never got waterproofing then.

Jo Broom (right) with daughter Elizabeth and co-lighthouse wife Kitty Kemp with her daughter Gale. JO AND LES BROOM

Post-World War II, the Kroenings found amassing even the few personal belongings they were to take was not simple. Jean: Mr Smith [the Marine Department secretary] said we'd need three months' supply, our own personal linen and household goods, and of course, being at the end of the war, everything was rationed. I didn't even have what we called a glory box. So I was dependent on my gifts from my friends when I got married. Had a kitchen evening and got my basics — what you could buy at the end of the war. George's sister gave us what we called a robinwool blanket, my grandmother gave me a pair of double blankets. Two friends pooled their clothing coupons and gave me two pairs of sheets and pillowslips, my grandmother looked through her cupboards and gave me knives and forks and spoons, some pots and pans because she was a widow on her own, didn't need them, tea towels, anything she could spare. Food — more or less tins of peas, corned beef, salmon, anything we could buy in tins. We went to the Farmer's Co-op and went along the aisles. We couldn't take much butter, bacon, eggs, anything perishable so when we arrived on the island we had nothing really, not even a pound of butter. With George leaving the sea, I think it was about £110 he had. That was quite a bit of money in those days but buying tinned things was expensive. But having that little bit of savings in the bank, it carried us on until the wages would begin. We never lived beyond our means because not being able to go to the shops you made do with what you had.

Barry remembered advice on food mostly from local sources — particularly Brian Pickering, skipper of the Picton Harbour Board launch Enterprise, *that tended to the Cook Strait lighthouses during the 1950s and 60s. Some information came from the Marine Department.* It was mainly dry stores. It had been explained that I had the right to purchase the outgoing keeper's stock, approximately 50 sheep, two cows, 25 hens, a third share of the station bull, and a third share of the station boat (£3 6s 8d). From memory the cows cost £5 each, which was a price fixed by the department and the sheep were about 10 shillings each. I know the chooks cost 2/6 each and I had to pay for the remaining bag of wheat and pollard.

The Enterprise *on a rough day at the Stephens Island loading block, 1955–56. Timing was critical for those operating both the boat and the crane.* BARRY LANGMAN

Chris set off for The Brothers with his duffle bag. In those days being a modern-day gypsy I didn't have much gear, travelled light.

But for families such travel was impossible, and joining the Service meant planning, organisation and amassing the piles of food and equipment needed, packing it in boxes or bags for easy manhandling, and making sure any hens were in regulation-sized coops. Then, with everything packed as secure and as watertight as possible, they set out in a variety of transport to where they embarked for the lighthouse station.

CHAPTER 2

Arriving at the lighthouse station

There are no records of what earlier keepers and their wives felt when, green to the job, they arrived on a station. Again, we turn to the twentieth-century oral accounts.

George Kroening: We reached Portland Island by train to Nuhaka, and from Nuhaka through to Waikokopu – a port between Wairoa and Gisborne for the sheep farmers in the Mahia vicinity where Richardsons Shipping Company ships used to come and lie offshore in Hawke Bay and they'd lighter the bales of wool out to the ships. But they'd stopped going there during the war. Then on to the little launch *Mermaid* to go out to the island. It was an open-cockpit, 26-foot fishing boat, rather small in those days even, and it had a temperamental engine – a power-kerosene engine, that's how far back it was! Being an open-cockpit boat a lot of our stuff was lashed on the foredeck, if you can call it the foredeck. Someone was sitting on cases in the cockpit and when a keeper moved from Portland Island if they could get everything on the launch, they would, but if they had to tow a dinghy with other stuff they did it.

Alan Wright was first appointed to Portland Island as a relieving keeper in 1958, did stints on The Brothers with Chris Staley and finally left the Service in 1963. He flew in to Portland Island on the newly operative airstrip, but one can see from his comment why towing was not always advisable: I flew across with Billy Cookson from Wairoa, the topdressing pilot. He had this little three-wheeler Cessna and he was always praised because he could take off or land in 25 feet. Everyone used to think, going from Waikokopu to Portland Island it'd be like a millpond. But it wasn't. There was always that little gap between Mahia and the wharf on Portland Island and that could be as rough as hell.

After a couple of days' crash course at the Meteorological Office on weather forecasting, Chris Staley arrived at The Brothers, a rock in the middle of Cook Strait, frequently beset by tidal

Some 15 years after the Kroenings, the Langman family (Alison, Wayne, Sandra at the mast and Barry's wife, Marge) made the same trip in the same small launch.

BARRY LANGMAN

rips and its landings inadequately sheltered. The way he moved seamlessly into the present tense (and other ex-keepers did this too) suggests a reliving of the excitement of the moment. Chris went by ferry from Wellington to Picton. I probably stayed overnight in a hotel in Picton, because that was the normal routine, and then the *Enterprise* used to leave early in the morning, eight o'clock something like that. It was about 45 feet long, skippered by Brian Pickering.

There are two ways of landing on The Brothers. On the north side we had a crane from which the guys on the rock swing a cargo net out and we throw cargo in and then you just get on the net and hang on — for grim death. Round the south side there's a concrete block stuck on the side of the island. The likes of Brian Pickering would nose the *Enterprise* in and then you had to take a flying leap on to this concrete block and then run for your life up the steps in case another wave came in. Brian was pretty good at handling that boat. He'd get the bow right in and then you'd jump. And then of course you'd have to stand on the block or on the bottom steps while they tossed up urgent stores that you needed. You had to catch them, pass them up the steps.

Barry Langman reached Stephens Island, his first station: I never got over the excitement. It was big adventure. I enjoyed it for the whole time. I wouldn't mind going back and doing the same again, if circumstances permitted.

TOP LEFT *A view of the southern landing at The Brothers in calm weather. In 1953 a keeper described it: 'about four feet square and four feet above high water level, and with big seas breaking over it, it tends to leave a slippery surface.'*
CHRIS STALEY

TOP RIGHT *The southern landing in a storm taken during a hurricane. 'Normally,' Chris Staley recalled, 'we can walk across from where the shot was taken to the rock behind the wave. That rock is about 60 feet high.'*
CHRIS STALEY

LEFT *The Brothers' northern landing in the 1950s. In any sort of sea the shelter offered by the outlying rock is pretty minimal.*
ANZ (WGTN) ABPL 6779 1C

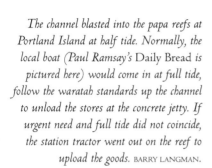

The channel blasted into the papa reefs at Portland Island at half tide. Normally, the local boat (Paul Ramsay's Daily Bread *is pictured here) would come in at full tide, follow the waratah standards up the channel to unload the stores at the concrete jetty. If urgent need and full tide did not coincide, the station tractor went out on the reef to upload the goods.* BARRY LANGMAN.

On arriving, the men were almost immediately whipped off with the team of keepers and into the job; the women were left to sort out themselves and any dependents largely on their own. Their accounts illustrate the novelty and apprehension that made the move such an adventure.
Jean Kroening: Of course I started to realise, once I left civilisation and got on this little boat and headed out to sea — I've never been a lover of the sea — and then gradually rounding the peninsulas, and then seeing the island — oh dear! To get to the little wharf there was a channel cut in the papa rock. You did a few turns, I was looking over the side of the boat, and then everybody on the island, Cynthia, Graham, Harold Young and Ron Corson were there to meet us. I think having come from a social little township it didn't worry me meeting strangers and I was able to talk to them. Anyway, Cynthia was a very quiet girl and good value and I owe a lot of my accomplishments to Cynthia.

So then away we go up this track — but they call it a road — and went along looking at the sheep each side that were owned or leased out by these Maori and then got and looked at the house and I thought, well, miners' houses in Rununga, very cosy and well kept, are palaces compared to these. Mostly miners' wives were workers; their homes were their castles they'd say. Going in the first thing I noticed was this long passage — bare boards — turning into a scullery, quite a fair-sized one, lovely lot of cupboards. The house had been renovated, bare floor. Me, who'd never scrubbed a floor in my life! I made the mistake of scrubbing it with sandsoap every day which meant every mark

showed. I went into the kitchen with its one table, two chairs, one couch, and a stove and the brown lino. They'd closed down the upstairs bedrooms and added three on to the back. The laundry was out the back with a canopy between the house and the laundry – the wind could come through the two sides. Laundry was tubs and copper. But I was used to that – Mum never had a washing machine – and wooden scrubbing boards, no glass ones during the war.

Cynthia Young was absolutely wonderful. She was the 16-year-old daughter of the principal keeper, and I felt so ignorant and useless! There she was, house-keeping for her father, doing secondary education herself, helping her 12-year-old brother do school work, and she was cooking for the Ministry of Works men on the island. And there was me, didn't know how to boil water!

With George whipped off to start lighthouse work, Jean faced unpacking on her own: George had taken the nails out of the packing cases and everything and I just looked at the boxes and thought, now, what do I do with these? But, on your own, you just do it. So I unpacked, put the mattress on the bed and put these tins on the shelf in the storeroom and then thought, we've got no butter – or eggs. So good old Cynthia, she came over with eggs and butter and bread and a bottle of her potato yeast to make bread and her recipe.

I just had to do it, trial and error. The first meal I cooked was hot milk on weetbix for breakfast. George milked the cow. Toast, I didn't have a toasting fork but George twisted up some wire and made a toasting fork and toasted bread on the coal range. I was used to the coal range 'cause there was one at home. The first potatoes I cooked I put too much water in and they disintegrated

Newly-appointed principal keeper Peter Taylor, and his wife Marita, with Stephen (on left) and David, arriving at Nugget Point 1961, their third (and one-man) station. Transfers were an occasion, and at that time people tended to dress for occasions. MARITA AND PETER TAYLOR.

and I would go down the paddock to where the men were working and say to George, 'How do I cook this?' He'd been at sea, he knew all those sort of things. He came from a family of cooks and bakers, so I learned from George. Because we ordered in bulk, we had these great big tins of dried fruit, and having made butter, I thought, oh well, I'll bake a cake. I looked at the oven and got it up to the right temperature, read the recipe — bake the cake for so long, leave it in the tin till cool. I did this, took it out of the oven, put it on the cake rack which George had made me out of wire, 'cause we had no cake rack, those weren't even thought of, and it slowly sank. I was so frustrated I just sat and cried. George came in. 'What's the matter?' And I said, 'Look at my cake.' But he just got a piece of thin tea towel, dampened it down, floured it, put the cake in it, got my biggest pot, put it on the stove — and that was our pudding. And next day we ate cold sliced fruit cake!

I was on my own so much with George in the lighthouse and then in the mornings he'd be working those two or three hours. I don't know whether it was my Lancashire or my Scots ancestry — and I sat down and I thought I Will Do It. So basically I learned the hard way and eventually, whether it's just what a woman does, I got used to doing the things and thought nothing of it.

Shirley and Alan Martin and their two small children arrived on Mokohinau by the steamer Hauraki. *Shirley:* It might have been only 60 feet long. It was old, it had been built round the turn of the century, and was originally a sailing boat and they cut the mast down, put diesel engines in it and it used to roll like a sick duck when the weather was not very nice. You used to have this trip where you'd go as far as Great Barrier, stay overnight in Tryphena with the nurse, usually the district nurse. [She made regular visits round the Gulf islands to check on inhabitants' health.]

Mokohinau didn't look as big as I had thought it was going to be and I must admit I was a bit apprehensive. I don't know, I must have been quite naïve in those days. You went and did these things, that was it. Arriving there it was a beautiful day, I remember that. My eldest son had been a wee bit sick — there was a bit of a roll on, that was OK, and we were taken up to the principal keeper's house while they did the unloading. Alan was helping — you didn't go ashore and stand and look decorative, you got stuck in. I was wearing a pair of light-coloured trousers — I knew I was going on a boat so I was wearing trousers, but they were light-coloured — and a little short, sporty top. My hair was all done up in a bun — I had long hair in those days — and I was definitely the city girl out for a ride. The keepers' wives were wearing sun frocks. I still remember climbing up this ladder, children being carted up by the sailors tucked up under the arm.

The landing at Mokohinau, looking much as it did when the Martins arrived, although the photo was taken 40 years after they joined the Service.
JEAN AND GEORGE KROENING

The boat landed off, you were put into a dinghy, everything was brought ashore in the boxes, coal, the whole lot. They had a hand winch with which the men had to wind up all the coal and swing that on to the trolley which was on a railway line. The trolley was pushed round to a certain spot where it was hooked on and there was a diesel winch right up at the top of the hill. It could be a very hard job by the time you'd unloaded several tons of coal and anything else. We were shown our house and I just had to hang around until everything was brought up and we could unpack. The others gave us a meal. Lighthouse hospitality is unparalleled, really. You'd step ashore and you were given a meal. If anybody went off on leave and came back you'd always have a meal ready for them, whether it was lunch or dinner, a cup of tea, morning tea.

Even in 1962 not all lighthouse families enjoyed electrical mod cons. The Martins were lucky.
Shirley: The first house that we went into, the second assistant's, was a two-bedroom wooden cottage that must have dated back to the late 1800s. It was immaculately kept. The furniture was old and nothing matched! There were two bedrooms, there was a kitchen, a big dining room, and a living room, bathroom of course and the toilet was in there – flush, we had a septic tank – and the washhouse was outside. The power supply was 110 DC and I'd been told I wouldn't be able to use a washing machine or anything like that, sort of going back into the dark ages. I had my own wash board, I was prepared to do hand washing. Then when we got out there we were told that you can

W. H. RAINE

get a motor for a washing machine that runs on 110 DC. And the same with an electric jug and an iron. But the power was only on so many hours a day and you did your work round that. After a few weeks I actually got a motor for a washing machine.

The organisation and the novelty of arriving at that first station were a foretaste of what would become a familiar routine as families undertook what was an integral part of lighthouse life. Transfers to different stations, which by the later twentieth century came roughly every three years, were to help dissipate tensions that could arise in the small station communities, familiarise staff with the different equipment at the different places, and share out the time at the less favoured places. The novelty of getting to one's first station would become dulled by experience, the necessary planning and the battles with head office over travel claims and reimbursement (often months late and not necessarily covering the full costs of damage or loss) for the inevitable, though surprisingly few, accidents while in transit.

James Clark arrived at Nugget Point in May 1875, replacing William Cunningham who had acted as principal keeper since Alex Carnochan's departure on 27 March 1871. Clark's comment on the road, hazardous, narrow, precipitous and prone to slips, is the first intimation of what would become over 50 years of struggle. I have the honour to acquaint you that according to your instructions as per Telegram, I removed from Tairoa's "Head Lighthouse" on the night of the 6th en route for the Nugget point "Light". I arrived at the latter Station on the morning of the 7TH Inst. Also family furniture and a small quantity of Stores which ware landed on the beach just above high water mark.

I may mention that it was necessary for me to employ a horse and cart to convey the above articles from the beach to the "dwelling house."

This I obtained from Mr. R. J. Campbell for the sum of one pound ten shillings which I consider is a very reasonable charge taken into Consideration the time engaged Which was two and a quarter days on account of the "Road" being so Slimy through the previous wet weather Otherwise they would have had to lay exposed for an indefinet time I hope you will allow this Amount to be paid ...[1]

J. Duthie, Waipapa Point, October 1913: I have the honour to acknowledge receipt of your Memo 543/257 re damaged stores & to state that the list of stores I sent is correct & was made up from my storekeepers a/c & the items were fully examined as taken from the cases. The 2nd officer is in error in his statements. Three cases of stores were opened in the landing store & the 4 items mentioned were all large parcels & the 2nd officer made a note of them & told me to make a list of whatever else was damaged. I drew his attention to a large number of other stores & took them out of the cases but he did not

Landing stores at the little bay on the north side of Nugget Point, 1934. In bad northerly blows Roaring Bay, on the southeast side of the point, was sometimes used. A small shed was erected there for storing the goods until they could be taken to the lighthouse station. It was not a trouble-free landing — Henry Philips, crewing on the lighthouse ship, was dumped in the surf there a number of times.
ALAN AND SHIRLEY MARTIN

A surfboat approaching the Cape Saunders landing, its fenders out and its anchor over to prevent the surging swell causing any mishap. Difficult landings at so many stations make the relative paucity of complaints of breakage a testimony to the skill of those handling the boats. Until the Second World War most things (and people) arrived by sea. HANSEN COLLECTION.

put them down on paper. He did not stop in the store above five minutes & the flour, sugar, pollard & wheat was laying down on the beach at the time, two bags of sugar being so wet that it was all melted & oozed out of the bags so was thrown away. We tried washing some of the fruits but did not improve it so threw it out. I am only asking that my stores be replaced or their cost refunded to me & I took every care to see that I did not put down any item in excess of the damage done. The stores are useless to anybody & therefore a dead loss & the greater part of them are still laying in the landing store & can be examined by anyone.[2]

W. Cameron and his family moved to Centre Island in 1922. The battle for reimbursement was ongoing some 10 months later. I have to state that when my boxes were brought to Centre Island per Hinemoa in April last I pointed out to the chief officer the condition in which they were landed, some with lids broken off others with sides staved in, which goes to prove that they must have been roughly handled while on transit from Cape Egmont … The personal effects, referred to in your Memo brought overland by myself from Cape Egmont, some of which got broken on the way, have nothing whatever to do with those for which I made my claim, as they were not included in the list of broken items which I forwarded for your perusal. Under these circumstances the decision is most surprising, as I consider the Dept has been wrongly informed … regarding the true facts of the case. The claim in my opinion is very reasonable as the same articles could not be bought to-day under twenty-five pounds. As I am not now in a position to replace them I respectfully ask that the Dept will reconsider the matter. Hoping for a favourable reply.[3]

Jean: When we got to Mokohinau and unpacked our possessions one of our crates had fallen into the sea when it was being unloaded at Waikokopu. We had packed our wedding photos in between our sheets. When we unpacked, it being so long before they came out to Moko, all the rust marks had gone through all the sheets. We had to claim. We got one pair of sheets and two pillow slips — that's all the Marine Department would pay us.

CHAPTER 3

Watching and cleaning

Arriving at a station entailed immediate work getting supplies and equipment ashore and safely stored. But the most important job lighthouse keepers did was to ensure their light shone out brightly. For most of the 150 years of the Lighthouse Service, keepers did that on shift, alone, watching the light in a spartanly furnished tower, ensuring that a kerosene-fuelled flame (kerosene superceded colza oil from the mid-1870s) burnt brightly and economically and that revolving lights turned steadily to give out their distinctive flashes.

George Kroening remembered his first time on watch, the evening he arrived: I went up the lighthouse with Harold Young and he stayed with me, showed me how to light the light, showed me how to wind the weight up, of course, and possible faults that might occur, how to keep the pressure up on the kerosene, and about half an hour afterwards he said, 'I'm going home. Do you want anything? That's my phone, you put the plug in here to ring me.' And away he went. I stayed there until midnight. It was quite exciting. Here I was, it was one of the lights I'd been past several times and I was finally operating it.

Two of the towers in which George worked were wooden. They were very heavily constructed, beautiful kauri timber and we know because we had to paint them. Akaroa and Portland Island were hexagonal; Portland Island had buttresses, probably 10 inches square, kauri beams put through it and they really anchored the place down.

There was a hexagonal-shaped room, wooden floor, lino — government lino of course — and on the ground floor cupboards etc to hold spare equipment. You climbed to the middle floor where the cylinders were for the air and kerosene and then the copper pipe led from there into the lamp room. It had storm panes, temporary panes that you could fit in from the inside of the light if a pane happened to get broken with a bird or something — never happened the whole time we were there. You went on up into the lightroom itself, up a tapered ladder. The further up you went the less room you got.

Then up on a little steel ladder on to the grating where you could go inside the lenses to light the light. The wooden towers especially were fairly draughty. They had ventilators round in the walls in the lightroom so on the still nights you could open the vents — they had gauze over them naturally — and let a bit of air in to get rid of the fumes. The rollers that turned the lenses were about four feet above where you sat at the small desk. It was only a small table, probably about 30 inches long, 18 inches wide, with just the lighthouse journal on it and the pen and ink, no ballpoint pens.

Chris Staley described The Brothers lighthouse winding apparatus used, post-electrification, only in training and emergencies. The wind vanes he refers to were known as governors. It was quite an intricate thing. There was a large weight that goes down the centre of the panel, you have to wind that up and it works rather like a big cuckoo clock, turning the lens around at the correct speed — well, you have to set that by the little wind vanes on it so that it flashes at the correct sequence — and it's the weight falling down, gravity, that turns the clockwork. It was a beautiful piece of equipment, all the clockwork stuff. It's all brass, old stuff, very very nice.

In the first decade of the twentieth century, incandescent lights that burned kerosene under pressure began replacing the old unpressured kerosene lights (innovations in their day). Barry Langman, on the last watch at Portland Island before a new tower was constructed, and the light electrified and automated in 1957, remembered the routine entailed in watching, and the 10 to 16 minutes pumping to get the pressure up if it had gone right down. The procedure was that you went up to the tower about half an hour before sunset, took a bucket of water, washed the panes on the outside of the lantern with a hearth brush and water (done every day, weather permitting) and then you went inside and drew the curtains and heated up the light and started the light.

You preheated the body of the light similar to lighting a primus stove. You filled the cup up with methylated spirits, lit it and let it burn out and by then the cast iron was hot enough to vaporise the kerosene. So you turned on the valve and let the kerosene come through on to the hot body of the light. It vaporised and went up in to the mantle and the mantle lit up and it hissed away all night. The collodion mantles were about six to eight inches long. [Collodion, a solution of gun cotton in ether, used for covering photographic plates and in the Lighthouse Service for coating the mantles, dried rapidly but made the mantles very brittle.] Once you'd burned the protective coating off them they were easily broken and you had to be very careful when you opened the door of the balcony that you didn't let moths in because they made straight for the mantle and into it and bust it and then you'd have raw kerosene going into the vapour and of course you had the ingredients for a good fire with that. It didn't take long to change the mantle. We had another

Lighthouse service maintenance man Henry Philips at Tiri, 1960s. From the 1950s Labour Department regulations forbade keepers to work more than 1.5 metres above the ground except on properly approved scaffolding and stages, and department maintenance men painted the towers. Philips and his co-worker, Joe Conlon, made a highly efficient team. Philips had long sailed on the lighthouse ships that serviced the lights, was a friend of the then Governor-General Sir Charles Fergusson who often travelled with Bollons, and later with his son Sir Bernard Fergusson. Conlon and Philips were always welcomed by keepers, and Henry, who told the children stories and made them propellers out of flax, was a special favourite.

MARITA AND PETER TAYLOR

mantle on the holder ready, all the time, and you just lifted it off with tongs and put the other one on and burnt the collodion coating off.

The light had to be exhibited at sunset. You stayed there until midnight. You wound up the weight – Portland Island about every hour and three-quarters – and you kept the pressure pump up at 70 pounds; you did your weather reporting, put down in the log book (which stayed on the station) what the conditions were. For example 'midnight, strong sou' westerly breeze, squally showers, sea rough, visibility down to five miles.' At quarter to 12 you rang the next person coming on the job. We just plugged on to the phone in their house and gave two complete turns of the handle of the old wind-up phone, party line, and it only went through to his house. He'd get out of bed and give one little short ring back to say that he was up because quite often you couldn't see the lights go on. You'd hear him come in the door near enough to midnight and you'd pass any comments, for example, 'A large ship went past going south, seemed a bit close in,' or, 'This wind started to freshen about nine o'clock,' little things like that, and you went home to bed. That was going off on midnight. The way we worked it on Portland Island you went off at midnight, went to bed, got up in the morning, milked the cows and did your station duties and then you went to bed soon after tea and got up and did the midnight to daylight – eight and a half hours on a wet day in the winter. This timetabling gave keepers every third night off.

Lighting the lamp was only the beginning. Trimming it to achieve an efficient and effective flame demanded skill and ingenuity. Fred Erecson, the first principal keeper at Puysegur Point lighthouse, reported on the initial lightup on 28 February 1879: I have the Honor to inform you that I have had the light burning for two nights, Feb the 4th and 5th. Keepers taking regular watches I used single wicks for the first night and double the last, and find that we can keep a far better light with double wicks, than can be kept with the single. the machine worked rather flighty, owing, I believe, to the want of the rollers in the steadying frame; but nothing to prevent me lighting up as instructed.[1]

Keepers experimented to get the best out of the equipment. Cuvier Island lighthouse was com-missioned in 1889 but in 1901 T. I. Cox still sought improvements: Soon after coming here I took out the damper out of the smoke tube and raised it about four feet higher up that is close to the Top of the apparatus and I am pleased to say [there] is a great improvement in the light and consequently a greater consumpt of oil as you will see by returns ...[2]

Each station's consumption of oil was carefully monitored by head office so that it could record monthly and annual averages. Over-consumption might denote a less-than-honest keeper or,

The winding machinery at Akaroa, typical of the beautiful mechanisms that were once in almost all of New Zealand's towers. The two small swivels at the top are the wind vanes or 'governors' that regulated the speed of the light's rotation. Weights powered the revolving machinery. These, which operated like those on a cuckoo clock, had to be wound up about every hour using a handle in a square-ended shaft. During winding an ingenious arrangement of pawls allowed the drive to be transferred to an auxiliary pinion so the speed of rotation remained constant and the light's characteristic was not altered. JEAN AND GEORGE KROENING

Samuel Hart with casual visitors to one of his lighthouses. Hart was at primary school in London with John Bollons who, together with John Fairchild, had a high reputation as captain of the steamers Hinemoa *and* Tutanekai. *Hart himself served under Fairchild on both* Hinemoa *and* Stella, *and helped erect a depot for castaways in the Auckland Islands. In 1888 he joined the Lighthouse Service as second assistant keeper at The Brothers. Principal keeper at Mokohinau in 1902, he subsequently served at Moeraki, Cape Egmont and Cape Palliser. He continued to exchange letters with Bollons and retired in 1926. His grandson, Roger Hart, a small boy when his grandfather died, remembers a jovial, likeable man.* ROGER HART

like under-consumption, a badly trimmed light. In 1921 at Cape Palliser Samuel Hart, called to account for oil consumption that did not agree with the station's average, set out the complex inter-related factors affecting oil consumption and demonstrated the skill and care needed to maintain a light at its full brilliancy. It seems to me that this disagreement of averages is partly caused by the rate of consumption slightly differing nightly by night. The full brilliancy of the light determines the amount of oil admitted to the burner, but what is full brilliancy is a matter of judgment and experience, there being no means of obtaining the standard of power definitely. Consequently the rate of consumption is greater or smaller according to the degree of brilliancy attained. This means that what is the average per hour for one night is not necessarily the average for another night, and for that reason the daily entries do not agree as to average with the average for the month.

When they do agree I think they may be regarded as coincidences, and not as being necessarily correct.

Other conditions affecting the rate of consumption are the age of the mantle, the state of the burner and of the interior of the vaporising tube. A mantle that has been used some time, a burner, or a tube, either of which is coated with the sooty products of kerosene combustion, all of these require varying quantities of oil per hour to realize the full light power than when the mantle is new, or the burner and tubes quite clean.

Of course these parts are changed as they become affected by use, still their condition is a cause of the rate of flow being uneven from night to night, and therefore influences the averages.[3]

The light had to go from sunset to sunrise. Falling asleep or letting the light go out or stop could mean instant dismissal, but the keepers' own professional pride was a strong motivator in keeping it alight during the hours of darkness. In 1901 J. Sinclair and Robert Carthcart both responded to one of the circulars the department used to send round publicising keepers' misdemeanours. J. Sinclair, Centre Island: It was a surprise to Centre Island lightkeepers to hear of some keeper departing to a certain extent from the instructions to lightkeepers in chapter 3/11 of instructions to lighthouse Keepers [Balfour's Instructions, which principal keepers were required to read aloud regularly to ensure the assistants knew their job] it must have been an inexperienced probationer that would in a careless fashion depart from such an important rule as to extinguise the light ten or fifteen minutes before sunrise such should not happen with keepers been 10 and 12 and 15 years at a real important public service that cannot be carelessly looked at with want of individual thought for the safety of seafairing men that might be in danger without a good light to guide them on their way such has never happened at my time either at Centre Island or Cape Maria van Dieman the light are kept burning regularly from sunset to sunrise . . .[4]

Robert Cathcart, Stephens Island: With reference to your Circular No. 492/III in which you "request that I will let you know whether there has been any departure from Clause I Chapter III of the Instructions to Lightkeepers, at any of the Lighthouses under my Control". And in reply I beg to inform you that this is the only Lighthouse that has been under my control, and as I am generally in bed when the Assistant Keepers extinguish the light, I cannot therefore vouch to the time they do so. At the same time I fully believe that they conscientiously do their duty, and would not extinguish the light before it was Judicious to do so. Personnally, I may state that I extinguish the light if a clear morning about sunrise, and some mornings when we have foggy weather, I keep the light going long after the time given in the Almanack for the sunrise ...[5]

However, identifying the exact time of sunrise was not as simple as head office assumed. Fred Erecson, Cape Egmont, 1901: I have the honor to acknowledge receipt of Circulars Nos 692/III & 693/III and beg to state that with regard to the 1st that so far as I am concerned there has been no departure from the rules refered to in the circular, so far as it is possible to comply with them. But the clocks supplied are not always reliable, nor is the time of sunrise and sunset given in the Otago almanac correct at places such as Waipapapa Point and Dog Island. These stations, lying so far West, the sun sets fully ten minutes later than the time given and for seven months of the year there is no opportunity to check the clocks by sunrise because he rises beyond high land and it is therefore necessary to use ones judgement when to put out the light, according to the state of the weather.[6]

Night watching had its pluses and minuses. George: I did my army education welfare service and a lot of reading. You could do hobbies to a certain extent, anything small, easy to handle, but the hardest thing was staying awake. On a good night you walked round the balcony, watched shipping go past, fishing boats that sort of thing. And wound up the weights and pumped up the kerosene usually every two or three hours.

 But in storms in the Portland Island tower, which had had to be braced against the wind, watching was a different matter. George: Especially in a good southerly, sou' west-erly – mainly because of the lay of the land – the tower would literally shake all night while you were there. The ventilator up the top, which was also a windvane, would rattle away, and even where the lenses were supported up in the dome with the shock rollers they'd be shaking. It didn't put the fear of God into you or anything like that, but it was spooky enough.

Bill Megennis was a relieving keeper in the Lighthouse Service in its dying days, the only sort of position open at that time: One of the great experiences I still recall – it probably

Alan Martin in the 1980s, beside the first order Nugget Point 'cage' of lenses, provides a sense of the scale of these things.
ALAN AND SHIRLEY MARTIN

wasn't the done thing — was to get inside the lens when it was turning at night time. It's just a wonderful thing, because the light's going through prisms like all the colours of the rainbow, and you see the light reflecting off these big solid pieces of glass — beautiful colours. I was at Cape Reinga, I had some friends come up from Auckland and I said to them, 'It's quite nice inside.' Well, three people inside the lens set off the alarm and the keeper who was on the station at the time came out. We'd actually come out of the tower, thank God, and he said, 'The alarm's gone off, what's wrong with the light?' And I said, 'Oh, must have been just a hiccup.' I didn't do that again!

Lives and merchandise were at stake if the lights did not burn well and regularly. Before electrification, each station carried a stand-by lamp, which was tested periodically; post-electrification, bulb changers automatically replaced a faulty bulb. Alan Wright: Lights in lighthouses have got two bulbs. If one bulb fails, the other automatically, by mercury, just flicks over. It's on a mercury balance and it just floats over and the light's only off for a few seconds.

Back-up options in the event of power failure were regularly rehearsed. Barry Langman describes the Stephens Island emergency set-up: Firstly we had two generating engines so that if one failed the other was there to carry on. The other contingency was the light operated secondarily from a bank of metal cadmium-plated batteries which were big alkaline batteries capable of holding about 150 amp hours at one and a half volts. So the batteries could run to a predetermined lower voltage before the engines had to be brought back into action. If the power failed we then could remove the bulb changer and put the mantle on, pump up the kerosene and operate on that. If that failed, we had a Captain Chance's lamp which was basically a kerosene lamp similar to what you find on a farm. That lamp was the last resort. It was a weak light but at least it was a light. Roger [Blanshard, the principal keeper] used to run instruction courses in handling the kerosene operation of the light, which we did at least once a month even though the station was on electricity.

Tower duties did not end with the final watch for the night. Most of the morning would go on day-to-day maintenance of the tower and its equipment. D. D. McFarlane's list in a routine monthly report from Castlepoint in 1941 indicates the range of regular, quite intricate work: During the month the lenses have been kept thoroughly clean and the lantern panes washed outside and cleaned inside each evening at sunset. The revolutions of the apparatus have been checked each watch and the right speed maintained. The oil pipe between the oil container and the regulating valve was blown through each time the vapour tube was removed for cleaning. All brass & steel work together with the lino on all floors have been kept thoroughly clean. During the months we keepers have been employed as follows cleaning lenses, brass & steelwork lino on all floors … oiled dome outside lighthouse … blackened grating round lenses …[7]

Steve O'Neill cleaning the lenses at Baring Head station in 1988, maintaining a long tradition. ATL: EP/1988/2211-F

McFarlane excluded the jobs and detail too small or too routine to need mentioning; George's memory of tower duties pre-electrification on Portland and Akaroa, which he and Jean visited some 40 years after leaving the Service, fills in the gaps. Normal station duties – you came off watch in the morning, put the light off, drew the curtains, came downstairs, opened the kerosene cylinder and filled it up again, you pumped up the air pressure, turned all the valves off and you went backwards down the stairs from the lightroom right out the door on your hands and knees wiping the floors with kerosene. It was government linoleum, about quarter of an inch thick, the old khaki-type, very serviceable, but not very impressive. All the towers stank of kerosene and it was quite nostalgic to go into the tower at Akaroa after all these years and smell it as soon as you walked through the door. You milked the cows if it was daylight and then did two hours' station duties Monday to Friday, mainly the work in the tower keeping the lenses clean.

The three of us would get up there and in a second order light there were 306 prisms so you had to clean the three sides of them. On a first order light there were 366 prisms. So it took quite a bit of doing. We used to order bottles and bottles of Windolene. The prisms get a smear on them from the kerosene fumes. We did them Sunday with just a feather duster and then as they needed cleaning – it depended on the weather a lot how much deposit got on the prisms. Occasionally we'd have a bit of a test on stand-by equipment.

Once the lights were electrified, the lenses were no longer cleaned daily. Bill: The Brothers, and other stations too, still had a weekly cleanup of the tower. Part of the duties on The Brothers: it was Friday, and if you were not on weather duties you'd be up in the tower cleaning it out. What I liked about it was that you were actually going up the steps and doing the same thing as they were doing 100 years ago, except there was a lot of work involved at that time, winding up the weights and such like. You were carrying on that tradition, and maintaining it as well. The lens-turning track had to be oiled, and it was the original old lens-turning track. The pedestal that held the lens was still turning on the same track since it was installed over 100 years ago. All the gear was there. The only difference was that it had an electrical motor turning it and the old mantle had been replaced by a 1000 watt bulb, about eight inches in diameter. Wonderful machinery. I just marvelled at it. And inside the lenses – that was a big job. You got to do the lenses about once a month. We used mutton cloth. There were people whose cleaning methods I didn't think were particularly good and it was an insult to that big lens that shines so brightly.

The rest of the tower also had to be maintained, though, again after electrification these jobs, over time, were done less frequently or not at all. George: The dome of the lighthouse is a copper plate all riveted, and the ventilator is copper as well, and sticking up above the ventilator we had the fork for the lightning arrester. From that fork there was a cable, two inches in circumference or getting close, that ran from the top of the tower down the side across the ground and down into the sea and onto a copper plate. Each month the procedure was you started off up at the tower and followed that cable right down into the sea to make sure the whole system

The Brothers tower, early 1960s. Buttresses, still in place, were added shortly after this photo was taken to strengthen the tower and provide greater stability.
CHRIS STALEY

The Brothers, with the keepers cleaning the outside of the lantern. The handholds used for climbing the dome are clearly visible.

hadn't been broken down in any way. I don't remember any actual lightning strikes on the tower. No doubt there were but they didn't register.

Cleaning the lantern panes and painting the dome with boiled linseed oil involved climbing on to the outside of the light on high towers, often at the edge of a cliff a hundred metres or more above the sea. George and Alan Martin both cleaned the dome. George: You had footholds and handholds, like stirrups they were, riveted on to the dome and after being up the mast at ships at sea it was a piece of cake really. You'd hang on with one hand, the system was one hand for yourself, one for the company and you always hung on for yourself better than you did for the company. You got all the sulphur deposit off, and gave it a coat of boiled oil. The theory was that boiled oil reflected in sunlight on the dome — and it did.

Alan: The worst job was having to climb right on to the dome. You can imagine being up there, 200 or 300 feet above sea level on this 12-foot hemisphere painted black, hanging on for grim death — it's quite a sight when you look over the side and there's nothing there for a long way down. You only had to do it once every six months. I do recall the first time — you had to climb straight up the lantern on the outside, reach one of these handholds, reach for another, bring your feet up and put them in the gutter round the edge of the dome. Then, of course, you had to keep going right up to the top, pour the oil on, rub it round with a piece of rag and gradually move around. The worst thing to do was the satellite, right on top, that knobbly piece with the wind vane on it and you had to get right up the top to put the oil on. We didn't go up in a strong wind, of course, because this thing had a tendency to swing around in all directions. But it had to be done, so we did it.

In 1936 at Baring Head, New Zealand's first electrified lighthouse, we see a new trend — outside technical expertise, rather than the keepers' ingenuity, being employed. R. S. (Bob) Wilson using, uncommonly for the time, a typewriter, carbon paper and headings, pasted the copy into the letterbook:

Switchboard
Flasher Contact [Flashers caused the make and break in the electric current

to give the light its characteristics, and at Baring Head and elsewhere they caused constant problems] on the Light panel having given trouble, through burning, a mercury contact was added, with the object of cutting this burning out. It had the desired effect, and gave satisfaction from the date of fitting: Sunday Oct. 8th until the 8th of Nov., when it developed another trouble, the contact failing to break and thereby forming a fixed light. A further experiment was made by Mr Tolly on Saturday, 21st inst. with another type of mercury contact, and this failed to operate. Finally, an experiment is now being made with the original copper contact silver plated, and in conjunction Mr Tolly preposes to fit a system of alarm should the light remain stationary whether it be dim or bright.

He goes on to describe the many interviews, discussions and trips into Wellington before the batteries could be installed. The lighthouse bulb needed replacing after six months, and bits of the tower and some station buildings were painted.

Truck

It was found necessary to have the radiator repaired at the P.S. [Public Service] Garage, on the 27th. These repairs were satisfactory. The Station truck has made the usual weekly trips for mail etc. and several additional trips in connection with the alterations. The undercarriage has been cleaned and painted; together with the mudguards, and the main body treated with solpah oil.

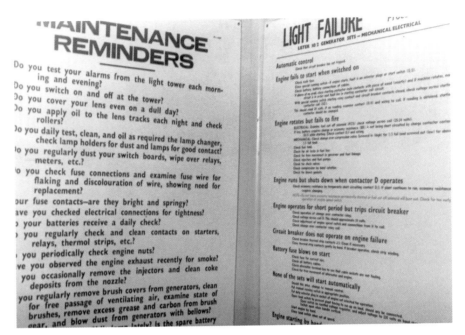

Maintenance reminders for the diesel engines. Following electrification, lists like these were kept in all station light rooms.

MARITA AND PETER TAYLOR

Reserve

Further mowing of grass with the scythe was carried out enabling the major portion of the enclosed ground to be cut with the lawnmower; the remainder being in plantation. Further tree planting has been carried out in the reserve, and the whole station kept in a state of tidyness.

P.S.

The following persons were catered for during the month whilst they were engaged on Government duty at the Station.

Mr. Tolly 21st Tea (employed on flasher contact)

Mr Warden. P.W.D. &

Mr Alexander. Battery expert in connection with the alterations to Power house. (Dinner)

Mr Bryant & Assistant 27th Repairs to Battery floor. (Tea.)

(2) Dinner Employed on alteration & change over of Batteries

Mr Alexander & Mr Bryant 30th (2) Tea & Bed

Mr Alexander & Mr Bryant 1st Breakfast.

M. Parker. Cory-Wright

Mr Sheltan P.W.D.

VIZ Beds	2 @ 2/- each ...	£.0-4-0.
Meals	17 @ 1/6 each ...	1-5-0.
		£.1-9-0.[8]

From the 1950s on remote and island stations, diesel engines charged generators for the electric power. The cleaning routines and procedures for the diesel engines were set out in list form and kept in the lightroom. Alan Wright: The Brothers had three diesels. That diesel today, that diesel tomorrow, that diesel the day after. You changed them around all the time, to keep them running well. The Lister diesel is about one of the most reliable little engines there is. The chances of them failing are extremely remote. It's just lack of attention and maintenance. As soon as you walked in the engine room, it's like any ship, you go in an engine room and you judge the engine room by the state of the room. If you can eat off the floor it's a good engineer.

You had a set routine that you read off every day before you did anything else, before you even looked at starting the engine up. You checked the oil levels, you checked the fuel gauge. Chris [Staley] and myself, we'd done our military training, so we were used to discipline and routine. But one chappie, a keen fisherman, came to The Brothers — he'd never had any routine or anything like that and you'd go into the engine room or the radio room, to do a weather or something, and you'd say, 'Have you done this?' 'No.' 'Have you done that?' 'No.' 'Well, there's the list!' After a while you do it automatically without thinking.

Alan Martin: In the radio room all three keepers would do the topping up of the engines, pumping up the fuel. When we first went to Moko the engines were 110 volts DC and standby in the back room were 110 one volt cells. Whoever was on duty would go round topping them up with distilled water. It came in great big carboys and we'd transfer it into a backpack with a little plastic tube coming down. You'd flick the tops off each battery and check to make sure it was up to scratch. When you put the light on, or the radio beacon at night, the engine that was on duty (there were two engines, you used them alternately) would be put on direct running — you weren't using the batteries, you were charging them. When it was daylight the engines were switched off and you drew from the batteries. As they were losing power they'd get to a certain point and an engine would cut in again and start pumping juice into them.

CHAPTER 4

Associated lightkeeping tasks

WEATHER

In 1873 the government set up a new weather-reporting branch in the Marine Department. At many stations lighthouse keepers were part of the national network of observers collecting local data and sending it through to a national office. By the mid-twentieth century, the lighthouses at Puysegur Point, Dog Island, the Nuggets, Moeraki, Akaroa, Cape Campbell, The Brothers, Stephens Island, Castlepoint, Portland Island, Cuvier Island, Tiritiri Matangi, Cape Brett and Cape Reinga had their weather data recording equipment, and three-keeper stations reported, as Alan Martin said, every three hours right round the clock seven days a week.

Cloud cover was an important component of the reports. In 1947 New Zealand's observations were recorded in line with international standards; Alan Martin learned these on Mokohinau: There were nine different types of cloud in three different spectrums — low, middle and high. So it's merely a matter of looking up there and seeing how much cloud — the sky was divided into eighths, and you determined which cloud was predominant and what it was doing, low cloud, middle cloud, high cloud and so on. As a new keeper you'd go up with the principal keeper and he'd look around and say, 'What's that cloud over there? Look at the book, are you sure? What height is it above sea level?' I think you were given a range of 500 feet, so it was not really difficult, it was just a matter of working it out. After a while it became second nature, especially if you're on a full weather station. Now when I go out, I usually have a look around, see what's happening. The guys down the coast say that since I've been taken off the Nuggets the weather's been lousy.

Electrification did away with night watching, but on weather stations weather duties were rostered. Barry Langman describes the Stephens Island roster: Because we were an important weather station in Cook Strait for the weather coming across the Tasman, we had to give a report every three hours night and day. Even though we slept at night because the station was automated with electricity, one keeper was

allocated to get up at nine o'clock at night, read the instruments, go back to bed, and get up again at 3 a.m. to do it again.

[The weather was radioed through] immediately to ZLW in Wellington. The second shift involved the other keeper getting up at midnight and also at 6 a.m. and doing the same. The third keeper was on the daylight shift from 8 a.m. to 5 p.m. We rotated those shifts and the duties that went with them — at night time it was just a matter of checking the operation of the light and seeing the frequency of the flashes was maintained and that the light was correct. We had to do it from the power house because the radio room was attached to the power house; the power house was next to the lighthouse and the instruments were all in the paddock beside the power house.

Alan found compensations for being on weather duties: Sleep wasn't too disrupted.

It is just after nine o'clock and in a somewhat contrived 1960s photo John Jepson radios through the weather to Wellington. Note the Morse key board to the right, by then little used.

ANZ (WGTN) AAQ 6401 A73471

Reading the weather at Cape Campbell, in the 1920s or 30s. HANSEN COLLECTION

It's OK in good weather, you'd get up, have a look around – Jeez, this is brilliant, this is absolutely brilliant! And then you'd get up and there's a storm blowing and the wind's doing about 60 knots and you've got to go up and do a midnight or 3 a.m. weather and you think, What the hell am I doing here? Even the dog wouldn't come out! Moko was the worst because you had to go right up the hill.

With the advent of radio, a number of the weather stations also unofficially reported on local conditions to shipping and yachties. The changeability of the weather made this service particularly important to the small boats cashing in on the crayfishing boom at Puysegur in the 1970s and 1980s, and those fishermen protesting against the station's demanning in the late 1970s fought vehemently for the service to continue. Bill Megennis: The extremities of the weather conditions at Puysegur Point and the inshore fishing meant a lot of boats working between Bluff up the coast to Preservation and boats coming from Milford would have occasion to use Preservation [Inlet] as a safety area. We tried hard to get weather reports over on the frequencies for the inshore fishermen.

On The Brothers after the Commission of Inquiry [the 1980–81 Commission which investigated the proposed demanning of the few remaining manned stations, including Puysegur Point and The Brothers] we were getting a hard time from the Marine Department – we were trying to update our duties. In the end, we got a hand-held VHF. The argument was that we needed it to communicate with Brian Pickering on the boat. We used it to communicate with Betty Baker [at Cape Jackson station she gave out local weather conditions and reports – a service yachties wanting to cross Cook Strait used frequently]. We'd talk to her at six o'clock in the morning and she'd say, 'What's it like out there?' for anybody listening on that frequency. Often she'd call us when she couldn't see the conditions from where they were, south of The Brothers. There was this network.

FOG STATIONS AND RADIO BEACONS
From the beginning of the twentieth century a number of stations were equipped with increasingly sophisticated navigation aids. Fog signals were the first of these.

Until the latter part the nineteenth century, fog confounded navigation. Fog muffles sound and obscures its direction, and beams of light get dissipated and absorbed by the particles of moisture that form the fog. But in 1898 came the first real breakthrough. A Slaughter's Cotton Powder signal was installed at Pencarrow station and Captain Fairchild, the esteemed captain of the Tutanekai, stood off Pencarrow Head to test the signals. His favourable report paved the way for similar installations at Taiaroa Head and Godley Head, later farther afield. Yet, a year after the signal's installation, difficulties with the button plate connected with fog signal was only one of a number of problems still to be sorted. Principal keeper William Cunningham remained sceptical about the signal's value. I may state that we have got over the difficulty of the wires sticking or hanging to the contact plates after the explosions by adding a lead washer the same size as the Bone Button.

I may state in conclusion that we cannot fire the Fog Signal in thick windy weather & the wires that carry the charges will not remain on the hooks & I dont think it possible to do so unless some expensive alterations are made & I question very much if the explosions could be heard half a mile to sea ward if the wind is blowing strong from the S. E. although it has been heard at Worser Bay & Days Bay when the wind is from that quarter. Of course when the wind is from the N.W. it should be heard an equal distance to sea ward.

I may state further for your information that the afternoon on which the "Tutanekai" stood off & on here for testing the distance the Fog signal could be heard to seaward there was a light air from the N.W. (Blowing towards the steamer) & everything was in favour of hearing the explosions to the best advantage.

Whatever substance you may send to make the new Button Plates of will require to be 3/8 or half an inch in thickness. [He wanted leather, as earlier, unsatisfactory ones had been made of teak, vulcanite, matai and ash].

I beg to remind you that you have not returned the new Steel Spring for the Fog signal magazine. I returned the broken one to the Marine Office some weeks ago.[1]

At Cuvier Island in 1909 parts of the newly installed jib-type fog signal were not up to the job. (Mr Scott was the lighthouse artificer, a job that combined the duties of engineer, overseer and foreman of works.) Robert H. Leighton: We are much troubled with the Air container pump as from the first time of using them while Mr Scott was here we have not been able to get the air pumped up without a great amount of work, this means that both pumps are being worn and become so heated as to burn the leathers which then crumbles away and so finds its way into the air pipes, valves etc.

My wish is to work the present light as well as possible, but it is useless to report all being satisfactory if it is not so. The pumps appear to be far too light for the work.[2]

In 1927, after years of discussion about new technology to assist ships to identify their positions, New Zealand's first radio direction finder was installed at the lighthouse station on Motuopao, off Cape Maria van Diemen; by 1940–41 radio beacons at Cape Reinga, Mokohinau, Cuvier Island, Baring Head, Cape Campbell, Stephens Island, and at Puysegur Point from 1943, operated continuously in conditions of low visibility, and in clear weather at stated intervals. Their signals extended over considerable distances. Chris Staley was on The Brothers when new radio beacons were put in. They were I believe the first air/marine beacons put

*Riggers on working on The Brothers'
towers. Chris Staley remembered, 'A
P&T rigger came out from Blenheim, a
foreman, and he stuttered badly, which to
me indicates that you're rather a nervous
type of person — I'm probably wrong there
— but he couldn't look at you and talk. I
looked out of the window and he'd gone
up the tower. It had a steel plate on top
probably 12 or 14 inches square and he was
standing on that, arms crossed, virtually
350, 400 feet above the sea. Which is
absolutely amazing to me. I wouldn't have
done that. He must have had nerves
of steel. Of course he was a rigger.
No margin for error.'* CHRIS STALEY

in in New Zealand. They could be used by ships and also by aircraft coming
into Rongotai. They sent out a continual Morse signal — Brothers Island, BI.
An aircraft could set a flight path say into Wellington, hone in on Brothers
Island and if you went off course one way you'd get a constant string of
dashes, and if you went off course the other way you'd get a string of dots.
So it was very simple to keep on course.

SIGNALLING PASSING VESSELS

*From the 1880s the lighthouse stations were progressively linked to the country's telegraph,
then telephone, system. At the end of the century the department had agreed with Lloyd's of
London that stations at Cape Maria van Diemen, Farewell Spit and Nugget Point would
fly a Lloyd's flag so that ships' masters knew they could have messages forwarded to, and
relayed from, those stations. S. F. Rayner at Nugget Point wanted his son employed to keep
lookout. In May 1900 he made a second attempt to convince head office that the position was
needed:* I have the honour to acknowledge receipt of memo No. 295/100 of
the 7TH May, containing instructions re signalling passing vessels, before
those instructions can be carried out, a flagstaff and signal box will have
to be erected either close to, or on the peak immediately overlooking the
lighthouse.

At present a telegraph pole in front of the dwelling houses is used as a
flagstaff, but it is not a particle of use to us, for during the three years I have
been at this station no passing vessel has ever taken a signal from it.

When Captain Blackbourne was here lately it was pointed out to him, and I fancy he will remember the position of the houses and the impossibility of keeping a watch from them that would be of any use.

The lighthouse is 900 yards away from the dwelling houses, the peak I mentioned nearly as far, they are the only suitable places for a flagstaff, should one be erected at either place a keeper would have to be on constant watch from daylight to dark to sight vessels coming from the south.

I therefore respectfully beg to ask, whether you would kindly consider the possibility of sending a third keeper to this station as I do not see how two keepers can do the signalling and lighthouse duties by themselves.

There is a mile or more of road to be kept under repair, which is away from where any 'look out' could be kept; and during the summer months a good many telegrams have to be delivered at distances ranging from 1 to 3 miles hence, a large number of visitors also keep one man in constant attendance.

In a telegram of the 13th Oct 1899 I mentioned that "two lighthouse keepers could not keep constant watch and attend to lighthouse duties".

I have always been given to understand that should Lloyds require any signalling to be done here, a third man would be sent to assist.

Nugget Point hillside. With the big double house (like the first Dog Island lighthouse home) snuggled down below the ridge, keepers had no all-round view. From that building the road zig-zagged up to (from far left to right) the signal hut, the principal keeper's house (built 1906) and, on the far right, the schoolhouse for the station and local children. In the mid-1960s the old double house had become an implement shed — a use to which it may well have been put earlier. The track running round the side of the hill leads to the lighthouse, a little under a kilometre away.

ALAN AND SHIRLEY MARTIN

A lightkeepers duties are monotonous as it is, on duty from night after night from years end without a break, and if they have to attend to this signalling they will have to be on duty all day as well.

At other signal stations such as Tiritiri and Cape Saunders where there are only two keepers, the signalling can be done with very little difficulty, as vessels all pass within sight of the dwelling houses & lighthouses and can be seen by all on the station

Trusting you will favourably consider this letter and be able to increase the strength of this station to three keepers.[3]

On 4 March 1901 David Scott, the artificer, arrived with materials to erect the flagstaff and another keeper had been employed. But there were still issues to be resolved. D. Partington, 1911: The Assistant Keepers and myself would respectfully request that you undertake to advise the Postal Department to appoint each Keeper at this station as Telephonist with a salary equal to what they are paying the Keepers at Farewell Spit, Stephens Island and probably Puysegur Point. Good business is done at this office in "Collect" and "Transmit" messages and we are required to be in constant attendance on three Telephones. Morse signalling will be established soon, and as messages cannot be sent direct to Kaitangata from the Lighthouse I or my wife must be prepared to receive or forward messages at any hour of the day or night.[4]

With telephones installed, keepers at signal stations had to advise of all shipping passing the station — an edict head office issued, again apparently unaware of the impracticalities of such a general demand. Charles Tregurtha Cape Egmont, 1900: With reference to your Memo. of the 21ST inst. I regret to state that the Tutanekai was not observed passing this station on the date mentioned. We were at work outside all the morning, and must have been at dinner when she passed It is impossible to see anything passing from the houses except through one or two small openings between the hills and through the clumps of flax. We generally take a good look around when knocking off work, and come out again after dinner to see if there is anything in sight, and I think very few vessels pass in the daytime without being noticed. About a month ago the Tutanekai passed one morning, I was about half a mile away from the lighthouse when I noticed the flag. Assistant keeper tried to find an ensign to answer the flag, not knowing that we had none, and didn't think of putting up the answering pennant till it was too late. I beg to suggest that an ensign be supplied to this station.[5]

At Waipapa Point, too, the instruction was impractical. A somewhat tetchy James Anderson, 1914: I have the honor to reply to your telegram dated Oct. 7th re reporting passing vessels. We have not had any instructions as your telegram would indicate. The Telephone Office is four miles away from here. It is closed from 5 p.m to 9 a.m. the following morning & with muddy roads & dark nights it would take a good time to get there and back at night.

Steamers pass so far off this point that the only difference we can tell at night is a big one from a small one. We could not tell their names.

If we had a telephone, it would be quite different. We would know when steamers were leaving the Bluff or Port Chalmers and that would help us a lot in telling their names. Of course we would be pleased to help in this if we knew how.[6]

Until phones connected automatically, simple possession did not guarantee service. Operators were essential; calling outside the local area could entail hours of waiting to be put through, and even then, the finally achieved connection only too likely to be lost. The time-honoured greeting, 'Are you there?' was not necessarily a silly question. P. Malthus, Stephens Island, 1921: We at this station are at all times anxious to carry out the wishes of shipmasters and their owners, and during the four and a half years that I have been at this station, I am quite certain that, with the exception of the times when telegraphic communication has been interrupted, we have never failed to pass on any message that we have received, nor failed to report any vessel that has given us its name & destination. The above refers

Men signalling from Tiritiri Matangi, c. 1902. The signal flags are flying, one keeper is signalling with semaphore and the other checks for a response. Signalling by flag and semaphore was a daytime activity, but by about 1911 keepers had to know Morse — the Lighthouse Service made prompt use of Aldis lamps, invented in the late nineteenth century. George Kroening remembered those lamps had 'a highly polished reflector behind the bulb in the body of the lamp. This produced a very concentrated beam of light. A sight along the top of the body enabled the beam to be precisely pinpointed. A pistol grip on the underside and a "trigger" tilted the reflector to produce an effect like the headlights of a car being switched rapidly from high beam to dip, except that in "dip" position the reader of the signal was presented with an almost total blackout. This made the Morse signal all the more distinctive.'

HANSEN COLLECTION

to daylight signalling. In connection with night signalling there is a point which I beg leave to bring under your notice. The office at French Pass closes at 5 p.m. and in theory Stephens Island office is through to Nelson all night. But nine times out of ten we cannot get Nelson as our rings do not carry through.

Sometimes a U.S.S. Coy's [Union Steamship Company] Collier will signal us during the early part of the night, and ask to be reported to Wellington. Once or twice we have managed to get such a message through, but only by getting hold of someone else along the line, and asking them to get Nelson for us. More often all our efforts have failed, and then when the French Pass office opens at nine the next morning it is no use our sending the message as the vessel will have arrived at Wellington long before that time.

… There is also this trouble sometimes on Sundays, when the French Pass office is closed. Our arrangement with Nelson is that as our rings (or theirs) do not carry through, we are to "listen on" between 9 & 9.30 a.m. and again between 5 & 5.30 p.m. on Sundays, and wait for Nelson to come on and speak to us. Usually this arrangement works well, but on some Sundays I put in half an hour in the morning, and another in the evening, alternately ringing and listening, without success.[7]

Life was not made easier by the general expectation that time off was time off. H. B. Jamieson, Cape Brett, 1938: In reply to your letters M8/9/300 dated 5th and 12th April re reporting ships bound to Opua to load meat, I have noted your instructions and we will continue to report these vessels whenever possible, as we have been doing in the past. Several boats have gone in lately on Sundays or public holidays and I could not report them as there was no one on duty at the Russell exchange. Also on two or three occasions the Harbourmaster was out and we could not get him until too late. Most of the vessels going to Opua come in from the North and pass about 12 miles from here so that if the visibility is at all poor we might easily miss them. If the Harbourmaster were to advise us of the appropriate dates of expected arrivals it would be of some help to us. He told me he had arranged it so that we could get him on the phone at any hour of the night or day, but my experience has been that we cannot depend on getting Russell on Sundays or holidays. they say they are not bound to be in attendance, but will put us through when the Postmaster happens to be at home.[8]

Eighteen months later and with the local Post and Telegraph man not inclined to make improvements, Jamieson wrote again, detailing his difficulties with getting in touch with one of three local exchanges that might be open.[9]

WRECKS

Keepers' observation and recording of shipping movements gave them a role in what today would be called search and rescue. There was the very occasional drama. S. F. Rayner and his men at Pencarrow in 1913 reported his experience with the Devon *and her ungrateful crew:* I have the honour to forward the following report of the recent wreck of the S S Devon at Pencarrow Head.

On the 25th at 7.30 p.m. Mr Edmonds who was on watch in the lighthouse called me up to inform me a large steamer appeared to be ashore on the rocks below the lighthouse. Immediately going to the tower I could see a large steamer hard and fast on the rocks between the 'Lower Level Light' and the landing. She was reported as soon as possible to the Harbour Board, yourself & others.

Soon afterwards the steamer which later proved to be the SS 'Devon' commenced firing rockets, the 'Wahine' passing south & slowed down and signalled to the Devon: from then on until some time after midnight the Keepers kept in constant communication with the 'Devon' but had considerable difficulty in reading her signals as her light did not shut out.

As I learned afterwards they were passing a hat to and fro before a large hurricane lamp to make the dots & dashes.

The following signals however were successfully sent and taken

Keepers: 'Are you breaking up'

Devon: The ship is breaking up aft alright.

Devon: Have you any rocket apparatus'

Keepers: 'No'

(All our signals to the Devon were taken quick and smartly I only remember having to repeat a word once.)

The Devon signalled a second time 'Have you any rocket app.

Keepers: 'There is no rocket apparatus here'

Devon: 'Can not you do something' and after a while Can you see the — over and over again but the missing word we could not read, imagining it to be 'line' I placed Mr Abraham (school master a thoroughly reliable and competent man) in charge of the light while Mr Edmonds and I went down to the landing where we searched the beach but were unable to find any line ashore We then signalled

Kprs: 'No line ashore'

Devon: 'Can't you do anything'

I was at my wit's end to know what two men could do and made no reply, but went down to the landing store opened a tin of kerosene & made two huge blazes which showed up the boat landing plainly. The Devon sent two rocket lines towards us but though we were nearly up to our waists in water the lines failed to reach us.

We then signalled

'Boat-landing in line with fires.

'Do you think of landing by boat'

Devon: 'No'

Keepers: 'Can you hang on till morning'

Devon: 'Yes'

Afterwards when the men were being landed some of them accused me of tempting them to certain death by signalling Boat-landing in line etc but the fires were made bright enough for the crew to see the state of the sea on the beach.

After their reply to our Signal Can you hang on till morning I considered it was not any use our staying there any longer and as we had both [been] drenched to the skin for hours and were half perished with cold we went home it was then 0.45 a.m.

A party of reporters arrived almost at the same time, they informed us Capt Johnson with a large relief party was at hand.

That was the first information I had received of Capt Johnson being on the way.[10]

The legend of Grace Darling, the whipper-snapper of a girl launching a boat into boiling surf and pulling for hours to a wrecked ship, had little bearing on the rather more modest reality of what lighthouse keepers could actually do. At Pencarrow in 1910, Ernest Parks, son of Alexander Parks whom we shall meet later, rescued and gave breakfast to the crew of a ship that (fortunately in calm weather) had gone on the rocks.[11] Most keepers were not so lucky. Jerome Sinclair, Centre Island, 1899: [A] bit of timber something like old wreckage was landed on the beach on the 28th inst three deck planks and a hold hatch frame piece were found early in the morning, as no name was seen on it and no particulars to hand to know the cause off such there were no need to send a wreck form when we hear full particulars then such may be sent ...[12]

D. Partington, Mokohinau, 1900, could do little to assist the ships he and his assistants saw in trouble. (The pigeons were a short-lived attempt to deal with Mokohinau's isolation.): I have the honour to inform you that a Barque having neither foremast or mainmast was five miles east of the Lighthouse at sunrise today. There was a flag flying but we could not read it owing to the mist. We watched this Vessel for several hours till we lost sight of her at the south end of "Great Barrier."

Both Assistants saw Blue Lights burning, no doubt from the same Barque, during their watches on the previous night. Had this Barque been off the Lighthouse on the following day nothing could have saved her from being blown seaward by the Strong South-West wind then blowing. In conclusion, allow me to remind you that this is now the second time, since I came here that Pigeons could have been usefully employed in carrying urgent messages to Auckland.[13]

Pigeons were supplied but were of dubious value. When Samuel Hart was at Mokohinau for a few years from 1902, one young keeper smashed his thigh after joy-riding on the trolley (a pastime the department then forbade). 'Not until eleven days had elapsed could we get a pigeon to leave the island.' The keeper displayed remarkable fortitude: '[H]e did not at all lose consciousness when he struck the truck, and he bore his pains while awaiting removal from the island without a murmur. His name was not Lyon for nothing.'[14]

Linked to the telegraph, Fred Erecson, at Cape Egmont in 1904, could play a useful role: I have the honor to inform you that the Barque Onyz passed Cape Egmont 10.30 a.m. on the 15th, from Dunedin to New Plymouth, about a mile off the land with a strong S.E. wind blowing, about 2½ mile past the lighthouse the wind fell to a calm & she was set in so close as to have to anchor. I then asked if she required assistance & was answered yes. I wired the Collector of Customs, New Plymouth, stating the position of the barque and got the answer that the Takapuna was coming down the coast & would render assistance if asked. This she did by towing her about 4 miles off the land.[15]

J. H. C. Conway, Cape Palliser, 1945 reported the aftermath of tragedy: I have to report that a person by name Jack Hale came to my dwelling at about 9 a.m. & said that he was off the "yacht' "Siren" & that she had been wreck on the rocks of the black reef, he informed me that the vessel struck the rocks at about 04.30 & that he got ashore before the light was out, which was about 06.00 he informed me he came ashore in the bay where we land our stores & seeing the landing store & no other building near he got into the landing shed to get warm, he must have been there two or three hours as it was 9 a.m. before he came to my dwelling, when he arrive there he was wet through & cold so I gave him some dry clothes & breakfast & a hot bath after which he went to sleep until about 2.30 p.m., in the meantime I had reported what had happened to the Police at Martinborough & to yourself, Jack Hale informed me that there has been two other men with him on board the yacht by name Fred Haywood & Friz Zimmerman but where they was he didnt know, so the other two men with me, at once went along the beach to look for them but it was not until 11.40 that Mr. R. Robson who was searching to the SE of the light, seen the body of one of the men in the water, then he signalled to me to come & lend him a hand to put the body upon the high water mark, when he went on with the search with Mr H Conway towards white rock but without results at about 3.30 p.m. the Police car being at the sand hill, the body of the dead man & Jack Hale left the station for Featherston or Martinborough The yacht appear to be broken up and the pieces are drifting ashore

The weather during the night was strong NW winds changing to W & SW, with heavy heavy rain visibility moderate & sea mod to rough.[16]

From about 1911 all keepers had to practise Morse and semaphore and know how to use international code flags for both general and emergency communications, but when in 1956 Barry Langman came to Stephens Island, radio had made these skills largely redundant: We sent a message off by semaphore to the tanker *Tania* and they responded by radioing up asking if there was anything wrong! We never had to use the international distress code. We had to sort out three ships on one occasion when heavy sea fog had them within the proximity of the island and they were sounding their fog horns and were working off the echoes. We could see the tops of their masts going through the top of the fog and we radioed them as to which one should go starboard or port. We had to know the regulations for safety of life at sea — the operation of the distress frequency, communication procedures — both for our radio transmitting licence and our signalman's licence, so that was another course we did. We heard of the *Calm* going ashore and we lost one small coaster on Cook Rock between Stephens and Cape Jackson, but the crew of about four just rowed off in their dinghy so they were quite happy. That was the only shipwreck we had while on Stephens. There was nothing we ever had to assist in.

'REPORTS, LETTERS, EXPLANATIONS, LISTS': THE PAPER WORK
As well as the physical work involved in keeping the station up to scratch, principal keepers had to do the station's book work. The monthly reports and other correspondence had to be written, and copied (sometimes by others), into the station letterbook, the bureaucracy dealt with, stores ordered and innumerable forms filled out.

Six days after The Brothers light was commissioned in 1877, James Nelson wrote one of the first letters from that station that must have been woefully ill-equipped when it was commissioned. Here, uniquely, the government provided the keepers' food. The Stella was one of the noted government steamers: I am sorry I omited the salt beef in the list of provisions of the 22nd instant the Stella came here before daylight and in the hurry I put the rong sheet in the envelop

The reason I did not return in the list of Stores the Water, Beef and Butter Casks. Butter Jars and empty Sacks was because they were down at the landing place along with empty cases that I understood was to be taken away by the next trip of the Stella after my arrivel here.

The preserved meat that is here is only 2lb tins there has been 4lb tins at one time I can see by the empties that are lying about.

The Stella arrived here at 5 a.m. on the 8th instant and landing the following articles for use at this station Viz.

35 lbs Mutton
200 lbs Salt Beef
112 lbs Sugar
50 lbs oat-meal
1cwt-1qr-9lbs Potatoes
56 lbs Butter
4 Knives
4 Forks
3 Table Spoons
6 Tea Spoons
1 Tenon Saw
2 Cwt white zinc paint
14 lbs Yellow ochre
3 lbs glue
24 Sheets Sandpaper
1 Weighing Machine,
    The Saucepan and oil can did not come to hand

I have commenced to take meteorological observations this month with the instruments that I have got and if you will be good enough to send some forms by next trip of the [s]teamer visiting this station.

Stores wanted by next trip of the Steamer

1 Sauce pan applied for before
1 Tea Kettle about 5 quarts
1 oil can about 3 gallons
Machine Brushes
Soda & acid
Hops
Matches[17]

J. W. Arthur's list from Waipapa Point in 1917 indicates some routine items:

1 Table Lamp with 1" Burner for P.K. House
1 Hurricane Lantern to replace Old one
6 lbs each 1" 2" 3" Wire nails
12 Linen Ribbons
12 Cotton Ribbons
12 Box wooden Matches
2 Gals. methylated Spirits.
1 Gal. Terebrine
1 Gal Turpentine
3 bags Cement for renewing floor in Asst. washhouse.
2 doz mantles
1 Gal Sperm Oil [this was for oiling the revolving mechanism]
20 Fathoms 2" Rope for making sledge and horse ropes
2 Hanks sewing Twine
1 Ball Binding Twine
4 lbs gum Arabic 2 hand saw Files
1 Tennon File
10 lbs Red Lead
12 Sheets assorted Emery cloth
6 Floor cloths
1 Squat shape Ink stand.
12 lbs whiting.
2 Coir yard Brooms
4 Tins Brasso.
2 Range Rakes.
1 Register for Ass. Range 3' x 9 ½ x 1' 7'½
1 piece Kauri 12' x ½" double dressed for making steadying Rollers.
4 doz ¾" screws
1 Gilpins Slashes
5 Gals Raw Linseed Oil.
4 lbs solder.
1 gal Tin Harness oil.
56 lbs White Zinc.
1 Riding Saddle & Bridle.
6 Prickers
6 Tube Brushers.
2 12' 4" x 1 Kauri for making door to keep flies out of Lightroom at night
1 piece fine gauze 5' x 2' made of copper or Brass
1 Jug

1 Basin & 2 Chambers to replace broken & missing pieces in toilet sets
1 cwt No. 8 Fence Wire
6 lbs Fence Staples 1 gals Tin cement for patching Malthoid Roofs
2 doz Two-monthly absentees Returns
200 No.12 Caps 100 No.12 empty Cartridges
10 lbs No.2 Shot
3 lbs powder [the last three bracketed together 'for shooting Rabbits']
2 Long handle hair Brooms[18]

Forms are an inescapable part of any bureaucracy but they proliferated within the lighthouse world – Anders Hansen reporting the loss of a single piece of paper is indicative of the highly centralised Marine Department. Puysegur Point, November 1885: I beg to state that one of the forms, re birds striking the tower was accidentally made unfit for use through being placed on a ring of Sperm-oil [used as lubrication] from a bottle of oil wich had been standing on the lightroom table. Any birds striking the tower in future I shall enter in a Ledger from wich I can copy on to the proper forms ...

Of the forms for recording birds seen about the station, I shall require a good many seeing that the number of native & acclimatised birds is considerable.

Of acclimatised birds periodically arriving at this Station, I have observed the following variety Skylarks, Starlings, Blackbirds, Goldfinches, Green Linnets, & Sparrows. These birds, I think, arrive via the mountains or highlands, for the reason, that they always comes when snow begins to cover the hills and leaves when the hills are bare.

Anders Hansen (on right) was at Puysegur Point station when in January 1886 F. A. Coxhead photographed the station. The tower, designed by John Blackett, was destroyed by fire some 60 years later.

HOCKEN COLLECTIONS, C/N SHEET 78A/5/A&B

Many of the native birds, go and come at stated intervals, such as the Wekas,[?] Parrakeets, Pidgeons, Tuis, and Hawkes.[19]

By the 1970s principal keepers were doing serious paper work: reports, letters, explanations lists, requests, requisitions; property registers (House, light 1; houses, dwelling 3; houses, fowl 2): log books, weather recording books, weather returns, drum returns, fog returns, reports on signalling arrangements, on septic tanks, on engine exhaust systems, on lightning conductors; reports on what chimneys had been swept, what medicines had been used, absentee reports, earthquake reports; returns on numbers of fowls, cows, heifers, sheep, bulls, steers, wives and children.

This pile of paper was filled out daily, weekly, monthly, bi-monthly, six-monthly, and annually.[20]

Chris Staley: There was a lot of writing, a couple of days a month of constant writing, extra letters to write many times, and then on top of that, of course, telegrams were the main means of communicating with head office. Most days we sent telegrams about something; a lot of it was to do with ordering things that we needed, and what have you. What was ridiculous, someone had a plan to reduce the number of forms used. And guess what? At the end of the month I had an extra form to fill in saying that I didn't require any more forms!

I even remember having a go at the mechanical supervisor over it. Every month I had to send these things in with the monthly report. One was for daily maintenance on the diesel engines. I had to tick little boxes and I said, 'Isn't this bloody ridiculous that one box I had to tick to say that the fuel tank had been pumped up that day?' If you didn't pump the fuel tank up the bloody diesel would stop anyway. I personally believe it was to keep somebody happy at head office, keep them in a job.

Keepers had to fill in fish, as well as the bird, forms but Anders Hansen made other contributions to mapping the country's flora and fauna. Hansen, Cape Palliser, August 1910: Re report of Curator of Portobello Fish Hatchery in which he mentions that had been unable to procure hapuka spawn, I would beg to state here, that while at Puysegur Point I was told by a Maori from Riverton that the hapuka spawned at the head of Preservation Inlet. If he told me at what time of year I do not now remember it. I think the maoris name was Jock Arnet, but cannot be quite sure.[21]

Hansen, Cape Palliser, February 1912: I have the honour to forward, under separate cover, a parcel containing a specimen of tussock found growing on a small patch of sandy & stony soil (but well watered by a spring), half-way between here and White Rock, about thirty feet above the sea, and distant therefrom a few chains.

I shall deem it a great favour, if you, Sir, will be so good as to give the specimen to Dr Kirk, Biologist to the Agricultural Department, asking him to be good enough to identify it.

It's peculiarity, to me, lays in its colour, which, (if it does not fade) you will see is reddish or crimson. The patch is only about a quarter of an acre in extent, but quite conspicuous. From inquiries made among the people living here, this peculiar grass or reed is not found growing anywhere else in the district.

Will you kindly let me know what Dr Kirk says about it?[22]

Occasionally other keepers reported unusual natural phenomena. H. B. Jamieson, Farewell Spit, 1948: Re my telegram of yesterday. Keeper Foster, after sending his midday weather, told me he saw broken water off shore, so I went up to the tower with him to have a look. There was a disturbance of the sea in a NNE direction from the tower, and about 2 miles offshore, or maybe further ... On Sunday the 8th we had a strong NW wind with rough seas, during the night the wind changed to SW and gradually decreased to a slight sea. What drew our attention was the fact of a disturbed sea surrounded by smooth water although the sea was rough right out the horizon, it being an off-shore wind. The disturbed area was local and did not seem to be coming with the tide. Anyway I thought it as well to be on the safe side and sent you in a report.[23]

Farewell Spit, with the tower bottom centre, 1948. In 1867 lighthouse engineer James Balfour noted the end of the Spit was 'some four miles' (about 6.4 km) from the lighthouse; in 2000 it was 8.5 km from the lighthouse. Measurements of cadastral boundaries since 1938 show the Spit has grown about 15 metres a year and in a northeasterly, rather than inwards, direction. ANZ (WGTN) ABPL 8848 W5221 ALBUM D

CHAPTER 5

Maintaining the station

There was a great deal more to maintaining the station than work on the tower and its associated equipment. R. S. Wilson, Cape Brett, 1927: Painted P/keepers roofs of dwelling, Wash-house and Fowl-house with one coat Red Oxide.

Also painted the Wash-house and Fowl-house and gates with one coat of White Zinc. The Oil Engine has been cleaned out, crank case emptied and fresh supply of Oil put in. The Crane has also received attention and the wire rope coated with Stockholm Tar and Goods for Shipment put ready for the Tutanekai.

… started work on tram-line repair Wednesday 29th June. Where the sleepers have been laid bare, I have had these tommed with timber, that I had gathered from the old whim. Stops to prevent the earth from being washed away down the hill have been placed at intervals across the wash-out holding back the and allowing the water to percolate through.[1]

A view of Cape Saunders station from the track up from the landing. In 1957 the tower, damp and running with rust, was replaced with a pre-fabricated galvanised structure, and in 1967 with the concrete and rolled steel structure. That in turn has recently been replaced by a low-maintenance rectangular metal structure.

HANSEN COLLECTION

J. D. Auld's list from Cape Saunders in 1940 identifies other jobs the keepers might expect to do — though even his list is not exhaustive. Horses, still on some stations in the 1950s, had to be shod; signal halyards on signal stations were checked; schoolrooms had to be repaired; water tanks cleaned out and limed; and when from the 1950s septic tanks were finally installed, they too needed the occasional clean. The coal sacks Auld mentions held some 70 pounds, and on boat day empties had to be returned — darned, cleaned, folded and packed nine to a bag in the proper fashion: Keepers have been employed during the month with the following duties: Signal practise, Repairing boundary fence, clearing Hedge clippings, repairing coal sacks, Painting Bathroom & scullery both dwellings, weeding & cleaning garden & paths both dwellings, clearing grass etc from fence P.K.'s. Swept A.K's chimney Aug 27th painting rust spots on Tower & A.K's dwelling, sharpening & repairing tools chipping iron grating Lt. Room, digging drains to take surface water away from tower, painting mantelpiece A.K's.[2]

Alan Martin, newly arrived to the lighthouse service in 1962, recalled the daily routine for moving through this steady round of work: There's a new keeper on station — that's me — so all three keepers have half an hour or so semaphore, signal practice, whatever. The principal keeper would get out the book of rules and regulations pertaining to keepers and he would read out certain paragraphs so we understood exactly what we were allowed to do and what we were not allowed to do — these were standing orders. He was training me up of course, this is what principal keepers did. And then he'd say, we're cleaning out the ditches, or we're doing painting, or we're doing this and that's what we did. We'd knock off at 12 till one – 12 o'clock was the midday weather of course – we'd go down and have lunch and then we'd start again until three or until the job was finished depending on what we're doing. Sometimes we'd work later.

Weather played an important part in determining what tasks were done when. Chris Staley: Of course you're under strictures from the weather. If the weather is bad you do indoor maintenance, if the weather is good you do outdoor maintenance. The paths have to be cleaned regularly so you can walk up and down safely, you have to maintain the railway track, and the crane had to be serviced on a regular basis, because it's very important when you're lifting human cargo to make sure these things are in good nick.

Jo Broom was brought up in the Lighthouse Service. In August 1949 her husband joined the Service and they were posted to Centre Island for two or three years, then to Puysegur Point to 1954, Cape Reinga to 1957, and to Moeraki. They resigned in 1959 and went to England, where Les had been born. As principal keeper at Cape Reinga, Les developed a different work pattern: The whole of these jobs is planning. Now, when I was up north, I'd go like hell for the first three months or two months, get all the blimmin' jobs done, then knock off for another three months. You can sit on your bum and do what you want to do, go fishing, as long as someone stayed behind to do the weather.

The men on The Brothers, without women to do for them, had to incorporate housework into the daily routines. Chris: There used to be a roster for the three of us. If you were duty cook you would get up around seven'ish and take over at eight o'clock. You had to do the cooking, the housework, and the weather reporting every hour. Now that takes a bit of time, you know. We used to have to send synoptic weather reports – cloud, sea conditions, wind, everything – every three hours and short aero reports every hour. They were used mainly for the planes coming in. Anyway, the duty cook did that up until 6 p.m. (actually I used to send the last report at six) and he'd have to get up at five o'clock because the first aero report had to go in at five minutes to five. He would stay on to get the breakfast ready until eight o'clock, and then the next guy who was going to be duty cook would take over at eight o'clock. Apart from the cook, the other two used to work in the morning until around lunchtime; afternoons were always kept free. General maintenance, painting, cleaning, maintaining machinery, all the diesel engines had to be serviced every day, pump the fuel up, check them, we used to change the engines over every morning at a set time. We had three, of course. The full maintenance was always done by mechanics from the Marine Department.

THE LIGHTHOUSE RESERVES

Each station stood on reserved land acquired, mostly through the Public Works Act, ostensibly to ensure access to the station and to allow the keepers to grow their vegetables and have a supply of fresh meat and dairy products. In fact, considerably more land than was needed was often taken. The work involved in maintaining the reserves was considerable.

In the exposed lighthouse stations shelter was critical, though the loss of records makes it difficult to assess how systematically planting was attempted at all stations, or its success. Later photos at Cape Egmont station show big flax bushes round the station houses, not the pines that Norman Simpson so laboriously helped plant. In this official report, Norman Simpson's private tragedy is almost an aside: [O]n the 8th received an Official Letter relating to 100 Pine trees 15 received a Telegram from the Collector of Customs to Inform me that the Pines would be at Pungarehu that day also Informing me that the

Les Broom (right), first assistant keeper John Hayes and an unidentified visitor in the Cape Reinga engine room, late 1950s.
LES AND JO BROOM

Pines had been some days out of the ground & that they were to be Planted as soon as possible. I brought the trees to the Station on the Morning of the 16 having to get the use of a Neighbour's Cart to do so. I beg to inform you that all the Taproots of the Trees were closely cut off very little roots being left the Trees were at once Planted in the gardens as the ground had been got ready for them at present the trees are very withered the Weather has been very severe much Frost & strong S.E Wind I beg to Inform you that the Spirits of Wine has only been used for cleaning the Lenses & Lantern glass Everything in the Lightroom in the Winter is very wet & without Spirits of Wine we could never keep the Lenses clean throughout the summer Months The Lightroom is infested with Flies & Moths so that it is necessary to use Spirits of Wine A party of A. C men [the Armed Constabulary had been stationed at the Cape during the lighthouse construction during the invasion and destruction of Parihaka and remained there during the repressive measures that followed] have begun to repair the Paddock Fence for some months past the Fence has been destroyed through Native Pigs The Paddock has been overrun with Native Horses & Cattle I have been given to understand that there is to be 10 acres securely fenced their is part of ground unsuitable for Cutting Sods for Bank Fences it is next to impossible to keep out Native Horses more so during the summer months

21st Watson Simpson Died Disease of the Spine Age 4 Years
Received 1 Copy of Marine Report[3]

European notions of productive land use were at odds with some perceived Maori patterns of usage and these exercised keepers at Cape Egmont. In 1889 Robert McIver reported that a Mr Rutherford, who was growing a commercial flax crop on the reserve, worried that, if the reserve is not fenced in it will not grow again, as the Reserve is overrun with Native horses and they will eat the young Flax as it comes up.[4]

In 1897 Te Whitu, a Maori chief, had for some time occupied part of the lighthouse reserve. Charles Tregurtha complained that the Maori made no attempt to halt the spread of gorse and he wanted the government to take over some of the land again so the keepers could feed and water their horses and cows: If we turn them out on the beach to find their own way to the creek, they are liable to be impounded.[5]

In 1907 Edward Wilson, supporting Mr Quickenden's request for use of the land, wrote: I have been given to understand that the Department gave use of a part of this reserve to a Native by paying a rental for it this Native has died sometime ago and since then several of the Natives lay claim to it they make very little use of it only for growing a few kumaras and are letting it get over run with Gorse.[6]

On Portland Island in 1881, where Maori land also adjoined the lighthouse reserve, Charles Robson, father of our diarist, worried about Maori and the reserve for different reasons: During the last month grass seed has been sown and raked in during damp weather and good deal of it is up but I find that the soil is so light and sandy that the high winds blow it away from the seed and then remove the seed also the rake not being able to penetrate deep enough a light harrow is much needed and indeed a plough also suitable for one horse with these I could get all the reserve into good grass and grow enough oats for the horse. The natives will not now sell us any sheep as they want the wool and we are unable to procure any from Mr. Walker except at shearing time since I came to the Island [the previous month] … we have been quite without fresh meat, if you will send me wire and standards with a few posts, sufficient to make 28 chains of fence I could enclose the whole of the Government land except the cliff sides and we could then keep enough sheep to supply us with meat, at present the sheep belonging to the Natives come round the ends of the fence and eat all the grass. At foot of monthly return I give a list of what is required to fill up the medicine chest though I hope you will send me the larger size asked for in my last letter amongst the other things in my list you will see 3 oz liquid ammonia I have to ask for this as there are a large number of Katipos in the drift wood which we use for fuel.

The Maori portion of this island is fast becoming overgrown by the cottonwood scrub and great care will have to be taken to prevent its overrunning the Lighthouse reserve I am now destroying all the old plants but young ones from seed are coming up very thickly in order to keep them down please send me a short-bladed scythe and a scythe stem.[7]

In 1936 at Baring Head where Mr Riddiford, the local land-owner, had donated the land for the lighthouse, keepers had to use Riddiford's land to graze their cows. The cows, R. S. Wilson reported, could wander: [Keepers lost] time spent in locating them; both morning and evening. To add further to our inconvenience, Mr Riddiford has placed 30 head of young stock on the terraces with our cows, and it is almost impossible to run milking cows under these conditions.

The land attached to the Lighthouse is taken up by the plantation and residential quarters, and the remainder is barren and waste, and owing to this I respectfully ask that another block of grass land be procured, adjoining the present reserve. This would ensure the Keepers independence, as the present arrangements are absolutely impracticable.[8]

Elsewhere keepers battled against introduced pests. At Cape Palliser in 1898 P. J. Vayle found that without rabbit-proof fencing the large number of rabbits made it impossible to grow any vegetables.[9] On Cuvier Island in the mid-1950s they shot goats. But rabbits were the main problem. By the early twentieth century, letterbooks, departmental reports and memoirs document rabbits in almost plague numbers at Waipapa Point, Cape Campbell and Castlepoint.

A 1965 view of Stephens Island station from the top of the tower — a community whose neatness and order contrasts with the drama of the setting. ATL: 92924½

J. H. C. Conway's report from Farewell Spit in 1935 identified a common problem: [T]he rabbit menace is spreading rapidly, great increase being noted even since my appointment, In addition stoats & weasels are fairly numerous and rats are very troublesome also wild cats.[10]

By the 1950s, on Stephens Island and without those introduced pests, Barry Langman remembered: We were fully and gainfully employed for the whole time we were there. Another job — we had no control over the station bull. When it came time to milk the bull would follow the cows into the shed and create a menace, chase the keepers' wives. We decided to divide the island into two main paddocks. That involved us in several weeks work as well, bringing all the posts and wire and batteries in on the launch and then laying them out on the fence line. It

was probably the most educative period of my life. What I learned there set me up as an entrepreneur for later on. If you didn't do it yourself it didn't get done. You had to be self-sufficient and you had to do some things that you may not have been prepared to tackle in ordinary life on the mainland.

The station work meant an investment of time and energy that could make transferring something of a wrench. In 1894 Alexander Parks pleaded poignantly against a transfer from Nugget Point to Puysegur Point, in part because of having to leave his hard-won garden behind: With reference to your Memo of the 14th. inst. informing me of your decision to move me to Puysegur Point, I must earnestly implore you to reconsider it, for it has brought dismay and misery to an otherwise happy and contented family.

In asking you to allow me to remain a few more years at this Station, please permit me to point out, that it is by no means an unreasonable request, as Principal Keepers have, (that is, Keepers with families and long years of service) frequently been allowed to remain at their Stations, for seven, eight, and ten years and in the belief that I am also a servant of long standing (and have never had any leave of absence, even for a single week, during twenty years of service) have gone to much expence and labour to establish myself and make a comfortable home, feeling sure that I should have a long stay to enjoy it.

The move to any Station means a considerable pecuniary loss to me, but to be sent to Puysegur after only four years at this station, during which time I have taken so much pains and labour to improve it, that dozens of old settlers that have known this Lighthouse since it was built, have remarked "My

ABOVE LEFT *A photo of Alexander Parks in 1879, about the time he became principal keeper at Akaroa Head. Born in 1847 in England, Parks joined the Merchant Navy and met his wife-to-be in 1865 while crewing on an immigrant ship. Nine years later they married and he became assistant keeper at Godley Head. After his promotion to Akaroa, he was transferred first to Taiaroa Head in 1885, then to Nugget Point in 1890, from where he made the much-protested move to Puysegur Point.* BETTY BENJAMIN

ABOVE RIGHT *The first house at Nugget Point, half of which was home for Alexander Parks and his family. Today the site is the car park for the thousands that walk along the now carefully fenced path to the tower.* ALAN AND SHIRLEY MARTIN

word I hardly know the old place, it is so much improved since I saw I last", would leave me a crushed and broken-spirited man.

When I came to this Station, after it had been one for twenty years, there was not even a garden. I have made myself a large garden on top of the high hill, where I could have a commanding view of vessels signalling to be reported. Prior to this, there had been frequent complaints of no notice being taken of their signals.

I now know most of the steamers passing here at sight and they get promptly reported by telegram to Dunedin. No troublesome complaints.

This garden is well stocked with gooseberry bushes, strawberry plants, rhubarb, early potatoes, peas and other vegetables. Am I so soon to be torn from all this and let another step in — and that other a bachelor — my junior in years and length of service?

In full assurance that you have not the least desire to use your authority unjustly, I cannot but believe you will withdraw the order for me to move.

My family await your answer in tears.[11]

Sadly, he was sent to Puysegur Point, where he died in 1896. The department, with a compassion it rarely showed, awarded his widow, Hannah, a year's salary and made his eldest son, Edward, temporary probationary assistant keeper at the station.

In 1956 Barry Langman was transferred from Stephens Island to Portland Island: Portland Island was a bit of a disappointment in that having spent all the time at Stephens Island painting, scrapping, refurbishing the houses, building fences, covering the wildlife such as tuataras and that — to arrive at Portland Island

and find a drought-stricken piece of land with no grass and no water, the cows were not in calf because there was no bull there and consequently we had no milk, we had no butter, and the gardens were in a run-down condition because the fences had broken down and the wild stock running on the island had destroyed the gardens, and the water supply as such – it was contaminated with dead sheep lying in it and that had to be cleaned out. And the station, apart from the new powerhouse, was in a rundown condition. To me it was a penalty. After doing all the work at Stephens I thought they must be sending me here for a punishment to start all over again.

STORMS AND SLIPS

Violent gales, extremely boisterous weather, severe storms — the letterbooks up and down the country are littered with such phrases. The result of such weather could be havoc. In 1895 P. I. Henaghan catalogued the work needed in the aftermath of a storm at Stephens Island: I have the honor to inform you that on the night of the 13TH when blowing a violent gale, the Sea washed away a portion of the tramway addjacent to the block, three lengths of rails and sleepers were displaced, and one of the wooden stays which support the derrick snapped in two, one portion of it was carried away & the bolt that secured it to the rock was broken. This storm which lasted for about four days was the Severest I felt since I came to the Colony . . .

Since the storm passed away we have repaired (or rather replaced) the break in the tramway and is now workable, but owing to the hand rails at the bottom being swept away, what we have done is only temporary.

In order that this may not occur again it will be necessary to have the sleepers embedded in concrete and bolted to the solid rock, to a distance of seventy feet past the block, the rails to be clamped together to the same distance, when this is done no sea can wash it away.[12]

Barry remembered the work after another storm, again on Stephens Island: There was some bush – I've seen it referred to as the Ruston Bush – on one part of the island; there was the area of bush immediately behind the first assistant's house and the principal keeper's, which consisted mainly of ngaio and taupata; and the rest of the island had odd patches of low coastal trees but mainly heavy grass. The island was divided in half with one long fence put in to keep the stock out of the main conservation reserve. I remember we had one particularly heavy rainfall when four inches of rain fell in four hours. It caused 26 slips. Now the slips that occurred all happened, except for one, in the reserve area because the land was not consolidated by tramping feet of cattle. The reserve had many many burrows from the dove petrels and it allowed the water to

One of the houses at Kaipara North, with the sand building up round it, an image that contrasts extraordinarily with earlier ones of the first houses, surreally planted on flat dunes. Reports have it that a boy was often employed to dig the drifts away. Unsurprisingly, after a short time the wives and families all lived at Poutu, with the men taking turns to overnight at the light.

HANSEN COLLECTION

go into the subsoil and to float off the rock or clay base underneath. Consequently it carried a lot of debris down through the winch tracks and we had to free all that up and get the rails back into position.

Cape Campbell station houses and the tower, built at the end of end of papa cliffs that stretch well back into Cloudy Bay. The hillock shows the fretting of the soil.

ATL: 92152½

Few records now remain of station life at Kaipara Heads or on Motuopao where the shifting sands of the great dunes could pile up drifts up three metres high round the buildings, or undermine others. But all over New Zealand, clearance of unstable soils meant land only too prone to slip. The lighthouse stations were no exception and the papa soils at East Island, Cape Campbell, Portland Island and Puysegur Point fretted and broke in drought and turned into mudflows in wet weather. While the keepers' accounts of the slipping on Portland Island and Cuvier Island below are some of the more dramatic, slips and the work entailed were a fact of life on almost all stations.

Lighthouse history, too, can also often open windows on other aspects of history. J. W. Cunningham's report on a huge slip on Portland Island in 1880 shows Maori actively engaged in local commerce: I have the honor to State that owing to the bad weather of late the Mouris have been unable to come over to the station for letters etc, it has been blowing & raining for Some days & nights with[out] stopping and it do not appear as if it was going to take up yet.

On the night of the 19th inst a tremendous Land Slip occurred on the N.W. Side of the Island Carrying Seven Mouri Wharries in its descent also a large whale boat, the Lighthouse Boat has met with the Same fate only a few pieces of either boats are to be seen, there is now about 20 foot of clay rocks flax etc where the Huts Stood no Mouris were in the Huts at the time or would have perished they left the "Howiru" a few days before it happened they were to have called for Several tons of dried fish which they were gong to take in their Boat to Poverty Bay. The road on the N.E. Side of the Island

The lighthouse station on Motuopao, on which the Cape Maria van Diemen light was built, was also notorious for drifting sand. Note, too, the long tramway up which all the fuel and any materials needed for the light were winched — by hand. AM WINKELMANN COLLECTION DU436.1111/C32, NEG. NO.1097

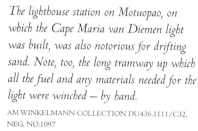

East Island station. In 1920 Captain Bollons reported that the island was gradually slipping away, that a further large fissure had opened a while before from the back of the tower, which had further subsided, and that it was only a matter of time before the station would have to be moved. Keepers and families, Bollons noted, were 'nervous and discontented'; staffing the station was difficult 'as keepers dread [it] owing to the unstableness of the land surface, the risky nature of the landing and the irregularity of the mail'. Two years later, the station was moved to a new site on East Cape. ATL: F12321L

has completely Slipped away, and the zig zag road on the North end of the Island has slipped away considerably in fact I can scarcely say yet whether we will be able to make it fit for the Horse to come up or not as it is not Safe to go near the face of the hill as it is [indecipherable] in a great mess, all round the Island is alike more or less, the ground about the Lt.house appears to be all right as far as I can see I find that the Slip was caused by a small creek on the top of the Island.[13]

A twentieth-century view of the Cuvier Island houses. The slip so recontoured the land that it is now impossible to see where the first homes were build. A railway, which enabled goods to be landed at Fairchild Bay, runs down to the bottom right. ATL: 112252½

Cape Palliser lighthouse, May 1911, and the fence to which the debris from the storm was washed. HANSEN COLLECTION

Edward R. Wilson, Cuvier Island, June 1893: I have to inform you that on the 7th Instant we had an easterly gale, with heavy rain which caused the hill at the back of Principal's dwelling to slip. It has filled the yard at back of dwelling, up level with window, and halfway up the water cisterns, also coal shed is blocked, there is no way of getting around the back at present as it is completely blocked. The bank in front of house has also slipped into the garden, there is also a slip come down at the back of 1st Assistants house blocking up the passage at end also, various other slips along the road to lighthouse. *He estimated repairs would take one man and the keepers three months, provided there was no more heavy rain.[14]*

Over the next four months and battered by another flood that brought down a large slip and badly damaged the tramway, the keepers worked steadily to move the slip — while the assistant's family apparently continued to live in the house. After about three months head office sent someone to help.

At French Pass the light had only just begun to function before the first lot of heavy, clayey soil came down; at Cape Palliser in 1910, Anders Hansen reported severe rain that brought down huge quantities of detritus from the watercourses on this hillside which in several places overran our fences, burying them nearly to the top.[15]

However, the Puysegur Point access road from the landing to the station had a notoriety of its own. Fred Erecson wrote the first report from the station on 14 September 1878: Sir! I have the Honour to inform you that I have in compliance with your instruction dated July the 17th 1878, taken charge of this Station. We landed on the 8th of August, since then the weather has been very wet & owing to it and the bad state of the road it has taken us (with the exception of a few odd jobs) to present date to get the stores etc to the station.

… I have found a place where I can get a large quantity of sandstone for the road, there is to much of a decline for the cart but I can easy lay down a temporary wooden tramway to connect it with the road if you would please to send me the truck wheels etc mentioned in my requisition. I would be obliged if sent by first opportunity.[16]

Five months later, with the light about to be commissioned, Erecson and his men were wearying: We have been chiefly employed at carting sand and metalling the road, since my last report, but it is such a long distance we have to cart, that it is but slow work – everything is ready for lighting up to morrow night.[17]

May 1880 and he was considerably disgruntled: I have the honor to inform you, that owing to the very heavy rainfalls we have had during this month (on one occasion close on 6 inches fell within twelve hours & on another 5.45 inches) our road has been completely blocked up by landslips, in one plase the whole sideling has come down & about a thousand yards of stuff is lodged on the road besides several smaller ones in different plases. We have had very hard work, and long hours, on this station ever since we arrived here, and to all appearance here is nothing but hard work before us. We have often to work in very bad weather besides being tormented with thousands of sandflies while working. Therefore I hope sir! That you will kindly grant us a rise of salary for each of us is doing our very best to deserve it.[18]

Fifteen years later Alexander Parks and his men, still being eaten by sandflies, still beset by the weather, continued the battle with the road on Puysegur Point. (A 'fascine' was a long pole used for engineering purposes, in this case attempting to provide firm base on which to build the road): We have cut large quantities of T-tree and fascined many chains of the road in the worst places, but it is dreary work trying to keep this road in order. There is no bottom to it and the weather has been very severe.[19]

Parks wrote about the impact of the work on keeper Andreas Sandager, to whose predicament he was obviously sympathetic – was this an attempt to get him off this 'punishment station'? I am of opinion that [Sandager's] health is now sufficient grounds to justify his removal to an easy Station. Without doubt, he would be fit to perform the necessary duties – less the road work and felling bush for firewood, this time. He can not work so vigorously as Assistant Keeper Semmens and myself and he informed me he has had to use an instrument for years past when making water.[20]

The never-ending roadwork at Puysegur Point took its toll. Andreas Sandager, 1896: I very much regret to learn that Mr Parks' illness terminated fatally. In him the Department has lost a good servant who never spared himself. Working as we have been for the last couple of years – practically night and day – could

Andreas Fremming Steward Sandager was born in Denmark in 1851. When and why he came to New Zealand is unknown, but he joined the lighthouse service and went to The Brothers as probationary keeper in 1881. After time at Tiri, Mokohinau, and Moeraki, where he became principal keeper, he was transferred to Centre Island in 1894. There he had problems with a settler, William Campbell, whom the department was attempting, unavailingly, to evict from the island; worse, Sandager was charged with drunkenness, being unfit for duty and being absent without leave — charges he denied and which rankled for a long time.

He was demoted to assistant keeper and sent to Puysegur Point in 1895. There one of his daughters met, and later married, Edward Parks. In 1904, having spent all the intervening years at Puysegur Point, Sandager retired on compensation from the lighthouse service and died in Invercargill on 5 June that year, aged 53.

BETTY BENJAMIN

not but be injurious to any constitution and if it did not cause it, certainly aggravated his illness. The task thrown on Keepers of maintaining — rather re-making — two and a half miles of road is mainly responsible for this, and anyone with the faintest idea of work can not but admit it is a case — not making bricks without straw but without clay, and no set of Keepers, even if they worked all night as well as all day will be able to permanently improve such a piece of road. In spite of all that can be done the work will keep on increasing for the obvious reason that the corduroy — laid down nearly throughout its whole length — keeps on decaying leaving the road without bottom, ready to engulf all the fascines of various makes that can be dropped in.

Sandager went on to suggest: [A] light tramway could without great difficulty, or expense be brought up the Wilsons River track.[21]

The work was still going on in 1917 when A. V. Pearce, suffering the effects of an earlier accident and at times in considerable pain, wrote: I might mention I have never given in with the pain or missed a watch in fact I cant remain idol I must be doing something but I am wondering if the continual heavy work as cutting bush for firewood and road work is rather much for me and thought I had better mention it to you, although I like this station as well as any I have been too, at a future date you may be able to place me at one not quite so heavy trusting my explanation is satisfactory.[22]

He continued to do heavy lifting despite a nasty illness, then cared for a wounded and ill miner four months later (see page 195), until his transfer to Somes Island about a year later in April 1918.

Nugget and Waipapa Points were two stations where questions arose over whether certain road maintenance was the department's responsibility or the county council's. At Nugget Point the issue simmered on well after S. F. Rayner's request in 1898: On the afternoon of the 30th a large slip came down on the road between landing store and lighthouse reserve. I telegraphed particulars to you, thinking that you might apply to the Clutha County Council for assistance to clear it away the same as you did before.

The road immediately on the other side landing store, generally called McKinlays road, is in a wretched condition and quite impassable for horse or cart, when fetching the horse feed home, as the sea was too rough to bring it round by boat to landing store by boat, it had to be carted through 3 or 4 sacks at a time and then we had to dig the cart out every now and again, since then large slips have come down, and, as I said before, the road is quite impassable …

The po[r]tion of the road I telegraphed about has I believe always been kept in order by the keepers at this station, except when a slip came down onto it, when, (I am informed) used Council men to assist in removing it.

It will take the keepers along time to remove the slip as the days are so short and the lighthouse duties have to be attended to.[23]

In 1928 a disgruntled H. E. Jamieson battled constantly with a portion of the Waipapa Point road to try to ensure cart access: The road between this corner and where the gravel ends, is in a disgusting state. The mud is a foot thick in places and the horse takes all his time to pull the empty cart through it. Our children have to ride through this sea of mud every day on their way to and from school. It is a public road and in summer thousands of visitors pass over it in motor cars and I think it is time some money was spent on it.[24]

BOAT DAY

Boat day, when the lighthouse steamers, or the other ships chartered in their stead, arrived with bulk provisions, brought news of the outside world and, if keepers were transferring, new faces. It also brought hard, sometimes dangerous, work.

Landing at The Brothers, as we have seen, was often a tribute to both ships' crews and keepers. In 1881 Thomas Frost, first assistant keeper, reported losing an 'entire Case of Preserved meats'. The steamer had arrived late, and bad weather had forced a change in landings: [I]t was almost dark before Keeper Davis & I commenced moving the stores to a place above high-water mark. I fell down while doing so, through not being able to see my foothold & the case which I was carrying rolled into the sea, myself only narrowly escaping following as the incline is very steep there.[25]

In 1882 there was a further loss: The *Stella* arrived between 4 & 4.30 p.m. on the 19th ... By 5.30 we had everything safe on the upper landing except for 7 bags of coal when it became quite impossible & unsafe to remain below owing to the darkness and the increasing size & frequency of the seas which were sweeping the landing. We were therefore only able to pile them on the ledge of rocks behind the derrick above high-water mark; notwithstanding this the sea broke so high upon the rocks during the night that all 7 were carried away by 9 next morning. The Keg of Beef was not landed and but 3 cwt of Potatoes. I have only put down 38 ruby glasses [for the small red auxiliary light that shone out over Cook Rock] as received because when Mr Acherson & I unpacked the case we found that 8 had broken in transit.[26]

Alexander Parks' dignified and quietly assertive response in 1895 to head office reprimands graphically illustrates the practical problems attending boat day at Puysegur Point of which head office (again) seemed unaware: With reference to your Memo No. 670/82 of the 25th ultimo, I bet to express my regret if some stores were damaged owing, as Capt Fairchild alleges to keepers not being at the landing place in time to help when the first boat landed, and my assistants & I are probably

A 1960s shot of the steep incline at The Brothers up which stores were winched.
GEORGE GIBBS

the greatest loosers in the matter. As I was not present when the first boat landed it is useless for me to dispute his assertion – but as matter of fact stores got wet in other boats when keepers were present. There was a nasty swell running up the beach among the stores before they could be got away. It was also raining.

I am of the opinion that stores would frequently be landed in a better condition were the boats not so deeply loaded when sent away from the ship's side.

With regard to the concluding sentences of your memo you may certainly trust Sir that I shall endeavour in future as I have done for many years past to be at the landing place with all reasonable despatch when stores are to be landed by the LtHouse tender; but at this Station during a portion of the year – from about the middle of April to the middle of August – Light-keepers can not reasonably be expected to be at the landing place before 9 a.m. without fail, and I would respectfully ask that you may be pleased to fix this as the time for keepers to be there when stores are landed during that period – during other portions of the year when it is daylight earlier, Keepers could get to the landing place earlier providing they are aware of the steamer being in the Inlet – but it frequently occurs that her whistle and even Siren can not make them aware of her presence owing to the roar of the wind and the surf[?] at the Station. 8.30 a.m. is too early to expect the keepers to be down on wet dark mornings remembering what a long bad road (the first beach well nigh impracticable under certain conditions of wind and tide to get the horse and cart along it) they have to traverse. On one occasion I am informed it took 30 diggers three hours to clear away large boulders and huge logs, thrown across the track by the heavy seas before the cart could be got round Rocky Point. On the morning in question the sea was in the cart and the horse only able to keep his legs with difficulty.[27]

By 1927 Dog Island keepers had complained repeatedly about the station boat, too heavy for the rocky steep landing and leaking due to dry rot. In May that year they must have felt their warnings justified: R. Haven: I regret to have to report that the station boat has been damaged owing to overturning on the boulders while attempting to land the mail yesterday April 30th. Owing to a bad easterly swell running along the beach and not straight on the beach, it made it very hard for the keepers to handle to boat. The boat was got off alright but in coming back again … a huge wave came up and lifted her up on to the boulders overturning her with myself underneath. The boat struck with such force that her stem was broken at the bow; she is also cracked in a couple of places … her bow is lying open on the starboard side having sprung from the stem.

Sir, I might add that a nasty accident was narrowly averted as when I was jammed under the boat I was cut on the head just above the right ear by a blow which might have knocked me unconscious I am also bruised on the right knee and right forearm. at midnight when going on watch I was so

An aerial view of Dog Island in 1967. Then goods and supplies were landed on the long beach where the Martins remember the gradient as easy. Did the earlier keepers use another beach? ALAN AND SHIRLEY MARTIN

A view of the relatively recently restored graveyard at Puysegur Point February 2008. The small grave is Ruth Pullen's (no other details are given); three of the remaining five are of Cromarty men who drowned in April 1895 when their boat overturned on the reef. James Cromarty's body was recovered at once and buried. The other two were found only two months later some way down the Sound. Alexander Parks and his keepers had to put their remains in coffins and tow them back for burial — the smell was too dreadful to have the coffins in the boat. BILL MEGENNIS

sore and stiff I could hardly drag myself up the stairs in the lighthouse. I could not get out from under the boat until Asst. Keeper with the help of the two women Mrs. Williams & Mrs Haven lifted the boat off the top of me. In doing so the two women got their shins badly bruised with the boat striking them and knocking them down. Needless to say almost everything in the boat got badly saturated with water. A 70lb bag of sugar belonging to the Asst. Keeper was completely ruined, that being the only total loss that I know of. I beg to add that the launch came at a very bad state of the tide being one hour from high water with the tide on the flood and the swell at its very worst The mail man has been asked repeatedly not to come just before high water as it is almost impossible for two men to handle a boat at that state of the tide.[28]

When Chris Staley was appointed to The Brothers the keepers were regularly rotated off the rock. Married men had homes to go to, though that was not paid leave; Chris, single and without a home in New Zealand, was among the first to use the time off as a paid reliever at other stations. He was at Puysegur Point when the government steamer Wairoa provisioned the station. Travelling overnight from Bluff, it would arrive in the early morning. On this occasion the wind was rising steadily. We decided we'd give it a go, get stuff through the reef — the reef is just a few yards from the shore but you've got to get through to get out into Preservation Inlet. There's a gap and it's quite dicey at times in bad weather.

There's a small graveyard alongside the beach of people who've perished on that reef. A new keeper was coming on to take over the station, they wanted to get him ashore. So they towed the first surfboat in through the gap in the reef — the motorboat has to tow the surfboat. During the towing process the propeller touched the reef, and got damaged. Anyway, we unloaded the first boat which had the new keeper on and most of his personal belongings. Then they decided they would get another load, but going back through the reef something else happened to the motorboat and it became totally disabled. In the strong wind it was heading off down Preservation Inlet out to sea. So the Wairoa fired a rocket launcher — they have these rocket launchers on the bridge that carry a line — beautiful shot, it landed right across the surfboat and the motorboat. The guys were able to haul themselves back to the Wairoa. But with the motorboat disabled, I was in a rather invidious position of having a relieving keeper on the beach, his gear gone in the surfboat, he was supposed to go too. The only recourse left was to take out the station dinghy — which was about a 14-footer. There was a gale blowing by this stage in Preservation Inlet. But we managed to get out to the Wairoa and get this guy off, and took off back to the beach. Willy waws, little mini-whirlwinds, were chasing around and I could see that one was probably going to catch me in the reef. I thought,

The entrance in the reef at the station's landing beach, Puysegur Point.
ANZ (WGTN) ABPL 8848 W5221 ALBUM D, P.54

well, I'm not going to end up in the graveyard too. So I just opened the motor flat out and roared straight through the gap in the reef and straight up the beach! Better a wrecked boat than a dead lighthouse keeper.

Care was always critical. Alan Martin: You've got to be very careful, especially if you were lifting stuff out of a dinghy. At one stage on Cuvier the boat came underneath – this particular gantry or derrick was motorised. We could lift, we could slew. We just got a couple of drums lifted out and the guy driving the boat took off forward and damn near took his head off because I couldn't get the drums up quick enough and they slewed to one side. We got away with it that time but it could be a bit tricky. It was all right when the empties were going back 'cause you just threw them into the sea and the men on the tender vessel had to fish them out.

The aftermath of boat day was long hours moving the stores to the station, compounded, at Puysegur Point as always, by the state of the road. The timber (see letter p. 185) was coming in for new houses. A. V. Pearce, 1917: We have had a very wet month and the road got very dirty with so much traffic however we kept constantly at the road work in all weathers and Mr Powell was enabled to shift from the beach some 30,000 feet of the very heavyiest timber leaving only on 1st about 5,000 feet

The Cuvier Island landing block and the crane swinging up the goods in the rock-girt landing place.

ANZ (WGTN) ABPL 8848 W5221 ALBUM E

of lighter stuff to be carted from boat shed so we will just about get it away before steamer gets here of course only ½ of it is right home and the other is stacked along the road we have had a lot of trouble near the landing where the crack is and with constant attention no accedint of any kind.[29]

In 1898 seas had swept the Stephens Island landing block taking with them coal and oil drums. P. I. Henaghan, principal keeper, had suggested that delivering 14 tons of stores at one time was not a good idea. Head office reprimanded him. Henaghan's ascerbic response also deals with a few home truths about driving horses: In reading the last paragraph of your memo, Myself & Assistants feel deeply aggrieved to find that the Department thinks we did not exert ourselves sufficiently in getting up the stores from the crane to the landing store on the occasion of the oil being washed away. I feel certain the amount of work performed by us on the occasion under discussion will compare favourably with what was done on previous dates ...

If the horse [the winch was powered by a horse-whim] when constantly at work and grain fed could pull this amount up to the landing store easily in two days, <u>it does not at all follow that</u> the <u>horse can do the same amount of work, in the same time, after being idle for a period of three months</u>. Any person familiar with horses will understand this. Mr Tutt who works the horse is a practical driver for he earned his living at it before joining the Lighthouse Service.

In Mr. D. Scott's days here [during the station's construction] I believe they used to put 14 hundreds [hundredweight?] on the truck each load, that was of course when the horse was constantly at work and fed up for the purpose. During my experience I find that 10 hundred is quite enough for a load, and if by any oversight this amount has been exceeded the horse shows signs of caving in. It is very easy to knock the horse up with this kind of work, but I hardly think the Department would approve of this being done [indecipherable] at the risk of more oil being washed away.

It is only just for me to state I have got more work done by my present Assistants at hauling up stores in a given time than ever was done here previously by the Keepers. The previous records have been beaten by two and sometimes three loads a day in the same time … We cannot however be expected to be able to compete in this kind of work with men whose responsibilities terminate at 5 p.m. − …

Another Source of trouble I find is the unsatisfactory state of the tramway at the point of loading just at the block. Owing to alterations made when repairing it a few years ago the truck is pushed up higher above the ground than there was any need for it to be. So that it is more difficult to load the truck now than previously. I pointed this out at the time to the workmen but my advice and experience went for nothing.

This is very hard on myself as I do all the loading up. About 6 tons of the last coals were landed in full sacks. It is true each of my present Assistants offered to exchange places with me, but as I undertook this stage of the work from the first, I mean to stick to it during the remainder of my time of Service on the Island.

In conclusion I beg to state that a change to a mainland station within the next year would be beneficial to me. If therefore any changes are to be made amongst the Principal Keepers I wish my case to be considered along with the rest … [30] *He was transferred to Waipapa Point that year, after four years on Stephens Island.*

The first stage of the Stephens Island landing platform on a fine day. From this photo it is difficult to imagine waves sweeping off 40-gallon (182 litre) drums of oil. ANZ (WGTN) ABPL 8848 W5221 ALBUM D

In the mid-twentieth century the Stephens Island station supplies had to be manhandled from one winch to another. While Barry Langman remembered boat day as a slog, his recollection pales somewhat besides Henaghan's account above: Once a fortnight we had to bring the stores up from the landing block — there are two distinct winch-ways, there was the crane to lift the goods off the launch — one winch-way took us 100 feet up the cliff face, the next winch took us another 500 feet and from the top on the sheltered side of the island we had a railway line which ran right round the island in front of each house right to the store beside the powerhouse. [At each point the supplies needed manhandling.] It was a railway line, narrow gauge, and we used to push the wagons after they were hauled to the top. All the coal had to be brought around, and the drums of diesel were pushed around on these trolleys and we then carried the coal on our backs up to the houses, and put it into the coal bunker beside each house. The goods were carried up the same way. The weight of a sack of coal was probably the worst — about 112 pounds; there were drums that could be tipped on their side and rolled so they were no problem; sometimes the maintenance required cement and shingle to be brought up so we had heavy bags of Wairau gravel, and cement. They had to be manhandled around. We'd probably spend most of the day waiting for the launch after it'd radioed through, then going down and unrigging the crane to get it into position; then it would take several trips to get the various items up to the top stage 600 feet above, and then move it around to the houses or stores. So launch day was basically taking up the whole day. And the rest of the time if we were quick and didn't have coal to unload we could have off.

In 1957 at French Pass, with no tramway to get the supplies up from the boat, C. H. Mallowes' letter again indicates the sheer hard work of being a lighthouse keeper:

Coal & Supplies: — Could all future supplies of coal be sent in by road? [This had just reached the Pass.] In the past all coal has been landed at the boatshed, and has had to be carried up a steep hill on the keepers' backs to the house. Owing to the grade of about 1 in 3, or steeper in parts, it is impossible to use a wheelbarrow for this, or the carrying of other supplies, and the barrow could be used to bring these things from the road. The kerosene and other fuel could be stored at the new shed.

I should also mention that the contractor will be starting the run twice weekly between here and Rai Valley in about a fortnights time, and he will know doubt be able to carry some of the supplies.[31]

Alan Martin recalled the ingenious arrangement that got the trolley round a 90-degree bend at Mokohinau. The stuff that wasn't going up directly to the houses would be unloaded and put into the boatshed — fuels were kept down there until the boat had gone and we'd deal with them later. The tramlines run flat along the shore, then make a right-angled turn to go up the steep hill to the houses and to just below the tower. A half-ton weight of coal was easy enough to push along the flat. Then, just before the corner, keepers linked the trolley to the steel winch rope that would take it up the hill. On the left hand side close to the bend there were two iron wheels on spindles about three metres apart. The steel rope pulling the trolley went round those wheels. As the trolley approached the corner they flicked the steel rope off the first wheel; as they approached the second wheel, they flicked it off that. Then it was plain sailing – round the bend and on a straight drag up the hill. If there was a load to be dropped at the houses, the winchman, who couldn't see the houses, stopped the trolley again when red lead paint on the rope reached the winch spindle.

We had a lot of fun with that trolley. I think I rebuilt it twice while we were there. We had the lighthouse inspector come on the station every year and there were certain things you were supposed to do. One was that when you finished with the trolley, which was at the top of the hill – it comes up to a slight flat in front of the winch head – you would chock the back wheel, unhook the wire and pull it into the shed. Normally we wouldn't do this, it's only that the inspector's coming. So the inspector's there and the principal keeper or the other keeper needed the trolley but saw the wedge behind the wheel and kicked it out. And that was it. The trolley took off.

The bend in the Mokohinau tramway and the spindles used for navigating it.
MARITA AND PETER TAYLOR

You can imagine, it's on a 45-degree angle and with a kilometre to go, she's really roaring when it hit the bottom.

So being a carpenter I had the job of rebuilding this thing.

LIZARDS AND BEACONS

Keepers could also find themselves engaged in a multitude of odd official and semi-official jobs, some peculiar to a station. When in 1890 the tuatara became protected, principal keepers on Stephens, Cuvier and The Brothers Islands were paid as 'lizard protectors'. The Stephens Island letters on the animals indicate a concern for them at a time when such responses were not universal and when the impact of collecting was too often ignored. In April 1901 Robert Cathcart, at the governor's request, had assiduously collected: a large number of tuatara lizards, and also twelve (12) tuatara eggs ... (I may state that I have since found a way to find the lizard holes without unnecessary digging) ... I have made a larger place for them ... that will hold about 100 lizards. As I consider that it is cruelty to reptiles to keep them in paraffin cases.[32]

In May Cathcart turned to the problem of the feral cats: Received ... Memo 830/111 informing me that "His Excellency the Governor, having directed attention to the destruction of Tuatara lizards on this Island by hawks and cats, and requesting me to suggest some means by which their destruction can be prevented." And in reply I beg to state that with reference to the hawks, I have no suggestion to make, as they are so very cunning and keep so well down the cliffs that it is next to impossible to get a shot at them, so therefore I fail to see how they could be destroyed. On the other hand I believe that it is possible to destroy the cats on this Island, as, in my opinion that is the only means by which the destruction of the lizards can be prevented. And the most effective way to do so, is for the Department to offer a reward for all cats killed on the Island. I therefore beg to suggest that the Department pay sixpence per tail for the first 50 Cats killed, and a shilling per tail for the remainder. And finally to have poisoned fish laid in a systematic manner around & about the Island, and if this is done I believe it will have the desired effect. And I believe that the Hope Brothers who have good Dogs for hunting cats, will undertake the work at the price [indecipherable], and also find the fish if the Department will send the poison ...

I beg to inform you that I have got 110 Tuatara lizards ready to send to Wellington by the "Hinemoa" when she next calls at the Island. His Excellency the Governor informed me that the Hon the Premier, suggested that we should collect 200 which are more than we can collect at this time of year.[33]

Bounties for cats and hawks were established, and initially 60 cats a month were shot. In 1907 George Greig reported: There are now very few cats on the Island and when one is seen it is invariably hunted down ... lizards are not numerous ... I could get the half dozen for the High Commissioner, but if they are to be saved from becoming extinct very few will have to be taken for several years. I can see no perceptible difference in their numbers since I first reported that they were decreasing.[34]

In 1928 hawks were still being shot, but efforts were being directed into fencing off the remaining bush. Meanwhile, F. Woodbury alerted authorities to new culprits: I would be glad if you would warn the Department of Internal Affairs that the Sea gulls that are nesting about the Island are destroying a large number of Lizards this year. They actually wait for hours at a hole until a Lizard comes out, grab it, no matter what size it is & fly to sea & back again, dropping it every now & then to kill it, sometimes they loose it in the sea: & that accounts for dead Lizards being picked up on Coasts near Kapiti. They are as bad as hawks & should be destroyed. This year we lost a [lot] of Lambs through them picking their eyes out, as soon as they were dropped. Several of the culprits were shot. They are thieving murderers & should not be tolerated where there is a sanctuary.[35]

Caring for the beacon marking the east side of the channel at French Pass was a routine task. The light blew out with monotonous regularity over the years, often could not be relit until slack water or until weather cleared, and ships collided with it at an astonishing rate. Charles Robson (our diarist) reported in January 1885: I have the honor to inform you that the Schooner "Reward" of Nelson came in collision with the Beacon at 10.40 p.m. on the 20th instant, smashing the lamp and gear and damaging the Beacon by splitting one of the heavy upright timbers and some of the smaller wood Mr Webber [a local employed as temporary keeper] and I repaired the broken wood-work and got another lamp up as soon as it was possible, the weather at the time was calm and clear, tide first quarter ebb. I have to request you will send another lamp and if possible one of the large size as the smaller ones get blown ou[t] in squally weather.[36]

Keepers at the Pass also had to manhandle the cylinders of gas that from 1927 fuelled the main Pass light. In 1957, with the road just in, C. H. Mallowes' ideas for cutting down the slog were not just limited to coal and supplies (see p. 94). The Pass light was electrified a few years later.

Cylinders & Coal Supplies

Now that the hut is erected at the end of the new access road, would it be possible to have someone explore the possibility of installing the cylinders in it, and running the pipe from the shed to the light. This would enable the cylinders to be brought in by road, and stop a lot of heavy and dangerous work landing them from the boat onto the bridge-work at the tower. Also the

CLOCKWISE FROM TOP LEFT *The 6.1 metre concrete beacon, erected in 1881–82, that Robson tended. While it was a substantial improvement on the iron-rod beacon that Nelson Provincial Council had installed, and more visible, the accident that Robson reports was not uncommon, and concerns about how well the Pass was lit led to the construction of the small rolled-iron tower on the mainland two years later.* WEBBER FAMILY
Wallace and Jack Webber in 1934 hoisting a gas cylinder up on to the current French Pass beacon. Webbers continued to help the keepers and descendents of the original family still farm at the Pass. WEBBER FAMILY
A view of the steps down to the little French Pass light and the swirling tide, impossible for other than highly powered craft to run against. ANZ (WGTN) ABPL 8848 W5221 ALBUM D
The French Pass light and, above it, the signal mast and a black ball used in a system to signal to ships the direction of the tide — another navigational aid for which the keepers were responsible. ATL 1931 NO NEG

weight and length of the cylinders made them very awkward to manoeuvre into the tower. They weigh over 200 pounds and if the step into the tower is wet, which is often the case, things are very slippery and a bad slip could cause a dangerous accident.

An alternative to the cylinders would be to electrify the Pass light [done four years later], and possibly the reef Beacon, using batteries such as are used at Okuri light. The batteries could be kept in the shed with a small diesel engine to keep them charged. This way I think would be a lot cheaper in the end as it would eliminate the necessity of shipping the cylinders back and forth to Wellington and the cost of recharging them.[37]

Other odd jobs were tacked onto the daily round. Again at French Pass, assistant keeper Charles Moeller recorded the ebb and flow of the tides in 1910 — critical work for establishing tidal phenomena properly: [T]here are two high & low tides at the pass, the tide flows inshore for over an hour after it begins to ebb in the pass, and ebbs inshore for the same time after it is flood tide in the pass ...[38]

With the station and light moved from Motuopao to Cape Reinga, the batteries on the new automatic light on Cape Maria van Diemen needed changing about every three months. It was a time-consuming task, undertaken in the face of long-standing head office reluctance to provide a decent horse. T. Harte, 1944: [A]t 5.30 a.m. on the 18th I noticed that the automatic light was not as bright as usual, when I telegraphed you, and got in touch with Mr Keene to try to arrange for an immediate change of batteries. Mr Keene advised that all his men had gone to Te Hapau, and though he did his utmost to get a man or two to return to round up the horses, he was unable to do so as the men although promising to come, did not turn up.

By the morning of the 11th, as Mr Keene could do nothing, I got in touch with Mr Bosselmann, D.E. P.W.D. Kaitaia, and requested the loan of two roadmen who work on our roads here. Mr Bosselmann very kindly put the men at our disposal, and the best arrangement I could make was as follows. The road foreman Mr P. Brown hired two very good medium draught horses at Te Hapua, and with his own two riding hacks, and the other roadman Mr L. Lazarus, he arrived at a point about three miles from the Station at 6 p.m. on the 11th. I was there to meet him with all the necessary gear, and the charged batteries on the new truck, and as I was anxious to get the job done, the men agreed to work all night ...

We started with our first load at about 7 p.m.; arriving at the Automatic at 10 p.m. ... It was necessary to make two complete journeys

By 2.55 a.m. we had the new batteries in place, and connected, and the light was set going at normal brilliance at 3 a.m.

At about 6 a.m. we got back to our starting point by the road, and the men rested the horses and cooked a meal before starting out on their return to Te Hapua. I was back at the Station myself soon after 6 a.m.

Before the change of batteries the visibility of the light was reduced to about 2½ miles … I would suggest; and I made mention of the fact previously, that we be supplied with a horse, or perhaps a better way would be to give me authority to hire a suitable mount, so that we could ride over to the automatic; say once a month, and test the batteries etc. Of course with the present staff of two men the position is difficult, but we can work extra hours willingly when required.

I enclose vouchers for the payment of Mr T. Muru, of Te Hapua for the use of his pack horses for two days at 15/- per horse, per day. To P. Brown; two riding hacks at 12/6 per day, per horse; two days to Mr Keene, one hack for one day at 12/6. The men being P.W.D. [Public Works Department] employees are paid by the P.W.D. but in view of their willing and good service I would request that they receive some reward from our Department and also that the Keepers here be given some consideration for the extra hours worked by us both. Mr Smith did all watches and Station work while I was away, and I request that if some overtime can be paid, equal consideration be given to us both.[39]

FORAGING AND FARMS, GARDENS AND GRAVES: SOME OF THE REST OF THE WORK

The variety of work expected of keepers seems almost endless. Wood-gathering is one of the better documented miscellaneous tasks. The free allowance of coal the department provided to each station was not always adequate; keepers were expected to supplement it with what wood they could scavenge.

The forbearing Alexander Parks wrote from Nugget Point in early 1892 'again' — a not infrequent word in keepers' communications to head office: I would again respectfully remind you that we are still not provided with a horse and cart at this Station, which, as we are expected to keep ourselves going with firewood, with no beast to haul it home from the bush, is very hard. You will easily understand that after twenty years drain on the Reserve to keep two families supplied with firewood, that have to bake their own bread, it means going farther affield for good wood. Moreover, it is 18 miles to Post Office and back — and then the difficulty of getting stores up when landed.

Please give this matter your early and favourable consideration. I could get a good sound horse to do the work of the Station in this district for about £15.[40]

At Waipapa Point in 1888 Fred Erecson found the expectation quite unrealistic: I … beg respectfully to state that it is possible to procure scrub with the dray but I do not know when to get time to do it and at the same time do the various duties required of us at the station. I know of no suitable scrub within 4 miles of here except in a swamp on Mr. Armandy's farm where I formerly got scrub with his permission, since then his land has been ploughed & put under cultivation & I can hardly expect to be permitted to take a dray across his fields, were it possible to do so for ditches.

We have 8 hours watching, each, of a night, and it takes us till noon every day to honestly do the work enumerated in the instructions to keepers. I will most willingly go away and procure scrub with the horse & dray in the afternoon if you think it consistent with the due performance of our night duties, but it will be impossible to get back by sunset.[41]

For Charles Tregurtha on Centre Island the same year, scrounging for fuel must have been almost the final straw: … 23rd, 24th & 25th furious Westerly Gales, hail & rain breaking down the protecting fence round the trees and I fear destroying some of the trees last planted …

We are also badly off for fuel in this miserable weather as [i]t takes nearly all our spare time in fine weather to get enough for our use, we have consequently to go in all sorts of weather to pull out roots etc which it is almost impossible to burn, after getting it home.[42]

In May 1914 at Cape Egmont Anders Hansen faced a different problem — advancing settlement. The Opunake County Council had stopped firewood being carted through the winter. While the lighthouse has received a supply of firewood which will see us through to such a time as the road can be carted on … the cheese factories take all the wood procurable, and the men supplying the wood to the Lighthouse are not at all anxious for the job. Rata is getting very scarce, and the price has risen, I understand, 5/- [shillings] per cord.[43]

Recalling the wood-gathering practice that lasted some seventy years, Les Broom, remembering his foraging at Moeraki, did not mince his words: The Marine Department used to reckon all these land stations could get their firewood off the beaches. So I wrote to the Marine Department, 'No wood here, you'll have to supply some coal.' Carting all these bloody logs up the hill — blow that for a lark.

The blowing tussock in this photo of Waipapa Point station evokes what, under the big Southland skies, can be bleak windswept plains. HANSEN COLLECTION

Swiss sharemilkers at Cape Egmont lighthouse further indicate the growing prosperity of dairying in Taranaki.

HANSEN COLLECTION

Keepers, in their own time and generally in the afternoons, farmed the reserve and cared for the sheep and cows that provided the major supply of fresh meat and milk and a varied diet (the poultry was generally the women's business). Barry Langman on Stephens Island: We had to shear the sheep with hand-held blades, we had to dip them as a requirement of the Agriculture Department for ticks etc. We had to do it with a semi-rotary pump by pumping out of a 44-gallon fuel drum and collecting the dip water and repumping back it through again. The milking was an acquired art, by hand. We separated the milk from the cream and made our butter from that.

But in later years they were not all farmers. Chris Staley went to relieve the Cape Egmont keeper: He was just hopping into his car, and he said, 'Oh, by the way don't forget to milk the bloody cow.' I said, 'I've never milked a cow in my life.' And he says, 'Oh, it's a peaceful creature, just milk it every morning, take what you want and then let the calf have the rest.' I got by. All these are experiences.

Shirley Martin was blunt about their generation of keepers' abilities as farmers, in that most of the keepers were amateurs and knew little about stock. The Martins' own experience with Muscovy ducks suggests a certain lack of experience. They invested in the ducks, on Dog Island, Shirley remembered, to vary the diet: We started off with half a dozen ducklings and a drake. The ducks hatched out 14 ducklings each — dear wee things — and we'd throw a bit of bread out the back door there. But little ducks grow into big ducks and Muscovies have huge feet and you don't like it when you turn round and find they've all streamed into the house behind you! The book that I got said ducks breed in September. Ours hadn't read the book. They bred three times a year and in 12 months we had 96 ducks! And they used to take off and I'd think, Oh, gosh, there they go! And they'd circle round and come back on to the landing strip and walk back home. They used to do that every evening.

We got to the stage where we'd give our eye teeth for a sausage instead of having duck. But the crew of the *Wairua* would come out and we'd say, 'Would anybody like some ducks?' And so we'd kill and dress them all and there'd be X number of ducks wanted for the crew, they'd come and we'd send off the ducks and it would be great!

Most keepers had gardens for fresh vegetables to avoid the expensive tinned ones that unduly stretched the budget, though in the 1930s head office had to remind keepers to at least dig over the plots so that their successors would not miss a growing season. George Kroening remembered reasonable soil at Portland Island: I believe that they did get small quantities of fertilisers but I don't remember buying any ourselves. Seaweed came up in the truck from down the landing. We've a photo of a cabbage – big as Jean just about! And the big thing was to get from the garden gate up to our house which was across the open paddock where all the stock was because they knew very well there could have been leaves of the cabbage or lettuce. So they'd congregate right outside the gate and virtually bail you up in the garden and you couldn't get out unless you dropped leaves off all the way up to the house! Trivial things, but quite humorous when you look back on them.

The sole cow at Puysegur Point, 1980s.
BILL MEGENNIS

Alan Wright: One of the biggest problems on any lighthouse was the salt spray. It was difficult to get a garden going. But Cape Reinga had some marvellous gardens. They were down in the flax, you wouldn't know there was a garden there.

Men and boys on Stephens Island rounding up the sheep. ANZ (WGTN) AAQT 6401 A73487

Lynne Kroening with silverbeet grown at Akaroa station, where the garden was a narrow strip between the station gate and the houses on the cliff edge, exposed to wind and voracious possums.

JEAN AND GEORGE KROENING

Not all stations were as fortunate. R. Downie, Cape Brett, 1956: Speaking for this station only I can say that not a thing has been grown here for at least twelve months in fact we have spent Pounds in plants etc only to have everything blown out or burnt down by the clouds of Spray salt sweeping over the station . . . [44]

Gardening may have also been a way of creating a sense of permanency in a job that demanded relatively frequent transfers (though the three-yearly moves that relatively regularly punctuated lighthouse life from the 1950s were less common earlier). On the inhospitable Brothers rock, Chris remembered: Someone had tried to put in a garden. They'd brought out soil from the mainland and it was in boxes with old window frames to keep the salt spray off, but there was too much salt for anything to grow outside. There was only a few bits of scrub, taupata bushes and things like that. The spray comes down like rain in heavy weather, so that the ground is impregnated.

At Waipapa Point keepers tended the graves of those lost in the wreck of the Tararua, at Cape Saunders the picket-fenced graves of two lighthouse children. In 1949 Tom Smith, unasked, restored the grave of the seaman drowned off Portland Island round which Charles Robson (our diarist's father) and his wife had built the fence in 1897. (Seven years later the station was demanned. By now the grave is probably invisible.): When the scow "Pirate" was wrecked here in the year 1897 one of the members of the crew was killed and the survivors buried him on the foreshore of the East side of the Island. A

The graves of the Henaghan twins. Thomas died of meningitis, Ellen in a fire. While keeper David Nelson's infant son also apparently died in the fire, his grave is not on the station. Cape Saunders' keepers were said to have a particular responsibility for looking after these graves. Curiously, the same is not stated about the other five children's graves on stations, and the grave of the seven-month-old baby that died at Kaipara North in 1909 has long been covered with drifting sand.

ANZ (WGTN) ABPL W5221 PHOTOS BOX 19

picket fence was erected around the grave and a board at the head, giving the man's name and date of his death.

The grave is close to the cliff and a few years ago a small slip demolished the fence and covered the grave with rubble. The frame and pickets of the fence were then taken to the landing where they have remained until recently.

During the holidays I cleared the slip rubble from the grave and replaced and repainted the fence. The head-board however, is badly rotted and the lettering almost weathered off, consequently it is not worth refitting. Would it be possible for the Department to replace this with a new one? If it is not possible to supply a Headstone, I would suggest a Totara slab about 2ins. thick with the lettering carved. I am forwarding here-under, the lettering as on the old board. The date of birth is too defaced to read, the date of death is correct and I have checked this with the visitors book in which are recorded the names of the master & mate and the date of the wreck ...

SACRED
IN MEMORY OF

KARL BERNER
BORN IN GERMANY –
DIED 16TH APRIL 1897
ON BOARD SCOW PIRATE
AT TIME OF STRANDING.[45]

Keeper Nicholas Sciascia who was fatally gored by a bull, and his grave on Portland Island. HANSEN COLLECTION

CHAPTER 6

Behind the routine tasks

Night-watching, routine cleaning and station maintenance, landing and hauling supplies, road-making, digging slips, weather reporting — but that list does not account for the time, effort and ingenuity needed to ensure that the light worked well and the station operated efficiently. Considerable resourcefulness, dedication and determination lay behind the factual reporting and requests for permission to carry out repairs to the centralised, bureaucratic world of which the Lighthouse Service was part demanded. They were often done in the face of apparent head office indifference — particularly before the recruitment, and even severer retention, problems of the 1950s, head office all too often apparently ignored requisitions for equipment or for permission and materials for often essential maintenance; if it did respond it often sent the wrong things. 'Having got you there, they left you alone,' said Victor Pullen, a lighthouse child in the early 1930s. In 1947 Frank Shepherd, with a frankness that was becoming increasingly apparent in keepers' communications with head office, described the monthly reports as 'a waste of time & paper'.[1]

We shall discuss keepers' relations with that distant department later. Now we turn to a small selection of reports on what seems like an almost limitless list of what could go wrong with the lights, other navigational aids and station buildings and equipment.

THE NAVIGATIONAL AIDS

Beautiful as the light apparatus appeared, it required careful adjustment. P. J. Vayle made the initial report from Cape Palliser in 1897: I have the honour to inform you that having taken charge of the lantern & lighting equipment from Mr. Scott, everything was got in readiness & the light exhibited for the first time at 6.30 p.m. on the evening of the 27th Oct. At 8 p.m. on the 28th Ultimo & 2 a.m. on the 30th Ultimo It was found necessary to stop the apparatus & remove two of the friction rollers that got jammed on the spindles & would not revolve. The apparatus in each instance was not detained longer than two minutes. Mr Scott made the necessary alterations & at present every thing is working well.[2]

Not for long. The rollers continued to operate poorly. Nine years later, after numerous attempts to get the right size ball bearings and two changes of rollers (the wrong size was sent initially), H. A. Wakefield's ingenuity found the answer (and gallons of castor oil were subsequently despatched to various stations): I am glad to say that I have found out why the rollers make the noise. The cause is insufficient lubrication Power of whale oil, it is too thin for these rollers & sloping track; in Proof of this, on the 16th I lubricated the rollers with castor oil & the result was astonishing, the thump, thump, thump, ceased also the jarring & everything ran as silently & as smoothly as a "bike" on an asphalt track; on the 22nd cleaned rollers & had to oil with whale oil again with the result that the rollers resumed the thump, thump, bump again.

I have enough whale oil for the machine, till the Hinemoa come again, but not for the rollers, will you kindly send me via Martinborough 1 gall castor oil.

I may add that after 6 days running under castor oil, the oil was quite clean & that there is not the slightest danger of the castor oil clogging.[3]

Sometimes time-consuming, fiddly repairs might have been avoided had the keepers themselves kept better records. At Cape Brett the huge cage of lenses floated in a mercury bath, lessening friction. This brought its own problems. In 1931 G. Sinclair reported the light was running very erratically and a thorough overhaul, involving drawing off and replacing the mercury, had not improved the situation. Sinclair noted that according to old journals, similar trouble had occurred but there was no record of how it had been fixed. The problem was finally rectified by finding a hard rubbery substance in an opening 1/8 of an inch wide. [It] must have been accumulating for years … If you could supply two tools as per sketch enclosed, they could be used each time the machinery is cleaned & overhauled., thus avoiding any accumulation of foreign matter in the mercury bath in the future. *Sinclair was careful to record how he had fixed the fault.[4]*

Worn-out roller tracks, vital for exhibiting the light properly, continued to frustrate keepers into the 1970s. The problems experienced with the Farewell Spit apparatus reflect service-wide issues with long-deferred maintenance and its repercussions. Frank Shepherd, 1951: Considerable trouble has been experienced last month with the revolving mechanism of this light, every night for the past two weeks it has been absolutely impossible to keep the light revolving under it's power, a constant watch has to be kept on the machine so as to be able to push it every time it stops and this is all to frequent, we have done all we can to improve the defect but so fare we

Cape Palliser tower, 1911, where the Hansen family had been for two years. But what the family remarked on was not the photo's elegant tower, but everyday happenings. Lena Hansen scribbled on the back of the photo to her brother Fred: 'Very glad to get your letter last week. The Hinemoa landed here on Monday, George & Mary & Annie came home by her. We are all that excited we don't know what we're doing. Mum or Annie will write next week & give you all the news. We are going along to pack home 4 little pigs from the "Rock" today. I think the big ones will be killed, next week. Were surprised to hear Tom was married. Give him our warmest congratulations & wish him all happiness. We are all well at home. I must knock off now. Love from all. Lena XXX'.
HANSEN COLLECTION

have not been successful, if anything, I think each night is becoming worse, even the new spindle for the Air Governor has made no difference, the rollers have been changed to different positions but the track is so cut about and grooved that it is impossible to find a smooth track, there is absolutely no room for any more weight on the wire rope, that should give you some idea of the terrible state of the whole mechanism.

Would it not be advisable to make this a priority repair job, if it breaks down all together, even as it is now the Keepers are objecting to having to push the lenses around. Hoping this receives your most Urgent Consideration.[5]

In 1902 the fog signal installed at Pencarrow Head was modified to fire every five minutes, instead of every 15 — an interval that might endanger ships. The change cannot have been welcomed on the station. Anders Hansen, 1904: I would here, beg to draw your attention to the urgent need there is for some means of communication between the Fog signal and the Lighthouse and dwelling houses. Now, with the greater frequency of firing, the signal requires unremitting attention. It takes the man in charge almost all his time to prepare the charges, cleaning fouling wires e.c. As a rule the lamp can be depended on to burn steadily for four hours, but at any time it may require attention. Accidents also may happen to the keeper in charge of signal or to signal itself, requiring the assistance of the keeper off duty immediately, and under circumstances that would well nigh prevent the keeper on duty from going to call him.[6]

When the lights were electrified, bells signalled any mechanical failure. Alan Wright on The Brothers, early 1960s: It's like a fire station, there's a gong that big underneath the bed and if the light failed the gong went off and you knew! You were out and off!

By then technology had outstripped keepers' technical abilities and outside expertise was sought for anything complicated. Alan Martin: I was first assistant at Cape Reinga. The alarm bells were ringing, it was in the middle of the night and so I hopped out of bed and grabbed my shorts and jumped into em and started running up the hill — my house was the farthest away — and then down to the light that had stopped rotating. The second assistant went into the power house to switch the alarms off. It wasn't until the principal keeper and I got down there that I found why I couldn't fasten my shorts — I'd got them on inside out! So having rectified that and thinking the alarm bells had stopped ringing, that the second assistant had fixed them, we examined the light. One of the rollers had seized up. We took that one off and away she went, quite merrily. It wasn't until we got home again that we found the alarm bells had been ringing solidly in all three houses while we'd been away.

We had a mechanic come up from Auckland. He had a look at all the rollers and said, 'We'll whip the lot off.' In one day they took all the rollers off, took 'em down into Kaitaia, had them refurbished, brought up, put back and we had the light going again that night. I do remember they lifted up the whole of the light, took the rollers out and then they ground the whole of this track and got it smooth again. Tremendous piece of machinery, absolute dream, nice to work on.

The rather more sophisticated electric beacons installed from the 1940s also frequently failed — but by then backup advice and assistance were available. Chris Staley remembered the experimental Brothers beacons: We had one helluva job with them breaking down to start with, teething problems y'know. Some of them we could fix. We had a system whereby I could get on the RT — radio telephone — to Wellington Radio and they would patch me through to a radio technician and he would tell me what to do. He'd tell me to read certain dials and change certain valves and what have you. We were only allowed to have them off — from memory I think it was for about one minute. If they were off for more than a minute we were supposed to put out a navigation warning.

Cape Reinga station in the mid-1960s. The road leads into the visitors' carpark; beyond that is the principal keeper's house. The buildings on the left are the workshop, the school, the school-teacher's house and the toilet block (built because of visitor numbers). As at many stations, emergencies at the lighthouse meant quite a dash.
ALAN AND SHIRLEY MARTIN

If, by the mid-twentieth century, keepers' ingenuity was no longer the mainstay of the operation, it found other outlets. Les Broom, Cape Reinga: We used to have the most trouble with the radio beacons. You could solve some of those problems by using a match, propping up a certain piece there and you can get it going. Used to be very handy if I was going to Auckland and I wanted a lift back I'd tell them at the Cape, 'Well you pull the match out at a certain date and tell them the beacon's not working.' Then I'd ring Auckland people up and the technician'd say, 'Are you going to the Cape? Well, come for a ride.'

Chris had left The Brothers to help with maintenance at Cape Palliser. One of his head office friends had instructed the keeper: 'Chris has been isolated on the rock for three months. He's a bit dry. You'd better take him down to the pub for a beer.' So we set off this Saturday afternoon in his car, old vintage model T Ford – and in those days, you had to ford the creeks. Anyway, we went to Lake Ferry, had a couple of hours in there, set off back to the station and one of the fan blades fell off the fan, damaged the radiator – we lost all the cooling water. So there we are stuck on the road. By a stroke of good luck I had got hold of a dozen beers in the pub to take back with us and I bought some chewing gum at the same time. So being resourceful lighthouse keepers we chewed up the chewing gum, and partially plugged the leaks in the radiator. Then we took one of the bottles of beer and thought well, we can't waste that. So we drank it between us, urinated in the empty bottle, poured that into the radiator and that was just enough cooling fluid to get us to the first creek. Then we could use the empty beer bottle to top the radiator up with water and get to the next creek – and so on. We did get back to the station but it was getting dark and the permanent keeper's wife, heavily pregnant, had decided to head off up the two or three hundred steps to draw back the curtains. She did it and I can't say she was pleased to see us when we got back.

THE STATIONS: 'I WISH YOU COULD SEE IT FOR YOURSELF'
Until the late 1950s, stations and station gear, like the light equipment, were often run down. Many letterbooks indicate a pattern of equipment not being replaced or repairs effected, adding hours to the daily work. Robert Leighton wrote from Cuvier in 1907 that the tramline turntable was worn out and disabled. Even the station horse, essential to station management until tractors in the 1950s gradually eliminated the need for them, was often unsatisfactory – again head office showed little interest. At Cape Egmont in 1917, P. W. Grenfell pointed out that the grey mare, purchased without the usual trial was: unreliable when driven in the dray owing to her frantic behaviour when the chains are rattling and her successful attempts to take charge, thus placing the keepers in a very undignified position and jeopardising their safety.[7]

At Cape Palliser in 1947 M. Todd set out in some detail just why they needed a new horse:
[T]he Station horse is absolutely "No Good" for working past the landing. She always playes up & wants to go her own way and if she cant get it she backs up & you have a job to do anything with her ... we had occasion to go to the sand-hill [the name for a wind-eroded shingle hillside] for fresh vegetables, and had to take the cart., but only got as far as the Little Mungi-Toi [Mungatoetoe] where she turned the cart over and broke the only good shaft ... This horse will eventually be the cause of some-one loosing their Life or having a serious accident. Should there be any Illness or an accident on the station this horse could not be used.

The womenfolk say they would not go out in the cart or let the children be taken out in the cart with this horse.

The age of the horse is Approximately 16 years.

The previous keepers have not used this horse past the landing, and mostly when they wanted a horse they used Mr. M. McLeod's horse Peg aged 26 and past hard work.

Mr. O'Leary, Tubb. and bucknell has seen this horse playing up.

If the Department could see their way clear of supplying this Station with a Dodge 1 Ton Front wheel drive Truck the keepers would appreciate the Departments action.[8]

Todd did get a new horse three months later. But complaints were no guarantee of action. In 1947 Pencarrow's principal keeper, J. H. C. Conway, and, very unusually, his assistant, G. F. Hitchings signed the following report on the Pencarrow winch — for a change it was not the diaphone fog signal that was playing up. Conway's letter was not the first on the subject; nor, typically, would it be the last: I wish to report on an event that occurred here to-day, at about 10 a.m. the Harbour boards launch came to the landing to service the low level light, when their boat came ashore they landed the following gear, one Battery charger, 1 bag wheat 3 boxes sundries 1-4 gallon tin of paint, on this gear being landed the Keepers proceeded to get it up to the dwellings, the truck was loaded up at the bottom of the hill & the Keepers went up the hill to the winch & started winching up every thing as usual ... then it was noticed that the winch was very hard to wind so I stopped ... to see what was the trouble as it's impossible to see the truck from the winch I went down the hill to look over & was very much surprised to find, that there was no truck on the line, it having left the line & gone over the side, & all the gear was at the bottom of the hill, excepting the Battery charger which was lashed to the truck ... Now Sir, I wish to say a few words on the winch, it have no collar or paw to keep it in gear & the paw racket that is on it is all broken, when the Keepers are winding anything up, one has to wind & the other has to be standing by the brake, to prevent the truck from going to the

Richmond George James Banks Smith, Jo Broom's father (and light keeper like his father) beside a Cape Maria van Diemen station winch in 1954. This was used to work the flying fox that carried stores to the island station from the mainland. By the mid-twentieth century it was frequently used by lighthouse families going on camping holidays. LES AND JO BROOM

bottom when the gears slip out which it does very often … Now Sir to cut a long story short; in my opinion this winch is dangerous to work with.[9]

The state of the winch reflected the state of many of the Lighthouse Service station buildings and equipment. The towers were no exception. It was common enough for requisitioned items not to arrive and for stations to begin operation inadequately equipped. But at Puysegur Point not even the tower's interior fit had been adequately thought through. The work fell on the keepers already working hard to get the station in order. Fred Erecson, 1878: I did not receive the copper nails and screws mentioned in the list of stores but I had sufficient boatnails of my own to repair the boat with. She is now in serviceable condition.

… It will be necessary to make some alterations in the lightroom, such as shifting the stairs & remove the position of the railing, so as to be able to open the machinecase doors, I will (with your permission) make those alterations, also finish the goods store but as I have some panel sliding doors to make, I would be obliged if you would sent me Fitplough & set of irons, neither me nor the asst have one …[10]

Other keepers faced more threatening problems. When first built (in 1865) the 39-metre-high Dog Island tower 'oscillated' in strong winds. Various attempts to stabilise it were still going in 1915 when lightning further threatened its structural stability (the conductors did not always prevent strikes). That year William Murray reported, with remarkable reticence: I must again report that the pillar in the centre of the lighthouse is not very safe, the lightning of June last seems to have followed right down and shattered the bricks where the ends of the stairs go through inside the pillar, and it appears to me to be getting worse … if the pillar was to collapse, all the rest of the brickwork in the tower would go as well.[11]

Equally remarkably, the department let months go by before doing further structural work. Even when properly stabilised, the tower on that low-lying island seems to have been something of a brooding presence — in the 1970s Shirley Martin worked out that if it fell over the house would be spared!

In 1915 at Cape Egmont, Anders Hansen, with little response from head office, was battling with the lightroom ventilation — something that had dogged the keepers since the light's commissioning in 1881: I would like again to draw your attention to the bad state of draught in this lighthouse. With Wind from all quarters but west and southwest the sweating of the lantern is very bad, and during thick rainy weather the water simply streams off the walls and panes across the floor; even the tower lenses get covered with water, and that too with all the doors and windows open. The light cannot burn without doors and windows open, no matter what the weather is like. During the whole of this winter keepers have not been able to keep clear of colds, sore throats, and bad attacks of neuralgia. We have to light the lamp occasionally to dry the lenses before we can clean them, and at times we cannot clean them at all; without making them dirtier and dimmer than if they were not touched at all.[12]

This time head office responded and a new cowl was fitted. Two months later Hansen described the tower as 'the best ventilated lighthouse I have been in.'

Increasingly, from one end of the country to the other, keepers reported towers in need of major maintenance. T. Smith, Waipapa Point, 1938: [T]he tower at is in urgent need of repair, and as there is a considerable quantity of water coming in I think something should be done to it before winter. [13]

J. D. Auld, Cape Saunders, 1940: Also wish to state that iron work in the Lt.Room is in bad state of repair. This having now reached the stage where the rust is beginning to eat deep into the iron. However, it will be noted above that keepers are endeavouring to rectify this by chipping to new iron & when finished will coat with fish oil & then paint.[14]

H. B. Jamieson, Cape Brett, 1943: The tower floor has rotted from the underside owing to there being no ventilation and is rotted through in several places, also the floor joists are affected where they come into contact with the flooring.[15]

Other urgent needs also had to be met, one of which was ensuring the stations had adequate water. Water was collected in tanks, fed from the roofs of the station buildings. But most stations were built before records had been adequately accumulated to allow long-term weather patterns to be appreciated, and the extent of summer droughts was not well appreciated. Keepers nationwide, whose inadequate water supplies were sometimes exacerbated by poor tank maintenance, faced the reality of long, dry summers.

Charles Tregurtha, Cape Egmont, 1897: [A]ll the watertanks at both houses are in a very advanced state of decay, and are leaking in several places they want cleaning out, but it is not safe to go into them, as the chances are, the bottoms would drop out. *A year, and a second letter later, he was still trying to get the department to understand that summer weather conditions meant two tanks per house were not enough.*[16]

P. I. Cox, Cuvier Island, 1901: The lantern is washed every time it is needed I cannot wash the lantern every night as there is not sufficient water at the

A close view of a water tank and its stand at the Little Barrier Island settlement, where R. H. Shakespear, the island caretaker for a number of years from 1897, lived a life very similar to that of the lighthouse keepers. Water from the roofs supplied the tanks. During droughts those on tank water would anxiously, and frequently, tap the sides of the tanks to ascertain water levels. AM DU 436.1182.

tower to do that we want another water tank at the Tower as the rainfall is very scarce in the summer when the house is put at the tower for Keepers & a tank put on to it there will be sufficient water for every thing but not before … *He wanted three more tanks.*[17]

At Moeraki in 1895 C. E. Johnson's discovery was not atypical. [One tank, nearly empty, had] water pouring from a large hole in the bottom of the tank connected with the zinc. The same tank I notice has been patched up with rags putty & paint etc. in several places this means has been resorted go again and there is now 15 inches of water in each of them. The pressure of water on the weak parts is however liable to force its way through at any time as they fill up and should it unhappily occur at the approach of a dry season it might lead to serious results.[18]

On some stations, water was still an issue as late as 1955. T. R. Welsh, Tiritiri Matangi: I wish to advise you of the position on this station re the supply of water.

This summer Keepers have been severely rationed and baths had to be used once a week and washing was a real problem specially with young children. Water was very short from November until the end of May when our so called spring began to gather a little more seepage.

He drew up careful tables to compare Tiritiri Matangi's water supplies with other stations in the region and pointed out the hardships faced by the women: Mr Clark, now at Akaroa, will confirm this and he will also be able to tell you that the previous year the women were doing their washing in the sea. A very bad state of affairs in this modern age!! …

I might add that of the 16 or so tanks available for water some five or six will not hold water for long. This has been pointed out to the M.O.Works but they just shrug their shoulders and say "What can we do?"

Trusting this will be given a priority.[19]

But in spite of Welsh's carefully marshalled evidence and his recommendation, the 1958 letterbook — the last of the Tiritiri Matangi letterbooks held by Archives New Zealand — ends three years later with no action taken.

Keepers' reports also document a dereliction (affecting both homes and stations) that cannot be attributed solely to delayed maintenance or wartime austerity. Some keepers were lazy, others lacked the necessary skills, some principal keepers failed to provide the necessary supervision and leadership —Peter Taylor, lightkeeping between 1958 and 1966, remembers one man who listed task after task in his monthly reports but 'did bugger all work'. Perhaps the department's cavalier attitude to despatching requisitioned items meant others again lost heart and gave up.

N. H. Harvey inherited Manukau Heads Station in 1926 from the Marshalls, who left behind an almost legendary trail of dereliction and neglect. (The department had begun occasional inspections again, after a long break, and had noted positive results. No inspector had recently been to Manukau Heads): I regret the Dept. has not seen fit to inspect the station. I have been at a few but have never seen a station so neglected & dirty as this one. I feel sure the Dept has no idea of the state this station is in. The oil store was full of old rusty tins cob webs & dirt, empties, not stacked but thrown down the centre of the store. The Workshop was in a dirty state, the

A new tank coming at Mokohinau, late 1950s. 'Nothing,' said Peter Taylor, 'was transported easily.' MARITA AND PETER TAYLOR

corners under the benches & paint locker I can safely say, was not swept out last year. The corners & paint locker being covered with rat droppings The paint locker was one mass of paint pots with small quantities of perished paint. The dry store, all the cupboards require cleaning out. The Lighthouse, the drawers require spring cleaning. The Medicine chest has no key and a lot of pills seems to have swelling in the bottles & are not fit for consumption, also bottles with no corks, & corks half eaten away with sand & mildew surrounding the neck of the bottles, also sand & dirt all through the chest which is detrimental to the health of the station. I have stated before, all the buildings & railings require painting. The road through the reserve is also in a bad state ... Neighbours are complaining about the black berries not being cut. The reserve which is leased outside our paddock is one mess of black berry. Asst Keepr Glass informs me that P.K Marshall left the station as stated Keeper Glass left the station in its present condition to allow me to see & report on it, as if he had framed a report he was of the opinion that the Dept may have thought that he had a grudge against his late Principal.

Seeing the light is being converted please inform me if the Dept wishes the station put in repair or whether it is to be left in its present condition.

I would be glad if the Dept would issue me lino as early as possible. I think I am entitled to a little consideration as my role of lino was lost overboard whilst being landed at Portland Island & I had made no claim as I thought I would not require it further. Keeper Glass has his own lino down & does not wish to lift it.[20]

If some keepers were lazy, head office, in failing to respond to keepers' requests, was also responsible for the stations' poor upkeep. In 1945 Mr G. T. Simmons retired from Cape Egmont station. From the early 1930s to 1945, he had run the place as if it were his own. E. Wylie, who arrived in September 1945 to take over, found a house bare of appliances, the station denuded: Every thing on the Station belonged to Mr Simmons Horses & Gates & all the dividing fences & crow-bar & when I arrived here there was nothing & he took every thing away. I have no way of getting mail or stores only for Mr Quickenden I would have had nothing as he brought Mail & Stores & Milk, my Children are frozen as it is impossible to get a Electric Heater up here. Would the Dept supply a ½ ton truck for getting Mail & stores & as there will be a lot of fencing to be done & a lot of shingle needed around the station, all the posts & wire could be carted with a light truck to where the[y] would be needed, otherwise I see no way of getting this place up to what I would like it to be ... I haven't applied for all the things required, but if all is supplied it will do to carry on with in the mean time.[21]

Wartime austerity notwithstanding, the department's response is difficult to understand — three weeks later neither the coal nor kerosene needed for cooking had arrived; the truck was refused. Wylie tried again. It is unclear from the letterbooks if he succeeded: In reply to your memo M.8/15/114 re truck. As a Truck is not going to be supplied, Will you supply a horse & gig & a sledge. If you want any work done I will have to have something to do it with as all the fencing post & wire will have to be taken out each day as it is used, as nothing could be left here at night away from the station & I have only a wheel barrow on the station to do any thing with. I don't mind a bit of hard work as I have been working from 60 to 70 Hrs a week since I came here, but I will never be guilty of doing a horse out of a job. This station has always had a horse & gig to take keepers children to school. & a sledge to do the work around the station. Mr Simmons used the gig to take his children to school when the[y] left school as he had no more use for the gig he let it get beyond repair, when the horse died 2 years ago he never got it replaced, that is why I am having all this trouble getting some conveyance to do work around the station for since the horse died there has been nothing done …

Mr Simmons should have left the station as he found it.[22]

In 1947 Tom Smith, whose father had kept Portland Island up to scratch during the 1920s, transferred to the island as principal keeper. His final paragraph of a very long letter to head office provides a wider context to what he reported – the station's state was not exceptional nor attributable to just wartime neglect, and head office had to expect negative fallout.

Report on Station

It is now a Month since I arrived and took over this station as Principal Keeper. Having found the station in a general state of dis-repair, with accumulated, essential maintenance work, which is going to take some time to carry out. I consider it my duty to forward you the following report. I have delayed this report until I became fully conversant with the running of the station and investigated everything fully. The following is the result of my finding.

Tower

The tower machine is in need of a complete overhaul. Prior to my arrival several stoppages were recorded in the journal, the cause apparently unknown. After making several adjustments … the machine … will now run continuously, but it is still erratic and occasionally develops a jerky motion which continues for about 15 to 20 seconds each time. This I think is due to the worn parts. Some of the bearings are so badly worn that horizontal shafts are not level, with the result that gears are not meshing true. The roller track is also showing signs of excessive wear. New rollers are on hand, but the installation of these is inadvisable until the track has been trued up.

The Smith Ford burner was dismantled on 16TH August last. Considerable trouble had been experienced with this, the light being put out on several occasions in order to prick the nipple; the internal prickers, including the spares, are all useless. The nipple holes have become enlarged and frequently become blocked. The burner was dismantled and replaced by a Chance burner before my arrival, so I have had no experience with it and can only quote Mr Corson who advises that the Chance apparatus is more satisfactory in every way. It gives a good light and is trouble-free, it is also more economical to operate than the Smith Ford gear. As there are abundant spares on hand for the Chance burner, I request permission to continue using it and will await your instructions concerning the Smith Ford gear.

Trouble has also been experienced with the auxiliary red light. The burner was leaking so badly that more kerosene was leaking away than was being burned. After checking over and fitting wicks a spare burner was installed and we now have a less waste-ful and better light; leakage is practically nil.

The tower itself requires painting. The walls on the south are bare in places and rust spots are conspicuous on all sides. The dome has not been oiled for many months and is dull and rusty looking. It will probably be necessary to scrape it before applying oil. During stormy weather the lantern panes leak badly. They are in need of re-glazing, perishing putty is constantly falling out of the astragals. The lens are in good condition but on arrival I found them covered with a coating of film caused by fumes. Mr Pullin spent nearly a week, working a full morning only each day, applying cleaner to bring lens and panes up to original brightness.

Whilst repairing the fence round the tower recently the temporary keeper noticed that the stay piles were showing signs of decay. On investigation it was found that most of them are in poor condition, two of them in particular. The timber was rotten to a depth of 3 to 4 inches on each side.

The letter continues, detailing the poor conditions and amenities in the second assistant's house; the borer-infested condition of most of the furniture on the station; the over-grown gardens; the fences that needed re-straining; the road, impassable in bad weather; the inadequate landing jetty, and rusting or rotting blocks, cable, and winch; and the fume-filled station truck that lacked adequate brakes. Smith, having reported the keepers' willingness to do overtime to get things shipshape, summed up: In conclusion, I wish to add the following. I have now spend 8 years in the Lightservice, during which time I have been transferred three times; on each occasion finding the station I am appointed to, in a similar condition to this. I am interested in the service and keen on my work, but to find one station after another in this condition becomes very discouraging. I consider it time something was done to improve the situation, for the benefit of those who, like myself, take an active interest in the efficiency and appearance of their station. I seem to have spent most of my time in the service not maintaining, but renovating stations.[23]

Smith's disillusionment was shared by Frank Shepherd, faced with a major clean-up at Cape Brett in 1947 (after, interestingly, the apparently hard work Jamieson and his men had undertaken): I don't how the other keepers put up with these conditions, it is a real heartbreak. I wish you could see it for yourself … [E]verything is in such a deplorable state that the bit we do is hardly noticeable … On looking back through the records there seems plenty of cases where the work under discussion has been reported, but it has never been touched yet, it seems a waste of time & paper as far as the P.W.D. are concerned all the work mentioned in this report is urgently required. What is required is for the inspecting Officers to dwell on the station, instead of the usual flying visit & then they could give everything a thorough inspection. I would save a lot of writing & fuss on the part of the keepers.[24]

Even specially commissioned reports elicited no action. George Kroening, newly promoted to principal keeper, was sent to Akaroa: Turner was in charge and he said 'We've had a lot of trouble with Akaroa. When you get there we want your idea of what is wrong with the place and why its keepers won't stay there.' He said, 'Pull no punches, we want straight from the shoulder.' I wrote eight foolscap pages and the last paragraph was, 'If something is not done to the lighthouse in the next twelve months we'll be the next to go.' And I wrote off tools and everything in the workshop – about three hundred odd items of equipment. The place was really run down.

The Akaroa station was finally improved. But by then George, fed up with no response to his report, had resigned. Even in the 1970s, the Martins were still having to get round the departmental propensity to cut back whenever possible. Shirley: They could be a bit stingy at times – if you wanted to order up paint you ordered twice what you wanted because quite often they'd cut the amount in half that they were going to send!

OUTRAGEOUS FORTUNE: THE EXTRAORDINARY MAINTENANCE

In 1942 a hopeful coalminer, thinking that the Puysegur Point tower was sending out signals that affected his brain, burned it down, along with other station buildings. The Beggs in Port Preservation *and Tom Smith in* Man the Light! *have already documented this dramatic event; I turn instead to the challenges (excluding the slips that were so much a part of life) that nature might throw at the keepers.*

Birds flying into the lantern, smashing it and possibly damaging the lenses were not unknown, but Anders Hansen's account of a lamp exploding is the only one I came across. One notes, too, in this account, his ability to observe and clearly describe (rather different from the

The second Puysegur Point tower under construction after its destruction by fire in 1942. LES AND JO BROOM

muddled accounts other keepers often sent in), as well as his conscientiousness with working through the implications of the incident for watch-keeping generally. Cape Palliser, 1911 ... On the morning of the 16th, a few minutes after five, the glass on the main lamp broke or exploded with a violence, never before experienced by me. The glass was shivered to atoms and scattered all over the service-table and light-room floor. Some of the pieces were driven into the linoleum with such force that they had to be prized out with a pocket knife. But what I particularly want to emphasise in connection with this incident, is the probability of the destruction of the lighthouse by fire should the keeper on watch be absent for even a short period on the balcony or lower rooms. I feel sure from the way in which the flame flared about & rose to nearly three times its normal height that the burner would soon have become hot enough to have melted the solder about the tubes leading to the wicks, when, or course, the oil would have sprouted up into the flame and caught fire. Under these circumstances nothing could have saved the lighthouse from destruction. In this case no damage was done as the light was lowered immediately and a fresh glass put on; the whole incident lasting probably not more than half a minute. I do not suppose that this is a common occurrence; but what has happened once may happen again.

This incident has deeply impressed me with the absolute necessity of unremitting vigilance on the part of the keeper on watch.[25]

At East Cape in 1923 fire threatened the station. Because of the distance down to the houses, the men on watch slept in the signal hut close to the tower. George Ager, assistant keeper (whose wife had recently died), explained to the department that he had lit a fire in the hut to boil water for scrubbing out the tower. With winds at gale force he went outside, very properly, to watch two Sailing craft taking shelter one of which I fancied was putting up a hoist. [Apparently] an extra strong gust of wind blew the Signal box door open ... & swept the hot embers out on to the floor setting alight perhaps the blankets in the lower bunk.[26]

T. B. Smith, Ager's principal, documented the fire's progress: I am glad to say that after strenuous efforts keepers, with the assistance of what other help could be got, fire was kept from destroying the bush on the cliff seawards although many flax bushes & dead tree caught fire all along past the engine shed ... It was blowing a Westerly strong gale, so much so, that when the flames which swept against the bottom of the tower so fierce were they, released the burning timber & iron it was dashed on the tower & away down the cliff blazing & the iron away out to sea ... Its a great misfortune ... as the hut was ... so handy to keepers to sleep in by night instead of having to negotiate this awful track by night & the loss both to the Dept & keepers is considerate as the personal list will show you, my overcoat alone costing £8. I respectfully request that Dept. allow some compensation for our lost.

The Tiritiri Matangi station tractor shed going up, mid-1960s. After deciding the previous shed was no longer useful, Peter Taylor and his assistants demolished it, poured on kerosene, diesel and old engine oil, and applied a match. The fire, lighting with an explosion that threw the keepers backwards, burned with such vim that Auckland radio received phone calls of a disaster on the island.

MARITA AND PETER TAYLOR

... Mr Ager who has had so much trouble of late, was quite broken up over the matter & if he had not stayed after putting out watching these craft it would not have happened ... it was his misfortune that he was on watch at the time.[27]

Station fires were not unknown. Alan Martin was on Mokohinau: We had a relieving keeper on station based in this massive great building at the top of the hill, near the lighthouse and the power house. It was a wartime thing with about six bedrooms in it, great big hall, wash house, all this kind of stuff. We had just finished having morning tea and were outside putting our shoes on when I happened to look up and saw smoke coming out of this building. Of course we went haring up there, but by the time we got there, there was not a great deal we could do. There were two 20,000 litre water tanks up there but no way we could get water out of them. All we could do was throw water over the side of the power house which was separated from this building by this concrete piece here, and push the walls in as they collapsed. The roof, incidentally, was asbestos. And that was it. Right at the end we could see the hot water cylinder gently bubbling away and suddenly it took off like a rocket and it went up in the air and went right over the radio aerial at the top there.

I was on duty that day and I was coding up the weather report. In the ending comments I say, 'Unable to code up temperature due to proximity to burning building.' Which didn't even elicit a raised eyebrow from ZLB — they just took it and sent it off!

Six months after the 1923 East Cape fire, Smith reported another tedious and arduous task. Fortunately, the long track to the tower had been improved by the recent addition of galvanised iron handrails: I have to report that the light was more or less obscured during the greater part of the night, to the North, & North East, on the 3rd inst through been covered with Mud blown up from around the tower by the terrific gale that was blowing from the South West, & Keepers, although both in the tower all night, were unable to clean it away. The lee side of the tower is perfectly clay colour Keepers this morning ... cleaned the window panes having used 21 buckets of water. The frightful condition of mud around the tower in wet weather has been brought before your notice & requires immediate attention.[28] *In 1925 the area about tower was finally concreted.*

In 1929 the devastating force eight Murchison earthquake badly damaged the Kahurangi Point tower and destroyed station buildings. The shocks went far wider. A.V. Pearce describes the Farewell Spit keepers' almost heroic dedication to safeguarding the equipment against force seven shocks, and in maintaining subsequent watches. Numerous afterquakes, whose noise and rumbling seemed much worse in the tower than in the dwellings, were still being felt five months

FAREWELL SPIT LIGHTHOUSE
TYREE PHOTO 9069

later: I have the honour to inform you that on Monday 17th inst. at 10.17 a.m. we had a terrific earthquake at this station, causing some damage to both property & personal effects but in neither case extensive.

I may state when this shock happened the keepers were in the tower cleaning lenses and without any warning the lenses started to rattle and the noise became terrific then the apparatus started to jump and rattle at the most remarkable rate. Keeper Cooper and myself with all the strength we had, kept hold of them and pushed all we could against the direction she was swinging and kept the lenses on the rollers … the whole machine and case was working away from the bedplate … the whole machine and case jumped bodily nearly 7 inches in a S.E. direction and had it come another ½ inch the

The second Farewell Spit tower, shortly after its erection. By 1929 the vegetation had changed, but the photo shows well the frightening height above the ground at which Pearce and his men experienced the earthquake. ATL: TYREE COLLECTION 993

machine and case would have fallen to the S.E. and with the high apparatus and lenses on top would have over-balanced and fallen to the west without the slightest doubt through the lantern to the ground below it was an awful sensation for us but we remained during the whole of the severest portion of the shock and pushed to keep the lenses on the track … and no doubt it was Coopers & my own efforts by remaining and doing this that saved a great smash up, then when I saw it had only a fraction to go before coming over I ordered the men to get out of the tower at once at the moment the worst of the jumping was over.

We had great difficulty getting down the stairway owing to the heavy rolling motion, the large pine trees all bent over to nearly touch the ground and back again for 9 minutes but it was 33 minutes before the swaying ceased after the shock and it was most awkward to move about even hanging on to the rails

I then ordered the men to go home and see if their homes were safe and all were very much in an uproar wives & families were outside unable to move about things came down but not much damage was done … so far as I have investigated I can find nothing else broken & no structural damage to tower or buildings but kerosene and everthing movable was thrown in all directions in the store in the tower all spare gear rollers Etc were thrown over the floors but did no damage of a serious nature

The burner was lifted and thrown over the side of stand just hanging on by tail pipe, the bunsen burner & all other gear was wrenched out and thrown all over the tower floor, I have now fixed all this gear and the burners are all in good order again there being no damage to them that I could not repair myself

At 11.15 a.m. I went back to the tower to investigate damage … nothing further had happened to machine from the time we left as the severest was over but during that 6 minutes in the tower with Cooper & I pushing the apparatus against the direction of shake is no doubt what saved a very considerable smash up and it is very hard to describe as if it had come the other ½ inch and fell we all must have been killed on the spot. I mention Keeper Cooper & myself because Keeper Kelsey seemed bewildered & stood where he was at the time of the shock until I ordered all to leave the tower

I then sent you a wire reporting same and although I did not have any idea at the time that I would be able to rectify the damage in time to have the light functioning again that night I was able to forward a wire about 4 p.m. advising she would function as usual I did not get her correct to time until the second night she running some 3 seconds slow in a revolution of 8 minutes I found a screw or two loose next day and after second night she has run correct.

At 12.30 p.m. I went up and took timber Etc to use for toms and with aid of roller jacks I jacked the whole machine and apparatus back to within ¼ inch of position it was hard work with the material at hand but we are not able to lift the whole apparatus to replace the liners which are to level up the lenses on track these are pushed nearly out with jacking the machine back however she is nearly level on track but I have now left her until inspected … as I can do nothing better and she is now running at present while we were doing this work of getting the machine back we had several severe shocks but we stuck to it and we have had many severe shakes since and very many less severe ones totalling over 100 at time of writing Friday 21st a severe one at 7.17 p.m. again took place the next day after the severe shake (Tuesday) another severe one again threw the burner out of position which was found at light up time and caused a delay of 12 minutes in lighting up

At the time of the severe shock it was nearly low water but the sea all backed up to the usual high water spring tide mark and combined with very heavy rain flooded us all round the dwellings to 2 feet of water which makes the place a great discomfort to our wives & selves on Wednesday we had a heavy East gale & with the tide being so high the sea broke right over the bank below the tower & came over the bank in the house paddock scouring out great channels this kept like that when it should have been low water however when the wind shifted the sea moderated and has not come over the bank since but we still have the dwellings surrounded with water … [29]

In 1942 a series of earthquakes shook the Wellington region. D. D. McFarlane was in the Castlepoint tower which stands on a high narrow headland that drops steeply to the sea on one side and to a tidal lagoon on the other. On the night of the 24th June inst at 8.15 p.m. two earthquakes occurred one following quickly after the other. The first was slight but the second was rather violent. Mercury was spilled out of the apparatus bowl all over the machine and the Lighthouse floors. The apparatus stopped instantly and it was not until 9 p.m. that I managed to get the apparatus going again I cleaned up all the mercury and had the Lighthouse shipshape again when at 11.18 p.m. there was a terrific earthquake which lasted about 5 to 7 seconds. It broke the mantle and the mercury poured over the edges of the apparatus bowl of coarse the apparatus ceased revolving. I cleaned up a quantity of mercury but as there was more than I could cope with I called out Keeper H. Emerson. As soon as he could restore order in his dwelling he came to the Lighthouse and we gathered up the mercury but there was not sufficient to float the lenses we had to put about three pints more mercury into the bowl. Mr Emerson told me nearly everything in his house was down and broken When I arrived at my dwelling I found everything moveable & breakable broken … It was about 0-40 before the apparatus was revolving as it should … I had a most terrifying experience in the Lighthouse as I expected to see the whole lot go over Everything in the Lighthouse is now in good order but there is terrible disorder in the dwellings to be cleared up.[30]

Further quakes two months later did little to restore equanimity. McFarlane: Keepers here are getting afraid to go on watch in the Lighthouse at night time ... It is an unbelieveable experience to be in this Lighthouse in one of these earthquakes ... for about a fortnight I did not want to go inside the Lighthouse and I was expecting a shake every minute my body broke out in a rash all over owing to the shaking about my blood and nerves received.[31]

A year later another violent earthquake, which again spilt the mercury, jolted McFarlane into repeating a request he had made three months earlier, for a vessel to hold the mercury and a funnel to pour it back into the bowl. At present we are useing a tea cup for gathering up the mercury. Any vessel that has been soldered is no good for holding mercury because the mercury goes right through the solder. Then again we have to have a vessel for holding the mercury that has accumulatted in the mercury block on the driving shaft. This has to be emptied every two or three days. So I would appreciate it if I could have this vessel soon.[32]

WAR

During the First World War the department found recruitment difficult, but few existing keepers left for the front, and the extant letters suggest the tenor of the keepers' days was little affected by the catastrophic European events. Anders Hansen, for instance, forwarded to head office, for despatch to the proper authorities, a Bank receipt for £2.2.0, being Keeper's contribution to his Excellency, the Governor's Hospital ship fund.[33]

His assistant, George Odey, steps briefly into history: I wish to inform you that I am thinking of registering for service at the front if sufficient single men are not forthcoming. I should like to know if it would be possible for Mrs Odey & the children to remain at the Station while I would be away.

The Principal Keeper & his family would assist Mrs Odey in every way they could doing any work necessary.[34]

The aftermath of the war, not its waging, affected W. Tutt and his work at Pencarrow: On the 12th Mr Larkin whent to Wellington and found that his sister had died from Influenza got word from the Department that he was going to bury her, he caught it himself & since died.

Mr Millar took his place till the 22nd

Mr Holland arrived on the 22 & took Mr Millar's place as Temporary keeper, he had been working at the Marine store for a day & a half before coming to the Station But before that had been working at the Wellington Hospital handling dead people & loading them on wagons to be taken to the cemetery he was doing that for several days do you think that that was

right to send him to a lighthouse I must say that I do not considering that people are dying in Wellington by the hundreds, at the same time up to this he is doing his work well

May I hope that the next man is a keeper who has seen service, I have had nothing but Temporaries since I arrived at this station the parts[?] have been badly neglected & I want to put them in better order & with so many changes & bad weather cannot do much towards it.[35]

The Second World War was different. Almost immediately edicts were issued on economising, rationing came in, keepers enthusiastically complied. A. H. Saunders, Moeraki, 1940: Acknowledging receipt of Circular 1940–105 of 9th inst Regarding requisitioning for the minimum of stores necessary, I beg to mention that the necessity to economise was realised when preparing the requisition for stores for this station, but suggest some reductions can still be made at H.O. discretion. Cotton Waste, I still have 10lb. more or less on hand which can be made do, Coal we must have as very little drift-wood comes ashore here, & there

The Baring Head station, 1937. In a preemptive move that recognised the force of the wind at the site, the shelter hedge was planted during the construction period.

are three dwellings (one a coast watcher) to be supplied here now. Glass for repairing window panes is not a necessity. Also we can manage without the linen rubbers applied for and the filler for table lamp.[36]

As late as 1944 keepers were still contriving savings. T. Harte, Cape Reinga: I have to advise that when the coal situation became acute, and considering the high cost per ton for delivery at this Station, I drew the attention of the Keeper's Wives to the matter, and requested that consumption of coal be cut down as low as possible.

Fires are now allowed to go out for a few hours in the afternoon and economy is observed as far as possible …

No wood is available at this Station, and I have at times had to supply some coal to the mechanics for their use in the new hut.

You may be assured that we are keeping our consumption to the lowest possible, but the situation of the Dwellings, and the windy conditions at some Stations will give considerable variation in the consumption of coal. From my experience, Farewell Spit was the most economical Station, and a good supply of wood was available there for the copper, and sitting room fires. Here, the consumption of coal is more than doubled in windy conditions, and I am of the opinion that this Station is even worse than Baring Head for strong and constant winds.[37]

On 4 September 1939, when New Zealand had barely declared war, most lighthouse stations became part of a chain of coastwatching stations and keepers were instructed on 24-hour watching and reporting. The department employed additional men at some stations, but at Castlepoint D. D. McFarlane despatched a series of letters from October 1939: [E]ach watcher must keep watch from the Lighthouse balcony as it is the only place that commands an interrupted view of the sea ... They therefore could not assist with normal station duties; nor did all temporary keepers understand how to run a lighthouse station.[38]

Coastwatching took a lot of time. The loss of records now makes it impossible to ascertain whether D. D. McFarlane, still at Castlepoint in 1943 because transfers were largely suspended during the war, was unusually disgruntled, particularly outspoken or representing a more general take on the situation: I have to acknowledge receipt of your Memo of the 2nd August re roofing the Wash-house at the P.K's dwelling and in reply state that I will not be able to do this work or that of the iron Fence. The Marine Department do not seem to appreciate that we three keepers at this station are keeping 8 hr watches day & night seven days a week and have been doing so for nearly 4 years. The time I have off after keeping these watches is hardly enough to enable me to have a vegetable garden If there is anyone in the Public Service who should be paid overtime it is the keepers at this station. I will now endeavour to give you Sir, some idea of how we have to keep a constant watch at this station. I go on watch at 4 p.m. until midnight I have to rest before I go on watch and I have to have my evening meal in the Lighthouse. I come off at midnight and I have to be back in the Lighthouse by 8 a.m. the morning that is 8 hrs off I go on at 8 a.m. I have to have my

Castlepoint lighthouse. The long walk across the estuary and then up the hill on what was then a little-protected track added significantly to the hours keepers on watch were out of bed.

ATL: 11738½ GORDON BURT PHOTO

mid-day meal in the Lighthous. I come off at 4 p.m. and I have to be back in the Lighthouse at midnight that is 8 hrs off After doing 8 hrs from Midnight to 8 a.m. which is a very trying watch one must go to rest after completing this watch. This is the only way the watches can be kept here with three men if any other way was tried the men could not stand up to the constant day & night watches ... Hoping Sir I have given a plain statement of how constant watches at this station is maintained.[39]

Watching was not the only trial McFarlane had to bear. Being the principal government representative and caretaker of a strategic installation in a small community was not always a comfortable task: I have to acknowledge receipt of your Memo Protected Places together with five notices. I have erected these notices on boards in prominent places. I wish you please to advise me as to the position at this station or if the Inspector could visit here it would be better. It has always been the custom for people to come out here cross the footbridge and go fishing from the High Top as it is called below the Lighthouse and also over the reef People going to the Hightop to not go within 75 yards of the Lighthouse. I had no sooner erected the notices when three men came across the bridge to go fishing & I did not know if they were to be stopped. To stop all the people from going fishing here it would be necessary to have a sentry The case has arisen here when the Coastwatcher notified a visitor it was unlawful to take photographs he the visitor wanted to know where the Coast-watcher's authority was to stop him. You will see that we are placed in an awkward position here and your advise is necessary for us to know how to act.[40]

Worse was to follow. Fishermen walked past the notices, challenged McFarlane's authority when he told them to leave, the notices were cut down, and the Tinui police had to be called. A local resident's suggestion of passes raised tricky questions of who should and who should not be exempted, and the keepers, their authority continually challenged, acknowledged they were incapable of stopping trespassing at night. A fence was proposed — McFarlane had to point out that no-one went where it was planned to build it. By October 1942 the keepers, already fully occupied at night with watching and unable to leave the tower, were getting fed up: If it is necessary for the Minister to declare this is a prohibited Place then surely Sir is necessary to see that those orders are carried out by the defence authorities and not leave all the responsibilities to the Lightkeepers of this station. Please give me definate instructions about opening the reef & basin to the public.[41]

At Cape Brett, Mokohinau (from which the keepers were withdrawn until 1947), Tiritiri Matangi, Cuvier Island, Baring Head, Stephens Island and Godley Head stations, the Air Force or Navy manned radar installations; some lights were temporarily extinguished; those on Cuvier and Mokohinau were out until 1946 and 1947 respectively. Where keepers remained, the letterbooks carry surprisingly few references to the Forces. At Cape Brett, with the navy lending a hand, boat-day work was dramatically reduced, and with the tramline finally extended to the top of the hill (for the Navy's benefit), they could do all the haulage. At Stephens Island the telephone and alarm systems had to be overhauled to prevent all the signals going through the keepers' houses. Principal keeper L. E. Saint wanted the Marine Department to refuse the Navy permission to have a car on the island — in the interests of harmony. The Keepers would then be disinterested parties, and a lot of ill-feeling between keepers and Navey avoided ...[42]

A few months later he wrote again to the Marine Department: [I] advise the Navy and P.W.D. that the boat shed and siding should at all times be kept clear for traffic, and on no account should the keeper's dinghy be taken from off it's cradle.

For some time past, it has been the practice of both the parties mentioned to dump materials and fuel, etc., anywhere at all at the "Lister" landing, and this has caused considerable inconveniency to keepers when handling the dinghy. An occasional hour's fishing in this boat is our only means of obtaining a change of meat diet, recreation and relaxation from life on the station, and is therefore highly valued by the keepers and their families.[43]

With the war over, some stations faced a reversal to the pre-war provision of services. At Cape Brett Jamieson wanted the weekly mail service that had been instituted for the Navy to operate for the children on the Correspondence School programme: What was considered essential for single men should not be too much to ask where there are wives and families.[44]

A number of the stations became run down during the war. But the Tiritiri Matangi and Mokohinau letterbooks document a different magnitude of problem. We go first to Tiritiri Matangi in July 1947, which had reverted to Marine Department after being under Auckland Harbour Board control. C. Bowles and his assistants (among them G. Gilbert whose Love in a Lighthouse *is an amusing, highly readable account of his time there) arrived, poor weather set in, and Bowles took stock:* The Station, generally, is in a bad state — fences and out buildings have been allowed to fall to pieces, panes in the tower, and windows in most buildings leak. There are no paths, and in places the necessary tracks are only mud holes where it is impossible to keep dry feet.

Principal and 2nd Assistant's dwellings both leak badly, and in the first mentioned house there is no store-room or wardrobes, and very few cupboards. The other two houses are not so bad in this way. Stoves in two of the houses are burnt out, and there is no hot-water service, and a very poor bath in each of the three houses. At two of the houses concrete tanks are leaking badly and need urgent repairs.

A Public Works Inspector was here on the 11th, and I showed him some of the most urgent requirements which would help to make this station more habitable.

The keepers responsible for getting Mokohinau operational after World War II. From left: George Kroening, first assistant keeper; Norm Miller, principal keeper; Ernie Baker, second assistant keeper.

JEAN AND GEORGE KROENING

Will you please expedite delivery of linoleum, as the houses are cold without floor coverings, and two of the ladies are expectant mothers.

Also, would you arrange with the Rationing Officer for extra meat and butter rations until there are fences made stock-proof.[45]

Improvements, whether due to shortages or bureaucratic incompetence, were not rapid. Three years later Bowles was facing an Alice-in-Wonderland situation: New stoves and hot-water supply services are being installed without a water supply being allowed for, which is rather short-sighted. The tanks that are here are inadequate and in poor condition. I explained in my monthly letters that water was very short during summer months and before any appreciable rain came to ease the situation it would have to be carted.

I think that a responsible officer of the department should see just how badly repairs are needed and how far those buildings have been neglected before cutting expenses ...

The roof of the spare house is completely crystalised and during gale last week large hole was torn in it: other roofs are in similar condition, and quite an amount of the wood work is rotten.[46]

The Mokohinau light was closed down in December 1940 for the duration of the war, the keepers were withdrawn in mid-1941, and until 1947 the station operated as a radar station. Norm Miller, principal keeper, was the first to return after the Marine Department had retaken possession. His assistants, Charlie Emmens (first assistant) and George Kroening (second), would not arrive until later. Miller formally marked the station's resumption as a lightstation.

Letter Book.
<u>Commencing at Re-opening of Station 31.1 47.</u>
Moko Hanau
14. 2. 47

Sir
... I wish to advise, that I commenced duties as Principal Keeper at this station on the 31st January 1947 ...

[A few days before] an inspection of the power house revealed the fact that the batteries had not been topped up with distilled water for a long period (approximately 20 gallons were subsequently required to bring the electrolyte to a safe level above the plates.)

The engines were also being ill-treated badly in various ways, none of the P.W.D. staff on the island having any knowledge of the equipment.

... Although time has not permitted of a complete stocktaking it is already evident that the greater part of the moveable equipment, tools and stores, have disappeared, and requisition will have to be made for a large number of items, before the station can be restored to normal.[47]

Pages followed listing needed items. A brief excerpt from Miller's oil and fog return adds to the picture of what the Air Force had left behind.

Oil & Fog Return Feb 1947

This return is preliminary only, and some correction will almost certainly be necessary at a later date. Until Assistant Keepers arrive, and I am able to handle all drums and check contents, it is impossible to arrive at accurate figures.

A total of 68 drums, stored in various parts of the island, contain oil of some description. In most cases, drums are badly rusted, brands obliterated, and contents in doubt ...[48]

He reported again in March that repairs to the lighthouse were progressing well and noted his work for the month: I have been engaged in hauling effects and stores from the landing, cleaning and checking over equipment in powerhouse, repairing telephone lines, scrubbing out houses, laying linoleum, moving and checking over furniture, attending launch at landing, and attending to official correspondence, returns and requisitions.

Subsequent letters dealt with a possible outbreak of TB in the cows, the future of the naval buildings, and breakdowns of equipment. On 28 April 1947 Miller reported that the two keepers were working nights to try to get everything back to normal.

In July 1947 he wrote that the PWD men had left the station with the tower not fully painted and leaking, the tramline not fully overhauled, and while the new concrete block for the wharf had been put in, the ladder they had installed was unsatisfactory and the landing block was difficult to operate. In the post-war years the PWD was doubtless under considerable pressure, but the lack of liaison between keepers and the Marine Department did not help — Miller's remark is an acerbic comment on the department's failure to keep its keepers informed: P.W.D. All men and material left the station on the 26th June. Apparently no further work is to be carried out by this Dept. in the meantime.[49]

CHAPTER 7

The domestic routines

THE DAILY ROUND, THE COMMON TASK

In The Plot Against America *Phillip Roth writes of the 1930s lower-middle-class American women who 'worked all the time, with little assistance from labor-saving devices,' washing, iron-ing, darning, turning collars, sewing on buttons, 'polishing furniture, sweeping and washing floors, washing windows, cleaning sinks, tubs . . . stoves . . . nursing the sick, cooking meals' and tidying 'while simultaneously attending to their children's health, clothing, cleanliness, schooling, nutrition, conduct, birthdays, discipline, and morale.' Their focus, and it was one shared by lighthouse wives who mostly had even fewer labour-saving devices than Roth's women, was primarily, and inevitably, domestic. Yet, as the following brief excerpt from Hannah Parks' diary shows, within that focus, lives were varied by visits, visitors, home entertainment and keeping quiet while the men caught up on much-needed sleep — not easy in houses that even the department was acknowledging were cramped and flimsily partitioned. Hannah Parks wrote a diary in 1893 while at Nugget Point. The following are typical entries:*

Feb 16th Thu. Putting away preserves. Up in garden. S.S. "Pukaki" came into Bay for shelter. Officer came ashore. Working machine. Another wild night. Too bad for Arthur and Jack in tent.

Feb 17th Fri. Too wet for the boys to go to station. A lot of signalling to the steamer. It is still too wild for her outside.

Feb 18th Sat. "S.S. Pukaki" left the Bay and "Napier" anchored under Nug-gets. Anderson to dine with us. Jack's brother Tom came down . . .

Mar 6th Mon. Alex and Arthur working down at the rocks. Alex lay down for a sleep after dinner. M. Jackman etc. came. I walked with them. Laila and Jessie for mail. Lucy and I for goats. Mrs Ottaway and Martha up in evening.

Mar 8th Wed. Mr. and Mrs. Colley and family away for a ride. A hot morning and wet afternoon — only Mr. Colley returned late.

Mar 9th Thu. In garden gathering rhubarb and onions and doing a little work.

Mar 10th Fri. "Tommy" sledging firewood. Visitors while we were at dinner. Heard of Mr. Anderson's accident. Children went for mail, etc. and to see [words indecipherable] …

26th Sun. I lit fire for girls and fried tomatoes. Dear Edward did not come. Sat out in sun reading and looking for him. After dinner read and walked with girls. Alex slept …

Mon 27th Mon. Alex and I off quite early to Balclutha. I stayed at McNeil's. They were very busy but made me very welcome. Alex was a little later than he said and I found he had a very narrow escape of being hurt badly as "Tommy" ran away. It was a mercy he stopped. Very excited all the way home with the new buggy. Called at "Erlstoke" and reached home in a heavy shower.

Mar 28th Tue. Drying rugs and things. Colley's went for a drive. I busy washing.

Mar 30th Thu. Finishing my washing, mangling etc. and getting ready for Catlins. Kenny Campbell up with message. I wrote to Harry …

Apr 4th Tue. Usual duties. Teaching children and ironing. In the afternoon Alex slept and I went out with Lucy, Laila and Jessie to McKinlay's.

Apr 5th Wed. Making up the telephone money and sent Arthur with the mail. Hot and windy after dinner – sent the children to play to let Alex sleep. Teaching, making pickles. Early to bed …

Jun 30th Fri. Bought from Indian at door:
    1 apron 2-3d
    9 handkerchiefs 5-6d
    1 muslin pinafore 3-0d
    Wound the striking clock – got it to go …[1]

Elizabeth Hansen with two of her daughters, Annie on the left and Lena on the right, on the verandah of a Tiritiri Matangi station house, early 1900s.
HANSEN COLLECTION

Hannah Parks left no record of how she managed her domestic tasks or of her daily routine. For that we turn to the twentieth-century wives. Jean Kroening, in the Service before the stations' electrification, describes her day-to-day housework, which in her case included milking: There were times in the winter when George was on the late shift, the cow would arrive up at the gate. Well, I just automatically did it. It took a while but I milked poor old Cherry. I'd be up probably seven o'clock, milk the cow, light the fire, get in the wood and the coal, make the beds, you did your dishes, your washing. I used to have breakfast when George came in from the light and

Cakes were not the only things to be posted out from lighthouse stations where the chief postmasters were the principal keepers. Fred Hansen, recuperating from the war at Cape Brett early 1920s, posted fish and wrote on the back of this photo: 'The Cape Brett mail for Russell full of smoked fish. The last lot you got is in the bag & the man is Mr Pearce, the Chief Postmaster.'

HANSEN COLLECTION

before he went out to do his chores. The washing, the ironing took so long. I learned to use a flat iron — you heat it on the stove. I burnt a few things. I washed — just being the two of us we didn't have a lot. I would go down the garden, and get whatever vegetables there were. George did the garden. We had cooked tea. That was the old miners' basic instinct, the men being at the mine all day, cooked tea at night. Lunchtime would be scrambled eggs, boiled eggs, poached eggs, whatever eggs there were available. Out would come that can opener that I don't like and George and I would have some salmon or something. In the winter it was soup — that kept me busy. Not having a fridge you made it fresh every day or every couple of days. I think it was just the general housework that kept me busy. On my own I used to knit. My aunts would send wool and I'd knit for them. And I learned to bake. We were still able to get dried fruit. I used to make fruit cakes and put two in a five-pound biscuit tin we used to get and post that down to the Coast.

There was no corner dairy, let alone a range of shops, where essential household goods could be purchased. Jean remembered unpacking her stores at Portland Island for the first time: I looked at my three cakes of soap and thought, Oh dear, they won't last three months. I remembered my mum making soap. Every time a sheep was killed I saved every bit of fat and I made soap. I got the recipe from my mother and got the ingredients, boiled up the fat to clarify it, got all the bits of meat and everything out of it — strained it — put it in the copper with so much water, caustic soda went in last, so much washing soda, and I lined the wooden tubs with one of my best sheets and baled with a baler out into the tub and let it set. And then I cut that soap. I was so thrilled!

The first kerosene fridges went to Centre Island in the early 1950s. Twenty years later than the Kroenings, and with more household appliances, Shirley Martin's basic routine was still much like Jean's, though she had Correspondence School for two children to fit in, as well as the cooking for technicians who, as the lighthouse apparatus got more sophisticated, were frequently on the station. (The department paid the husband an allowance to cover food and board.) If my husband was on duty he'd be up before six o'clock to turn the light off and send the weather. He'd come down the hill. At Mokohinau he'd get the cows in for milking, light the fire. I'd get up say about quarter to seven. On Mokohinau the men milked the cows because the principal keeper was concerned that the women might get stepped on and you don't want accidents on remote stations — accidents used to happen to us at regular intervals. I'd have cooked a breakfast, got the kids all organised for the morning. When they started school I'd be trying to do the school and teach them at the same time, do the washing, put that out, come in, see if the kid's been doing his writing properly, and nip back out again. You'd be baking bread, preparing

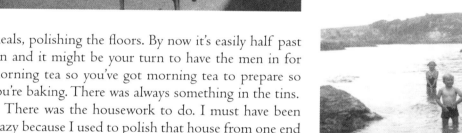

meals, polishing the floors. By now it's easily half past ten and it might be your turn to have the men in for morning tea so you've got morning tea to prepare so you're baking. There was always something in the tins.

There was the housework to do. I must have been crazy because I used to polish that house from one end to the other once a week; the windows, because salt spray got on them I'd be out there with methylated spirits at least twice a week. But I was young and fit and I was on the go from daylight to dark. The floor was polished. It seemed like half an acre when you're on your hands and knees. And it was red lino and showed every scrap of dust — old houses seem to be pretty dusty, and with a coal range of course. Twice a year the chimneys had to be cleaned, and that meant spring-cleaning. It didn't matter how careful you were with putting the sheet up round the mantelpiece, soot always escaped. It's difficult to get off with just hot soapy water and elbow grease. Yes, I seemed to have the mop in my hand all the time, trying to keep the dust down.

There'd be lunch, washing up, there'd still be the children to attend to with schoolwork again. After their schoolwork we'd probably go off and swim. Or we'd take them down fishing, give them a line to hang on to and show them things in the rock pools, take them for a row in the boat. And then it was dinner time and everybody's exhausted. We went to bed fairly early —

TOP LEFT *'Shirley Martin, local barber, at work on No. 1 son. Mokohinau 1960s.'* ALAN AND SHIRLEY MARTIN

TOP RIGHT *Linley Rodda on Stephens Island in the early 1960s, ensuring the family would not go hungry.* ANZ (WGTN) AAQT 6401 A73481

ABOVE *Children swimming at Mokohinau, 1940s.* JEAN AND GEORGE KROENING there was nothing much to do, you could play cards, we'd play Monopoly or something like that. The children were in bed by about seven o'clock. I suppose we could be in bed by about half past eight, maybe nine o'clock at the latest, because Mokohinau was what they call a full-weather station and that's weather every three hours and the men would work in shifts and Alan might be doing midnight to 6 a.m. so he wants to get some sleep because his sleep's going to be broken with getting up at 12, three, and then again at six. Also occasionally something would go wrong with the equipment and the big fire bells would go.

There were quite a few workmen, and you give them morning tea, you give them afternoon tea, dinner, supper, and it's like running a restaurant. All cooked in those days, you didn't just give them sandwiches, you made them a shepherd's pie or you cooked them something. Good heavens, it's a wonder we weren't as fat as bacon pigs. But out there you're doing a lot of physical work.

To busy housewives on Stephens Island the dovies (fairy prions) and mutton birds must, at times, have been almost the last straw. Barry Langman: There are vast numbers there, I would say millions. When the dovies come in they seem to come in about wave height and then they fly up a few feet above the land contour and they fly into the fences, they fly into the lighthouse, they fly into the houses. You couldn't leave your drop sash windows open during the night because the dove petrels would come straight through and they'd land and you'd hear them strutting around underneath your bed and you'd get out and find half the sea food they'd been eating and ingesting was scattered all over the floor. They used to hit the telephone lines and they go 'Spang' and the lines would vibrate into the house — they were a hell of a nuisance. I think the beams of the light blinded them. The most ever I found round the tower was 32 dead birds. That was in one night — they'd hit, then drop down, necks broken. Then they used to impale themselves on the top or second wire of the barbed wire fence, and hang there and die. The mate'd be anxiously waiting.

There was a small colony of mutton birds there as well, and they're a very solid compact bird — dove petrels, fairy prions actually, are a very small bird, but the mutton birds are a different kettle of fish. When they come in — if you get hit by one, it'd bowl you over. They fly about 40 miles an hour. The dove petrels used to flutter round and hit you on the shoulder. They were rowdy birds, all the time, all night long, you'd hear the females in the burrows calling out, 'Where y'been? Where y'been?' Where y'been?'

A Brothers keeper with a fairy prion, or dovie, chick. CHRIS STALEY

The Taylor children's Nugget Point playground. MARITA AND PETER TAYLOR

Caring for small children in particular devolved on the women, although Barry remembered his came with him when he was working near the house. At Akaroa, where the houses were on the edge of a 100-metre cliff, children were confined to the house garden. Even on the gentler slopes of Mokohinau, Shirley found childcare had its moments: They used to vanish as soon as you'd turn your back. You'd be pegging the clothes on the line and they'd go out the other side of the house and disappear. I was busy — must have been polishing the floors — and the phone rang at Moko and Mrs Johnson said, 'Did you know your boys are in the pig paddock?' 'No-o!' As far as I knew they were outside digging in the dirt, just outside the house. I was terrified of pigs. It was our first station and I was a city girl. Fortunately I couldn't see any pigs and I couldn't get to our back paddock fast enough. I took the belt with me and I yelled at them and if they slowed down their bottom got a pat, 'Get home, get home!'

As they grew older the boundaries enlarged — though the Martins, like other keepers, had strict rules. My boys when we were at Baring Head would think nothing of, 'Can we go off and camp down by so and so?' You'd say, 'All right,' and off they'd go with a sleeping bag and a little pup tent. They had a lot of freedom there, really. Cuvier, it was fairly rugged. We had a rule. I had to know which direction they were going in, where they were likely to fish and they had to be home at a certain time. They knew if they weren't home within half an hour of the time they'd stipulated a search party would be coming for them. Yes, we had rules, but they were very self-sufficient boys by that time. In fact it

David (left) and Peter Martin with the catch for smoking, Cuvier Island, c. 1980.

ALAN AND SHIRLEY MARTIN

got to the stage where we'd go out snorkelling and instead of Mum watching them they'd be watching Mum to make sure she didn't get into any trouble!

The early diesel engines used to power the lights (initially only they were electrified) were 110 volts DC and so were not suited to what Alan Martin called 'normal person things'— vacuum cleaners, washing machines, electric fridges. Then it was found that the diesels worked best if they were run all the time — and they generated 230 volts AC, suitable for household appliances. But worries about how much fuel was being used and other concerns meant restrictions on domestic use. Shirley: You could use your ordinary household appliances but you had the power on only for certain times because you were still running on diesel. Some principal keepers were very particular about when you could use the power. Dog Island, the principal keeper we had there, he didn't like you to use the electric jug while the light was on just in case the power surge was too great and triggered the alarm bells. By that time we'd been in the Light Service quite a long time and if it didn't make the bells ring it was all right to use it. But I remember him knocking on the door at seven o'clock one morning: 'You have the electric jug on!' I couldn't say no, because there it was, steaming on the bench. He'd been watching the voltage and seen it drop. 'But the bells didn't ring!' 'That's not the point.'

In whatever state it arrived, food always came in bulk. Jean on Portland Island: When they killed the sheep, we would have half and we made a bag out of sheet to wrap around it. We hung it in the alleyway between the old washhouse and the house. It kept maybe two weeks in the winter. But the first time I had that half-sheep put on my bench and I thought, Now how do I cut that? How do I cook it? So down the paddock I went, 'George, come and cut the meat.' And he did.

Shirley: There was a grocer we dealt with who was very good at telling you, 'Oh, you'll need 40 pound of flour, 70 pound bag of sugar,' things like that, and you took out a sack of potatoes and whatever vegetables you thought you needed. Meat, if you required it, was brought out in an icebox. You had a kerosene refrigerator with a bit of freezer space and you had to work round that. You had to grow things in the garden or you had no fresh food. It was no good getting much in the way of frozen foods. You got to the stage where you'd buy tinned food by the case lots — two dozen tins of baked beans, the same of spaghetti and vegetables.

Principal keeper Noel Proebstel dressing a carcass, Cape Brett, 1970s. STEVE O'NEILL

We didn't have any sheep on Moko. We had cattle and pigs and when we were going to kill a beast we used to get somebody over from Great Barrier to come out and they'd kill it and take half of it away and the other half would be for the three keepers and it was usually a fully grown steer, and there was an awful amount of meat on that.

I remember the first time it happened standing there with a book in the hand saying, 'Cut down to there, turn right at the next bone,' and waving the flies away! My husband would come home with this baby bath of meat and I'd say, 'What's this?' And he'd say, 'I don't know! Steak?' You ate that and all the nice bits quickly before they went off, and froze what you could.

Like Jean, Shirley learnt from the old hands: Phyllis Johnson [the principal keeper's wife on Mokohinau] taught me how to make bread properly, how to make my own bread starter instead of relying on yeast blocks — potato water and you start feeding it with sugar and flour each day, it made a very nice loaf of bread. Things to do with meat and how to cure it and how to do this and do that — if I had any questions she was always very good at answering them.

The Brothers keepers, faced with domestic duties, generally had even more than the women to learn. Chris Staley: I remember seeing one guy first day he was duty cook. I went into the kitchen and these pots were boiling on the stove. I said, 'What are you doing now?' He said, 'I'm getting dinner ready.' Well, this is round mid-day and we had dinner at, I dunno, half past four, five o'clock at night and he was boiling vegetables then. They'd be slightly overcooked by five o'clock! But they quickly learnt.

On The Brothers twentieth-century keepers had few opportunities to acquire butchering skills. Chris Staley was on one of his stints on a land station: I did steal a lamb one day, on one station, I won't say where. The local farm had plenty, millions, and these lambs were trotting around the station so I decided, I'll have a leg of lamb. So I shot this lamb and hung it up a tree but I didn't know what to do, to be quite honest. It was quite an experience. I think I ended up burying most of it. I took its back legs off and tried roasting them. But on many stations, Puysegur in particular, I shot many deer.

Alan Wright, on The Brothers with Chris, regularly listened to Aunt Daisy: So I wrote her one day and told her how we enjoyed her programme and after a while, once a week, it got into her patter: 'To my boys on The Brothers, here's a recipe for you.' It was for proper food, all sorts of things. We actually went over to see her, one day when we were on leave.

With Aunt Daisy to help overcome inexperience, The Brothers keepers did themselves all right. Chris: The food was all provided by the Marine Department. We had a wonderful storeroom, full of everything, so you could experiment. We had a huge stack of cookery books, we'd go through them. If you cocked it up, well, you threw it away and that was it, it was of no cost to us. We used to have a full dinner every night. We used to have a lunch too, when we'd finished work around one o'clock, that's when we'd have things like soup. People used to have a go at pasta, anything. The boat used to come on a regular basis every two weeks, so they used to bring out all these stores for us, bread, meat and veg, things like that. But also there were many, many times when they did special trips to bring out mechanics, electricians, they'd always bring us a couple of loaves of bread. We had our own fowls out there too, we had unlimited supply of eggs, excellent fish — cooked them, smoked them. We used to have quite a few roasts, lamb and beef and what have you.

By the 1960s alcohol was tolerated as long as it did not interfere with the job, and the men on The Brothers became experts in more than food. Chris: Skiffington [the department's personnel officer] could never understand why we used to get a sack of spuds every fortnight, a big sack, a hundredweight sack and six pounds of rice! We were exchanging sake with the fishermen and all sorts — a bottle of sake for a couple of crayfish.

Their nineteenth-century counterparts did not share Chris and his men's culinary experiences. In 1879, and two years after the station had been commissioned, J. W. Cunningham had to explain why he had 'issued rations in excess of scale'. This is the first intimation of problems that would persist, intermittently, until the 1920s: I now beg leave to State that the quantity of Flour used in excess was expendid but not used as the bag of Flour turned out to be bad and the bread made from it was sour and could not be eaten. Therefore we were obliged to use biscuits until such times as we

Chris Staley captioned the back of this photo: 'Alan Wright sleeping off the booze.'

got bread baked the potatoes were rotten … The quantity of Butter used in excess of scale was rancid and only fit for cooking purposes I issued Sugar and Tea in excess as I found I could not do otherwise not having any Oatmeal and being out of Potatoes.[2]

Growing vegetables on The Brothers was impossible, and for years the range of food was as limited as its keeping qualities. 1882 brought with it a series of problems. Robert Wilson recorded that, among the station stores, they had also received: 20 lbs Fresh Beef, 1 side 20 lbs Mutton, 1 Case 72 lbs Preserved Meat, 1 Bag 40 lbs Sugar, 2 Cwt potatoes, 200 lbs Flour, 6 Cabbages, 5 Bundles each carrots & turnips, 1 Vegetable Marrow. I regret to say the side of Mutton which came by last trip of Stella on the 17th inst was bad & had to be thrown away, although it was salted the same day as it came, The Fresh Beef was very little better, but we managed to eat it. Also the last three casks of Salt Beef that have come here have all been bad, some of which I reported in a letter on 27th Dec. 1881 there is 141 lbs on hand now which I will send to Wellington by next trip of Stella, for your inspection, as it is quite unfit for use.

Nothing of importance has taken place during the month.[3]

And again in July: We have exceeded our allowance of Butter in consequence of our being without potatoes for about a fortnight before the steamer arrival and our increased consumption of bread and butter owing to that deficiency.[4]

At times in the late nineteenth and early twentieth centuries, live sheep were hoisted on to the island for fresh meat, but they were inclined to fall off the steep rock, and fresh provisions

The flying fox, installed in 1886–87 to facilitate getting provisions and mail to and from the mainland to the Motuopao station. Samuel Hart, in an article in the Public Service Journal, *recorded that before wire was put in, Maori brought the mail from Parengarenga and the keepers came across to pick it up. 'The swift current and beam seas ... made these crossings wet and often risky.' Once the boat capsized; the men, hanging on to the keel, kicked it ashore, and managed to get back with 'one oar and the blade of another.' They had shed most of their clothing — as they returned, the station women, noting 'their abbreviated attire ... retreated to a discrete distance, preferring to greet us when clad more conventionally.' In the early days of its operation, the flying fox would break, and months, if not years, could pass before the lighthouse ships arrived to lay a new wire.* HANSEN COLLECTION

continued to be unreliable. William Tutt, 1912: The 120 lbs fresh beef that was landed was bad; it was stinking and alive with maggots after taking up the stores we thought what a treat fresh meat would be for our dinner we were sadly disappointed now as the meat was only on the Hinemoa 24 hours it must have been bad before it was received half of the Suet was alive as well through beasts crawling out of the bag. this sort of thing can easily be stoped if you would please ask the Steward of the Hinemoa to inspect the meat for us, the corn beef was alright but 2½ lbs short weight on the 25 killed a sheep 60 lbs.[5]

Attitudes on women's roles and the heavy round of domestic duties meant women were not officially involved with station work until the wider social changes in the 1970s. Shirley: At Cuvier when they were demanning my husband and I were the only people there. We were taught how to use the radio and send a weather report in case of emergency. And also how to turn the radio beacon on if the men were away working somewhere and there was a request for a signal. Particularly at a place like Baring Head where you've got a telephone line, someone might phone up and say, 'The beacon's required at such and such a time.' It only operated continuously at night and in fog. I didn't really practise. We were shown how to do these things in an emergency.

FLOODS AND FURNISHINGS, SCULLERIES AND STOVES: THE DOMESTIC WORK ENVIRONMENT

On paper the houses the Lighthouse Service built for its keepers look solid, if somewhat cramped, by today's standards. But the reality often did not match the design. What follows is a tiny fraction of the numerous complaints about housing and domestic amenities that litter the letterbooks.

In 1881 Charles Robson arrived at Portland Island station, commissioned only three years previously. Neither the daunting dereliction he faced nor the perception of the department's false economising would be atypical. I have to report the following articles deficient here, in the Principal Keepers house there is no double Bedstead … the only cheap double bedsteads now supplied to Lightkeepers will in the end be found more expensive than a stronger article as they wont last and I beg to suggest that in the future any bedsteads purchased by the Department should be put together at the store where they are bought, and so inspected before they are accepted … One dressing table and one chair belonging to the Principal Keepers house are in use in the Lightroom, and as it is necessary to have them there to accommodate the Keeper on duty, and to place the books and lamp on, perhaps you will be so good as to send others in their place, there is also no pillow for the Colonial sofa in the Principal Keepers house and no medicine guide … American leather cloth or other material is also much wanted to cover the mattress for Colonial sofa I find a number of tools broken and useless which should be written off, and there are a number of bottles in the medicine chest which are empty, on a future occasion I will send a list of what is required to fill them, unless you see fit to send me a chest similar to one recently forwarded to Pencarrow, and which would be much better suited to an isolated station like this (where there are a good many persons) than the small one we now have.

I have the honor to direct your attention to the bad condition of the Principal Keeper's and first Assistant's houses, neither of which are rain proof, on the second and third instant this station was visited by a severe gale with rain from S & SW , the rain penetrated the roofs of both houses in all directions to windward, and on the morning of the 3RD the kitchen of the Principal Keeper's house was found to have been converted into a pond, not a foot of it being even moderately dry, the varnish in this house never has dried and never will dry, owing probably to its having been adulterated with oil, and all the dust etc raised in sweeping is stuck to the walls so that they are in a shocking condition, clothing hung against them sticks fast, and the only remedy which I can suggest is to paper them, if you approve of doing so please send me some paper for the purpose as soon as possible or all our clothes will be ruined.[6]

Robson's letter did not end there. His situation was not atypical. At Centre Island in 1888, ten years after the light's commissioning, unsuitable building materials left Charles Tregurtha's poor assistant enduring more than scrounging for wood in execrable weather. Tregurtha: 1st Assistants house flooded in every room, clothing, bedding etc all wet. This house has always leaked in wet & stormy weather, and we have several times, endeavoured to stop the leaky places, but without much success. I think the

Centre Island under snow and the first lot of the station houses. LES AND JO BROOM

most of it drives in under the ridging and could be best stopped by substituting lead ridging for the galvanized iron. A great many of the weatherboards etc in that and the other buildings are quite rotten, and it will be necessary to do considerable repairs before long.[7]

The Centre Island houses were repaired in 1897. By then Tregurtha and his family were at Cape Egmont station, established 15 years previously. It was almost being out of the frying pan into the fire. There too they found dirty homes in poor repair and household items missing. Tregurtha, December 1896: On the 5th received 2 single iron bedsteads I found on arrival here, that 2 single bedsteads belonging to Principal keepers house, was in the Dry Store, but neither of them was in good order, being tied together with strings, [indecipherable] broken etc and the double bedstead is nearly as bad, several of the locks in the house will not work. I intend taking them off, and cleaning them, but hitherto I have not had time. One of the inside doors is off altogether and two hinges of the storeroom door are broken. I am asking for new hinges for these doors. The sash cords on nearly every window in both houses are broken, and I have had to wash the walls and ceilings all through the house, as they were black with smoke etc.[8]

By the 1890s the department had recognised that some of the station houses were 'barely habitable.' Upgrading began, but generally it was inadequate, and by the 1920s complaints escalated. Quite apart from the additional work, one can only guess at the frustration and heartbreak, that in 1923, poor William Glass's wife at Castlepoint (who was bringing up five children) had to contend with: During the light rains of Jan 14th, 15th, & 16th, the roof over the kitchen started to leak.

On the 15th inst, I examined the whole of the roof, & found the malthoid completely perished & pitted with holes. On going above the ceiling, I found 16 kerosene tins had been placed on the joists to catch the rain as it ran down the rafters. At places I could see daylight through the joints of the sarking boards. On the 17th inst, I informed the Principal Keeper & he instructed me to put patches over the largest & most conspicuous holes.

On the morning of the 22nd inst at 3.30 a.m it commenced to rain very heavily, & when I came off the last watch, & returned home, I found the roof had been leaking very badly again, damaging some of my private furniture, sewing machine & covers etc, which were standing in the kitchen ... I had to take up my linoleum in the kitchen ... I also removed all the furniture from the kitchen & my wife was fully occupied all day mopping up the water to stop it running through the house.[9]

Two months later Glass reported leaks in every room.

In 1926 R. Haven and his assistant on Dog Island were still in the original dwellings, built in 1865: I beg to report that Asst. Keeper Williams has moved into the house just vacated by Asst. Keeper Brown who left by the steamer on transfer to Centre Island

The reason for moving being that the roof of his house is in such a leaky condition that the water drips on their faces when asleep in bed at night making it very uncomfortable for them and also soiling the bedclothes, their storeroom also leaks very badly.[10]

No. 33—Dog Island Lighthouse

Dog Island station in the early 1900s. The old double house, just to the right of the tower, was where the keepers lived until new houses were built in 1926. In the 1960s the double house became the powerhouse and new state-house-type homes were built. Pip Aplin, assistant to Alan Martin, described theirs 'as solid as a brick shithouse' and ice-cold, in spite of the insulation they installed.

ALAN AND SHIRLEY MARTIN

New houses at Dog Island, begun in 1927, presumably ended the discomfort and the tedious, frustrating and back-breaking work of hand-washing and drying sheets and heavy blankets with which poor Mrs Brown must have struggled. At Moeraki station in 1928, Mrs Johnson faced a situation that need not have arisen. (The condition of the house was symptomatic of the station. The crane, the non-working electric bells, water tanks, rotting coal bins, sagging fences all needed attention, and the steady programme of work, which the two keepers undertook, was still going on into 1931.) J. C. Johnson: I wish now to inform you that at the time of Steamer's last visit, Captain Bollons inspected station & houses & one of the items was condition of wall papers on bedrooms; one room in P. K's house been in the worst state, scrim & paper hanging from walls. The suggestion was for me to pull it all off, & see what it was like below. This part I have done & though it is patched & not clean looking, it is better than the state room was in before:—

The under coats of paper have no scrim at all & paper has been pasted to bare boards ... there was 5 or 6 different coats of paper ... the last lot having been put on with scrim as well, & this work very badly laid out, for it (scrim) had simply been tacked to walls ... the result was that the scrim between weight & air draughts pulled over tack head & lose everywhere, billowing down into room ...

We have not yet put in a winter here & am unable to say how cold the draughts may be or what rooms may be like in winter In my opinion a much better way than papering to have stopped the trouble in the first place, was to have procured supply of those light woods such as Maxwell or Beaver boards or the 3ply variety & lined the rooms in panel style. This would have been effective for it could be fitted close & properly nailed in place, – seams covered by board slips, it would take away so very little room space, & would last any·length of time when it was done. also it could be oiled varnished, or painted any colour similar to rest of house.[11]

The state of the houses do need to be seen in a wider perspective. In the 1940s a teacher on country service in a remote rural district moved into an Education Department house that had sacking over the windows and when he asked about a lavatory, the locals pointed to the nearest bush. Jeanette and Pip Aplin remembered dry rot and unfurnished accommodation in their orchard-supplied house. But the Marine Department's propensity to skimp on cheap materials and solutions and its perennial reluctance to address the problems resulted in considerable frustration. In 1954 Jo Broom at Cape Reinga had put up with badly leaking windows for over two years. Les wrote the first letter in September: In reply to your Memo 8/63/3 regarding windows in the above dwelling ...

The Ministry of Works official mentioned one of the biggest faults was the windows were glazed on the inside, this allows the rain to drive under the glass and spray the whole room with a fine shower of Rain. The only

way to stop this is to draw the blinds. These are now becoming rotten with the wettings they have been getting in the past years and are really in need of replacing … until some decision is reached I would appreciate it if the dept would supply towling as this is the most effective way of coping with the water for the moment.[12]

In May 1956, after MOW had informed him of the impossibility of doing anything at all with the windows, Les ended yet another report somewhat plaintively: This will be the 3rd winter of this, and my wife is fed up to the teeth with it, and at times makes my own domestic life rather hard. Even though I like this station very much it makes one feel like asking for a transfer to a station at least where the houses are waterproof.[13]

Not until 1 April 1957 were new windows installed.

If leaks and draughts were not enough, a number of the early homes had not been built with families in mind. Although from the 1890s the department recognised that many of the original houses were too small, the upgrading and enlarging programmes lagged behind need. In 1937 T. R. Tennent describes his second assistant's house on Centre Island: [It's] a 3 roomed bachelor cottage, the rooms being very small, pantry & scullery being merely a lean-to. When 5 of us are in the kitchen there is no room to turn around. This means that we have had to pack most of our belongings & store & bach. We shall have to try & borrow furniture from the other houses as there is only two beds, & one chest-of-drawers. This house has been occupied by temporary keepers, for a number of years, hence no complaints before this, & they have been practically baching.[14]

Additional duties not envisaged when the homes were built created further pressure on available space. Principal keepers mostly had homes larger than those of their staff; on school-house stations it was they who boarded the teacher. Until the post-World War II renovations, the post office operated out of one of their rooms. Wives lived with the public having constant access and the frustration of having their space taken over by an official function. At Cape Brett in 1944 H. E. Jamieson adopted a fairly peremptory tone to try to get departmental approval for the long list of necessary renovations and maintenance: Next there is the question of an office. In the Principal Keeper's front porch, measuring 5 ft x 4 ft, is crowded the Post & Telephone office, including barometer, barograph, telephone, letter-box, all the usual Post Office paraphernalia. There is no room to sort mail, and no room for people who want to come to do telephone business. Also we cannot use the porch as a porch, or for getting in or out. It is quite obvious that this cannot continue, therefore if the Dept. does not sanction a sleeping porch to offset the use of back bedroom for office, I suggest you give me permission to take the oil-store from near the Tower and set it up by the Principal Keeper's dwelling.[15]

Increasingly, too, sanitary arrangements came in for criticism. In 1922 Fred Lovell, somewhat unusually for a second assistant keeper, wrote to the department to draw its attention to defects in his Stephens Island house where his wife was bringing up five children: I have … to draw your attention to the fact that the privy is placed in my washhouse forming a very unsanitary arrangement. My house is the only one here fitted in this way. The other two have baths placed in this division and in view of the size of my family I am asking for a similar concession. Will the department please supply me with a bath and sufficient timber etc to build an outside WC also material to ceil the bathroom.[16]

As sewerage systems were progressively installed in rural populations, the keepers' long drops and kerosene tins were increasingly at odds with what the rest of New Zealand was becoming accustomed to. Cape Brett acquired its septic tanks in 1944, Stephens Island in 1954. But even in the 1950s, good sanitation was not assured. Familiar and long-standing problems with departmental liaison appear in T. R. Welsh's letter from Cape Brett in 1953: I wish to report the poor condition of my septic tank since my arrival at this station. We have been unable to flush the lavatory properly since we came here and the odour that comes through our kitchen window and through the drain pipes of the wash house is such, that with a small baby and a child of three, my wife and I dont feel like living in the house, especially with the Poliomyelitis around. All water from washing has to be carted away by bucket and a tin in the shed serves as a lavatory

We also have dozens of rats that we would like to pass on to anyone who has not experienced our plight, in fact we are not very happy about it at all.

The 1st Assistant's also is leaking at a broken pipe that leads from the tank itself and is causing him & family some unnecessary smells.

The 2nd Assistants could also do with a check over

After our telephone conversation and telegram to say Works have been advised, I rang them to inquire when they would be out, but they knew nothing about the tanks and informed me they had no men to do the job until after the 19th January

Sir, may I suggest getting some private firm to do the job as I dont feel like putting up with this too long.[17]

Four years later, further sanitation issues exercised Welsh, by then at Tiritiri Matangi. With reference to your memorandum re drains etc may I draw your attention to the following statements, which I hope you will give a little more consideration to.

Firstly, your statement that you cannot accept my statement, that cracks and leaks in a bench top bring one into direct contact with filth & disease. May I point out to you that this <u>is</u> so, as any person who has the public health at heart will point out to you.

If you are still in doubt, may I suggest that you have a talk with Dr Turbutt, who gave us a talk on health at the conference. Frequently he has mentioned items as these on his radio talks. *(In the 1950s Turbott, the well-known and influential public health administrator, gave radio talks on health as part of a drive towards health education.)* Secondly the cracks in the benches have been sealed before, but, because they never get a chance to dry out the compounds do not give a satisfactory join.

As regards having linoleum as a cover for a sink top well we all know this is bad, if not worse for tops, because the edges can never be sealed off properly. I leave this item to the women on the station as it is they who have refused to have it on their bench tops. The Assistants is twice as bad as mine.

Eight years earlier the drains had been described as 'putrid.' There had been little change, and Welsh did not welcome the suggestion that the keepers do the work. Remembering the hours of work done by [a previous keeper] and comparing our present hours of work, namely 4 hours a day and twelve hours fog watches for <u>seven</u> days a week per man, does it not seem a little unfair and unreasonable to suggest that we now do the <u>same</u> ourselves.[18]

The department provided major items of furniture, but in 1920 second assistant keeper William Glass at Castlepoint describes his dwelling's bare boards. Apart from gender role perspectives, the letter indicates just how much had to be transferred from home to home to be assured of comfort. Glass had not brought his own linoleum on transfer because he understood the department supplied it. His wife was probably not ill, but pregnant: It is about 12 months ago since I had that promise from the Dept, & during that time, my wife (who is in ill-health at present & has 4 young children) has had to scrub bare boards every day. Sir. Is that a fair proposition to ask any woman in ill-health to do? The Doctor advised her not to scrub the floors in her present state of health. What will be the consequence? Disease … Sir, Will it be expecting too much to say the linoleum will be here by the next trip of the "Hinemoa"?[19]

Jean Kroening was fairly scathing about what she inherited at Akaroa in 1950: If you could call it furniture! Akaroa had a huge kitchen. All that was in it was a long wooden table which you had to scrub to keep white and I can't remember how many chairs, I know they were real old-fashioned chairs — and a colonial couch — wooden ends, wooden back, a bit of a swab, a wire mattress swab, and I don't know how old it was. That's all I sat on in the kitchen at night because I never bothered going into what was the sitting room — two easy chairs and a little table, that was the sitting room. With George being on duty, at night I'd sooner sit in the kitchen in the warmth than in the very cold — there was only one window in it, it was a very small room and it wasn't worthwhile lighting the fire just for me.

The coal ranges often malfunctioned, causing the women hours more work. In 1909 Sam Hart at Cape Egmont reported: The range in Assistant's house is almost useless for baking purposes. What should bake in two hours takes five, and then has to be finished next day![20]

Percy White (a big man whose table was shaped to accommodate his stomach, Victor Pullen remembered) was on Stephens Island in 1921, and like Les Broom apparently goaded into writing, voiced what was by then a common complaint: I wish to draw your attention to the poor cooking qualities of the stove in the house I am in being No 21st Assts. When I first came the wife started complaining about how long it took to bake the bread. I didn't take much notice as I thought she did not understand it properly and so did not complain. However, I find the stove is to blame for instead of cooking the bread in an hour or 1½ hours it always takes 4 to 5 hours to bake a loaf … While being sort of cooked on the top the bottom is quite doughy. This to a woman with a family of five healthy hungry children is very annoying on baking day and of course I hear a great deal about it. The stove to outside appearance looks A1 but you cannot cook bread or pastry in the oven. The top of the stove gets red hot but the bottom you could hold your hands on at the same time.[21]

White tried to rectify matters, even offered to buy a new stove himself — though that, he pointed out, would have to accompany him on transfer. While what happened is there unrecorded, the stove at Akaroa and the department's attitude about getting a new one contributed to the

Kroenings leaving the Service. Jean: The soot and that stove! The hole between the oven and the firebox and the wind – the wind would blow the soot down the chimney. It would come out of the oven if you had the door open. And here's me with a newly bathed little baby, and in those days it was all white gowns, no modern jump suits. I would lift him off the table, put him on a rug on the floor to take the bath water out – and turn round and he was covered with soot. And I would have to start again. George wrote [to the department] about all the things that was wrong with the station and they came out and inspected the houses and the stove and turned us down! No new stove. You had to keep on trying to bake bread in it. I do think if the Marine Department had done a little more for us they would've kept their keepers. I called Akaroa Lands End, other people called it the penal station.

But working well, the coal ranges were remembered fondly. Shirley: There was a coal range [on Mokohinau] for cooking on which I had never had anything to do with and neither had Alan. Still remember our first morning and we were busy trying to light the fire and nothing would work and because there was no smoke coming from the chimney the Ministry of Works carpenters came all steaming in the door: 'Why isn't the fire going?' They showed us how to do it and once we got the hang of it, it was good but nobody had told us about the fact that if the fire was very hot the water in the hot water cylinder was going to boil and I could hear Bump, Bump. I was *terrified* until I realised what was going to happen.

It was quite interesting learning to cook on the coal range. What's the secret? Well, you get your fire going and just keep it ticking over nicely and get your oven up – the oven had thermometers on them, weren't really old-style coal ranges. But they're excellent for cooking, there's no doubt about that. You've always got heat there and you've got lovely good cooking surfaces which you can cook umpteen things on at once, and I generally did. But when we moved to the first station that had an electric stove [Baring Head] I'd have mixed up something and I'd have forgotten to put the stove on because I was so used to having heat there and you'd shove it straight in and there it was cooking. But yes, the stove was excellent once I knew how to sort it out, run the dampers and things.

Chris preferred The Brothers' coal range to an electric one: Once you got used to it we produced some of the best food I've ever had on that island, because doing duty cook every third day you tend to, how shall I put it, compete with each other to see who can cook the best food. There was some wonderful food cooked, absolutely wonderful. I used to bake lots of cake. I can see a Dutch chap now. He was a little conscious about his weight and I used to make these cherry pies with loads of cream on top, and he loved them. 'Cherry pies again, I'll have a bit more!'

As with the run-down stations, it is difficult to read the correspondence on the poor housing and amenities without asking how this state of affairs came about. Materials unsuited to the rigours of the weather were used; maintenance and upgrades, deferred in the face of repeated reports, created a cumulative problem already exacerbated by poor liaison between the Marine and Public Works departments. Other factors were also involved. H. E. Jamieson, who struggled to get the Cape Brett station in order over the war years, also suggested more specialised expertise was essential. Keepers here are willing to do any work within their capabilities, but there are some items on the list which it is not advisable to leave to the keepers … As we are exposed to storms … this work needs to be done by experienced tradesmen, not amateurs.[22]

In 1923 William Glass, wanting a transfer from Castlepoint after it had been made a two-man station, added a largely unvoiced perspective, but one that must have been felt at the large number of similarly manned stations. [S]ince being made a two-handed station, I might add, that in the interests of common humanity & future keepers who are sent to this station & wish to lead an honest life, that no two <u>honest</u> & <u>conscientious</u> men can carry out the work of this station, as required by the Dept. & also the Book of Instructions to Lightkeepers (parts of which are being repeatedly quoted to keepers) & retain their health. I can procure a Doctor's statement to the latter effect if so desired. Have the Dept. considered the amount of sleep that keepers can get during the night or day, that there is a half-mile walk to relieve the man on watch, another half-mile walk before the man on watch can get home, so that he is fortunate if he can get 3 hours sleep at a time. This means 5 hours on & 3 hours off duty. Also, if the Lighthouse duties are complied with, that station generally must get out of repair, as the two duties cannot be done properly to-gether.[23]

But, as some stations' state indicated, not all keepers were conscientious and considerate. For instance, Babbage, at Castlepoint before Glass, had put buckets under a leaking malthoid roof rather than repair it; the Johnsons at Moeraki inherited shoddy work. Some families' scant regard for later inhabitants must have left houseproud women on transfer wondering why they bothered.

In 1921 Assistant Keeper Fred Lovell was transferred from Cape Maria van Diemen station to Stephen Island — pursued by A. V. Pearce's complaint. Below is both the initial letter, tucked into the Stephens Island letterbook, and Fred Lovell's response. If distance allows us to enjoy its delightful insouciance, one's sympathies should probably lie with the Pearces. I have the honour to inform you that when I put the temporary keeper into the room Mr. Lovell vacated I found the door of the bedroom missing.

I have searched for it and cannot find same. Mr Lovell must have taken it off because I was almost certain it was on the dwelling when I went through on taking over this station, however, he has not had my permission to remove any doors and has not told me it was taken off.

Would you please ascertain from him when he arrives in Wellington why he took it off without my knowledge, where he has put it, and why he did not tell me about it; while I was searching for the door a carpenter here told me another door was off and he put it on himself in an upstairs bedroom.[24]

Lovell replied in July: In reply to (copy) of Principal Keeper Pearce's letter to you, dated 6th ultimo I beg to submit the following: –

Para 1;– I presume that Mr Pearce means that the door was <u>not</u> found and was therefore missing. He will find it doing temporary service on one of the outbuildings allotted to his personal use.

Para 2;– Mr Pearce's deductions and remarks are out of order. I am <u>quite</u> certain that the door was not in my dwelling when Mr Pearce took over. It's present location will prove this.

Para 3;– The punctuation being somewhat irregular I am unable to be certain of the meaning of this paragraph. I append the following statement which should clear the matter up.

When I entered into occupation of the first Assistants dwelling, two of the doors were unhung; one of them being missing. The other could not be hung on account of the distortion of the door jamb. Before leaving Cape Maria I (not the carpenter) rehung and refitted this door (which was an upstairs bedroom door).

I respectfully suggest that subordinate officers should be protected by the department from the annoyance of perusing garrulous epistles.[25]

His later apology was carefully phrased. 'It was not my intention to give offence and I beg to withdraw and express regret for any portion of my letter that appears disrespectfull.'[26]

During the 1960s and 1970s, when the Martins were being transferred, conditions had decidedly improved. The houses themselves had largely been renovated, senior ex-keepers carried out regular inspections and the department was more responsive. Alan Martin: They were actually upgrading stations and it looked like it was going to be a lifetime job. The houses were being upgraded. Instead of having paint on the walls we were able to put wall paper up. On Cuvier I was putting down floor tiles. Things were much easier. New engines were being put on the stations. They started the lighthouse keepers school to upskill the staff.

Even so, houses could be still be left with little regard for future occupants — the Johnsons (see p. 148) were not the only family to be faced with major spring cleans before moving in.

Shirley: We did strike the odd house where the people that had gone out just didn't bother and didn't clean – blood from meat in the refrigerator just all hardened on the underside of the racks and things, and smelling something horrible, the kitchen cupboards were so filthy my husband had to paint them before we could put our things away in them.

A later transfer took the Martins to Cuvier Island, not a prospect that Shirley looked forward to with any enthusiasm. (Kitty was inspector Bill Kemp's wife.) When I got there the house was so dirty that with a wet cloth you could write on the white doors. So I complained to Bill Kemp, 'Something has to be done about the state of things or I'm going.' I was getting quite anti. And Bill said to me, 'Now Shirley, you know you're fairly fussy.' And I blew my stack and I said, 'Would Kitty like it?' 'No, no, I suppose not.' So – within twelve months they'd sent out new lino and we had carpet tiles down and we got wall paper and paint and it cheered me up no end.

CHAPTER 8

Children's education

Before the advent of the Correspondence School in 1922 expanded opportunities for primary schooling for those unable to access local schools, their children's education and future exercised the keepers. In 1880 Richard Tregurtha at Nugget Point had, like all public servants, suffered a 10 per cent cut in his pay, he was smarting about the internal relativities, and he put starkly the educational impact of his job on his family: With my present pay (£99) I fail to see how I can do justice to my family. You are well aware sir, that nearly all the Lighthouses are far away from any schools. I now have a boy that should be at school, but with <u>free</u> education it would cost me £40 a year for board etc.

This it is plain I cannot afford to pay; therefore my children must grow up in ignorance. This also tends to perpetuate the two classes, to which I have referred, as principals with large Salaries <u>have</u> the means of giving their children a good education, while those with very low salaries have <u>not</u> that means.[1]

Particularly from the 1920s the issue fuelled many requests for a transfer. The following are typical. W. S. H. Creamer, Castlepoint, 1921: I have to acknowledge the receipt of your Letter of the 20th instant 9/9/198 No. 183 161, informing me of my transfer to Cuvier ... Now Sir, I wish to state my position. I have been upwards of Eighteen Year's in the Light Service and this present Station is the first schooling my children have had, my Eldest son was eleven years of age, when I first came here, and in two and a half year's he has been rushed through the standard's till at present he is in the Sixth, is that Sir, a fair Education for a Boy, who will very shortly, have to start out and fight Life's Battle. I have six children and five of them of school age and three of them are now just at the time, when their Education mean's everything to them.

Now Sir, a school station from here, will finish four of my children's Education, or I should say Three, and the other two would not matter for sometime, and I would then be perfectly willing to go to a non school station.[2]

The Creamers went to Cuvier, where there was no school and where his son, interestingly, got permission to teach his younger siblings.

In 1922, when R. S. Wilson asked to be moved from Mokohinau, the families of The Brothers keepers boarded in Wellington and the men had set periods on and off the station. In reply to my application to you Sir, for a transfer to the Brothers Light, or one as favourable with a view to Education. It is imperative that something must be done in the near future for my children. As now they have, about reached the age, when they will have to shortly begin earning their own living at some trade or calling.

The Brothers Light, is the only Lighthouse in the Service where the Lighthouse Children may have the guide and care of their Parent's in a City; and for children of the Lighthouse Keepers' to be sent to town backward in education and devoid of all knowledge of city life it is nothing less than a sin for it to be allowed. Especially that a station now favourably situated, as that of the Brothers should be in charge of a single man, when there are married men in the Service whose children are now being deprived of the only opportunity they have, under such favourable circumstances. Sir, I sincerely ask of you for the welfare of the children of the Lighthouse Keepers, that make the Brothers Lighthouse one with a view to the above effect. Thanking you Sir in anticipation.[3]

In what seems like an increasingly desperate string of correspondence, Wilson applied for a transfer again in January and March 1923, then in July 1923 on the grounds of his wife's ill-health, and again in 1924. He was finally moved in February 1926, presumably too late to benefit his children.

The advent of the Correspondence School in 1922 did not solve all primary schooling problems (and the issues round financing secondary education were not resolved until the 1970s). R. S. Wilson, a month after his first attempt to get transferred from Mokohinau, spelt out one of the difficulties with correspondence lessons: I Beg to state that advantage is being taken of the Education Depart. correspondence class, In regards to my Daughters Education. This to my Eldest Daughter's disadvantage through not being proficient myself to render assistance. As I am not versed in modern methods of education, together with that of English & Arithmetic for Std VI, in which my Daughter is studying ... I am not in the position to send them away, & nothing is done in regards to Secondary Education by the Education Department in the way of correspondence. It is entirely in the hands of my own Dept.

It is my duty to my children, to write to you to explain my case. This I have done, and spoke straightforward and genuine.

Sir, I place my case before you & respectfully wait your reply.[4]

At some stations schoolhouses were built, but schoolrooms did not ensure adequate education. Attracting teachers was one issue, as George Thwaites, on Stephens Island in 1909, found. There another teacher had just left and, on £24 a year, replacing her was not going to be easy. I also wish to respectfully remind you of the necessity of getting my children to school. We have had very bad luck with school teachers during the six years that I have been at aided school stations. During that time we have had 8 teachers and I doubt if school has been open half time. Consequently my children are backward.[5]

Moreover, as the Marine and Education departments both refused responsibility for funding the children's education, keepers had to pay for the teachers' board while the principal, with the biggest house, absorbed further cost in boarding the teacher. Even where the local school boards (and few followed Southland's example) were prepared to make capitation grants (these, providing funding related to roll numbers, assisted with the teacher's salary and sometimes school equipment), schools were only viable if numbers were adequate. Keepers at school stations had a vested interest whether those joining the station had school-age children and would help with the funding. W. Colley, Centre Island, 1896: I would also state that I made application to the Southland Education Board for assistance to educate the children at this Station, and they have been pleased to grant capitation allowance at the rate of £4 per pupil in attendance, subject to clause 87 of the Education Act of 1887.

If it could be arranged for to have a few more Scholars it would be an inestimable advantage and complete success. I would respectfully ask you to take this into consideration as it is one of the greatest difficulties that we are under at this class of Stations.[6]

On Stephens Island in 1916, P. Malthus found the department's parsimony a serious concern — for a number of reasons: I respectfully beg to submit the following matter to you for consideration. I have three children of school age. The eldest is over seven, and has had only five months school at Castlepoint, so he needs to be kept going, as he is already behind other children of his age. I thought that as there were other children here, we would be able to get a teacher without having to make up too much out of our own pockets. But W Sanders declines, for his own reasons, to have anything to do with the matter, and W Smith says that as W Sanders declines he intends to do likewise. As the Education Board will not grant Capitation unless the teacher receives £52 a year and board, (and that is surely little enough) this places me in the position of having £34 a year to make up, besides keeping the teacher. That is altogether beyond my means, so apparently the children have to go without any education as both my Wife and myself are too busy to devote time to their instruction.

There is another matter I wish to mention. In the Public Service List for 1916, it is stated that the Principal Keeper at Stephens Island receives £10 a year as telephonist, and £5 a year as Lizard Protector. When I say I was coming here, I reckoned on those two sums to help solve the education problem. But now I find that the telephonist's salary has been cut down to £2-10-0 a year (an absurdly petty sum considering the constant tie and amount of one's time the telephone work takes up) and I am informed that the £5. a year as Lizard Protectors has been taken from us under the plea that it is to help pay for the mail service.

I respectfully beg to ask if the Department can give me any assistance in the matter of the school, failing which my children will be handicapped for life.[7]

On the mainland, keepers recognised their community responsibilities in helping to keep the local school going. C. E. Johnson, Moeraki, 1895: Arrangements are being made for a social on the fourth of July in aid of the school funds, which I regret to say is owing to the scant attendance but poorly provided for. As I should like to be present for an few hours would you please grant me leave for say 24 hours, on me placing a trustworthy man in my place here for that time at my expence. The school being two and a half miles from the station it cannot be accomplished without making a breach of the rules laid down for Lighthouse Keepers guideance.[8]

Although some women found the Correspondence School a further and unwelcome task, that view was not universal. Shirley Martin: I liked it because I knew exactly what the children were learning and what they were up to. It was excellent. They did very well at Correspondence School. My eldest son went through to University Entrance at Correspondence School. They had a couple of goes at school. One was at Cape Reinga where we had our own school, because there were nine children there. The teacher we had at Cape Reinga – that was primary – was excellent. Tom Clarke [the principal keeper] actually borrowed one of his nieces, I think it was, to make sure there were nine children on the station. We were between teachers once and I wanted to put my two on Correspondence School, and he vetoed that idea. The children were transported across the most terrible roads to Te Hapua school for the mornings and about half the kids had been car sick because the road was like a snake and they'd be too sick to do anything. At the end of the term I think my youngest son knew absolutely nothing. A new teacher arrived and he said, 'David knows two words.' I would have preferred them on Correspondence over that time. Once the new teacher arrived and sorted them out they did really well.

Some Correspondence School children had opportunities to be immersed in an actual school situation, but for the Martins distance made that impossible. Shirley: They did have sports days where they were involved with other schools in the Northland area. But Te Hapua was the little Maori school at that settlement, about 21 miles, and the next school was about 29 miles away at Te Kao. After that it was Kaitaia, so that's 70 miles. It is just too much. The roads were unsealed, full of pot holes, hazards like roaming cattle, pigs and anything else. Down towards Houhora the road was very sandy and you sort of fish-tailed along that part and hoped you didn't meet anybody coming the other way.

CHAPTER 9

Wind and weather

GALES, STORMS AND DROUGHT

Lighthouses are almost always built in exposed places, and New Zealand's are no exception. Some stations offered relatively sheltered spots where the dwellings (to use the Marine Department terminology) could be built; at others the only shelter came from shelterbelts planted after the stations had been established; almost everywhere families found themselves enduring extremes of weather. Months of bitter cold, gales and rain could be replaced by drought.

In June 1888 Charles Tregurtha on Centre Island reported that sudden violent hailstorms, driving through the ventilator, broke the glass in the table lamp; in 1891, with summer barely past there had been two months of successive heavy gales with hail and rain.[1]

The wind there did not abate over the decades. Jo Broom: One time it took Les three goes to get up to the lighthouse because he kept sliding down and the wind

The Cape Campbell houses, 1965. As at Pencarrow, the hill offers a degree of shelter from the prevailing and insistent nor'westerlies. ATL: 92146½

At the lighthouse site, the Spit provided little by way of shelter. The pines, today such a feature, were planted in 1873, with further planting in 1889. They must have made a dramatic difference.

was blowing him over and it was so muddy he was sliding in all the mud. So three times he had to come home and change. It can blow at Centre Island and there's not much shelter there, not where the lighthouse is right out on top of a cliff.

Puysegur Point in particular was well known for its wet, its wind and its sandflies. Some keepers loved their time there, but in 1895 Alexander Parks made no secret of his loathing for the place. He had been working on the road at the time (see p. 85): The weather has been very depressing (as usual at this place). 29.80 inches of rain having fallen in the month. The few days on which it did not rain or blow hard we suffered torture from sand-flies. A few fine days we had to stay indoors with every window and door closed the torture from sand-flies being altogether too horrible. [2]

Nine months later, and at the time of the Russian scare, Parks' ironic letter to Wellington demonstrates the extremes of weather met at Puysegur Point as well as his loathing of the place: With regard to the red flag to be shown from daylight to dark at Lighthouse Stations in case of war being declared, please allow me to point out to you that it would be impracticable to do so with an ordinary bunting flag ... as there would be nothing left of it at some Stations after the first day, at <u>this one</u> I feel sure I am within the mark in saying that on most days of the year there would not be a shred of it left after six hours flying. If ... the flag is to be exhibited irrespective of weather – please supply an oblong sheet of zinc painted red – about half the size of the bunting one – for stormy weather – should the undesirable occasion arise for exhibiting it at all.[3]

Chris Staley also suffered from the sandflies: Puysegur Point has got sandflies. They just about defeated me. They're still shocking. Some guys can handle them, I can't. You could see a person and it looked as if he had a halo round his head like smoke. That was the sandflies. Some people just ignored them and got away with it. I couldn't ignore it. I got out as soon as I could. There's nothing you can to about it, suffer in silence. You had to cover yourself up all the time, but they can even bite you through your clothing.

Akaroa station was notorious for its bitter weather. George Kroening, who remembers spray being whipped up over the lighthouse, some 100 metres above sea level, got caught in a southerly coming back from Akaroa township. My first horse ride was from the lighthouse station into town and back. I read an episode there where some chap [William Black, overseer, 1879] was coming back from Akaroa and he curled up and went to sleep and didn't wake up. I can well imagine how he felt because the same sort of thing happened to me with the horse. I came off watch at sunrise, milked the cows, got on the horse to go into Akaroa and get the other mail and some stores because the truck [Cooks Freighters had brought in the supplies from about 1939] hadn't been for about three and a half weeks. It couldn't get out because of the weather, the snow. We were getting short of meat. Coming back I got almost up to the top of the hill and the wind changed to southerly and when we were coming over the brow of the hill to come down on the lighthouse side I couldn't sit on the horse. I had the reins through the crook of my arm and was pulling the horse and it wanted to turn back, and I wanted to turn back too and I thought no, got to keep going. Then the snow started and I've never been so cold in all my life. I could have curled up behind a couple of rocks and just gone to sleep. I got down to Phelps's farm, I had some mail for them too – we always did that – and Frank Phelps says to me, 'You'd better come inside and have a tot of whisky to warm yourself up, you look frozen.' Which I was. I said 'No, I'll keep going because if I stop I don't think I'd get going again.' I got

A 1940s image of Puysegur Point station. The new houses were set further back from the point than the first ones but Bill and Kitty Kemp, there in the 1950s, remember milk being blown from the billy. ATL: F22240½

Marita Taylor, born in Australia, looks out of the Nugget Point kitchen door for her first close-up of snow and her first real intimation of how bitter the Nugget Point micro-climate could be.
MARITA AND PETER TAYLOR

back to the lighthouse, took the pack off the horse, fed it and Jean had a hot mustard bath ready for me, first time she ever put mustard in the bath. I was freezing. Went on watch that night, until midnight. And that was the worst trip I've had on the lighthouse. I'm not romancing. It was just fair dinkum! The southerly was just screaming up that hill.

At Portland Island the lie of the land accentuated the wind and only the specially planted taupata trees gave any shelter. George Kroening: My wife crawled from the garden up to the house one day, southerly. It's hard to visualise or to imagine what it's like in a real blow and in some of these places, the lay of the land with a slight slope on it, it just adds to the fury of the wind. All the stock'd be getting in the hollows, behind the houses, behind the sheds.

Until the 1970s, when adequate tanks went in, many stations besides Tiritiri Matangi station experienced drought. Jo Broom, for instance, was at Cape Reinga: We had 14, 15 people staying in the house at the time. One of us women would wash our hair in the basin and rinse it, only one rinse. The next one would wash in that rinsing water and have clean water to rinse it.

   Barry Langman: Water was a big problem on Stephens. Stephens didn't have any streams, but it did have a big collecting area from the old naval barracks which we called The Palace. During the war, when the radar station was installed there, this was used as the living quarters of those manning the station. Its roof catchment area was used to put the water into a reservoir. From that we had a water trough to keep the cows and sheep OK and the surplus we'd pump up to the houses into our underground holding tanks and to our water tanks on the pedestal at the back. There were four 400-gallon square tanks for each house, and the underground reservoir. We got to the stage where, because of a drought one summer, we had to use the washing water to flush the toilets. And the cattle – the last amount of water I put into the water trough I did by standing in the bottom of the reservoir and throwing it over to be put into the water trough. Roger [principal keeper] said, 'We'll give them a week without water and then we shoot 'em.' Fortunately it rained – the sheep can get a certain amount of juices from the grass, but the cows need a lot of water.

When that happened to us, Henry Philips [one of the painting team that by then routinely toured the stations] said back in the days of the *Tutanekai* Stephens Island ran out of water. They sent out water, put the water off the *Tutanekai* in surf boats in drums, they lifted the drums up on the crane, they took them up on the winches, they rolled them up the hill to the houses, they lifted them up and tipped them into the tanks, and when they were all finished and sat down for a welcome meal – then the rain came down in torrents.

The weather was not responsible for all water shortages. Anders Hansen's request provides one of those fascinating windows on social history that the Marine Department records provide. Cape Egmont, October 1914: I have to request that you will be so good as to ask the Collector of Customs, New Plymouth, to send us out a small common lift pump for our well. I am asking for this pump because I am afraid we shall be short of water this season. No rain of any consequence having fallen since the beginning of August. What water we have in the tanks we want to save for cooking purposes. We have been dipping the water out of the well with bucket and rope, but it agitates the water so much that the clay from the side of the well gets mixed up with it and makes it unfit for either cooking or washing. The river water is so poluted by filth from milking sheds and the cheese factory as to be quite unfit for domestic purposes.[4]

'WHAT THEY CALLED A ROAD' – ACCESS AND ISOLATION
The lighthouse sites not only brought extremes of weather, they often brought isolation. Even if there were roads, they were often in terrible condition. At Cape Egmont in 1885, carting in essential supplies for the lighthouse's vital service could become impossible. Norman Simpson: I beg to inform you that on the 22nd June their arrived at Pungarehu 111 Cases oil next day I went to cart the oil to the Station I found the Road in such a

An undated photo of the road to Cape Palliser, east of Putangirua, where it hits the coast. Today, huge retaining walls attempt to hold unstable papa cliffs in place.
HANSEN COLLECTION

bad state that I had to return without the Oil at this time of year to bring a small load requires more than one Horse when the last 40 cases of Oil were left at Pungarehu I found the road unsafe & had to draw the attention of the Road Engineer to the broken Culvets etc I then had to wait untill the road was repaired & at present time the road is about as bad as ever.[5]

Poor roading was not restricted to the nineteenth century. Away from the towns, roads bogged in mud in winter, white with dust in summer, were commonplace well into the twentieth century. Today access to Cape Palliser is possible only by foot, bike or four-wheel drive. In 1945 J. H. C. Conway had also to battle wartime petrol restrictions: I wish to bring to your notice the difficulties that Keepers their Wifes & family have in getting away from this station & back again. There are two ways via White rock & the sandhills. White rock is 8 miles away along a rough rocky beach & if any keeper goes that way he has to be up at 4 a.m. in the morning & go by horseback & as most of the Keepers are in their fifties & sixties its not a pleasant trip to look forward to. Now Sir there is a person by the name of J. Hunter of Martinborough who says that he is quite willing to come out to the sandhills which is only two miles from the station & pick Keepers up, but owning to the restrictions on benzine at present he is unable to do so on his allowance therefore I respectfully ask that this man be granted a permit to refund him the amount of benzine he may use on any trip he may be called on to make to this station, when considering this request I wish to bring under your notice that some of the farmers on the coast here, are allowed 15 to 20 gallons per month for going to town for their stores & etc

& as the light service is just as important as farming to the country I think that my request is only fair.[6]

Access to East Cape station was problematic. Weather conditions, of which a current sailing guide warns in a page of all capitals, made regular stops difficult; the landing place had to be approached through papa channels; severe storms swept away the landing shed and parts of the tramway; and getting the stores up from the landing to the light had its own problems. One local carter, putting in his bill, noted: [D]ray and 4 horses cannot shift what I had reckoned on owing to heavy sand and papa rocks, time lost through tide having to wait low tides & not being able to work in-coming tides.[7]

Getting to and from Te Araroa, the little service centre, by land was bedevilled by slips and flooding. The passing of years did nothing to alleviate the problem. Acting principal keeper H. R. Bateman, 1947: Mr Walters P.W.D. overseer of Te Araroa kindly made it possible for transport to be carried out and had to engage 5 extra men and a bulldozer to do this. Keeper Olsen & myself left Station at AM to clear boulders etc. and make tracks to enable the trucks to approach as near as possible to the station, this took us 3 hours. Trucks were only able to proceed a short distance along the beach past the landing shed, necessitating the engagement of two carts to finalize the journey. Mr C. Goldsmith & Mr J. Tai were engaged. Unfortunately both trucks sank deep into soft sand and had to be dug out which proved to be a 2 hour job. May I suggest Sir that it is not advisable to transfer keepers to this station between the months of May & Sept. as conditions have to be seen and experienced to be appreciated.[8]

Akaroa lighthouse was accessible by road in the 1930s; in 1950 the journey was often hair-raising, even without a gale blowing. The Kroenings had bought an old Model A car in Greymouth and driven to Akaroa township — in those days, a trip in itself. From Akaroa they set out for the station where George was taking up his first position as principal keeper: We were quite overawed by the road out to the light, in the old Model A. It boiled twice on the way before we got to the top. You go from ten feet above sea level at Akaroa township to 2,172 feet at the top, to about 300 at the lighthouse. So going up the hill was quite a pull, but going down was quite an easy ride, mainly across grass paddocks. There was no road as you'd call it from the top of the hill right down to the paddock. It got terribly slippery when it was wet. It was 14 miles from Akaroa, seven gates — opening the gates was the passenger's job while you sat there handbrake on, your foot on the footbrake to hold yourself on the hill, and then you had to drive through the gates and the only way to stop on the downhill side in the paddocks was to turn the car side on to the hill. Otherwise you just kept going with the wheels locked, just like a sledge and you could

The Kroenings' car, children and grandparents. The steepness of the country — and the proximity of the houses to cliffs not really suited to small children — can be easily seen. JEAN AND GEORGE KROENING

finish up straight over the side, a fair way down. Fortunately the track wasn't close to the edge until you got down near the light.

Poor roading meant ships provided many coastal settlements with their primary link with the outside world. With weather dictating access and timetables, there were inevitable delays. One keeper waited 13 days in Picton before a boat and settled weather allowed him to return to The Brothers. At Portland Island in 1905 where keepers hitched in and out on local coasters, Thomas Turner, like others, was thwarted not only by weather but also by local shipping arrangements — quite apart from the worrying question of how the department would view his enforced leisure: With reference to my being overdue on my leave, I beg to state, that I arrived in Napier 4 days before my leave expired. I was unable to get a steamer to return by account of bad weather & two Home boats being tendered by Messr Richardson & Cos steamers "Weka" & "Fancy" These are the only two boats that will land at this station The Union Co. steamer "Haupiri" left Napier for Gisborne & I tried hard to get back by her, but the Manager said it was irregular for them to land at Portland Island as Richard & Co. steamers did all that work. I could not get via Wairoa as the S.S. "Tangaroa" was in Napier over a week through bad weather. I reported myself to the Collectors of Customs, Napier, & he admitted I could do no more, but wait until one of the small boats left, which I did & landed here on the 24th inst. I might also state that 5 days prior to leaving Wellington I sent a reply paid wire to the agents in Napier asking when the "Weka" or "Fancy" would be passing Portland Island They did not reply, as they said on account of the Home boats in Napier their steamers would not be

Paul Ramsay's boat, Daily Bread, *leaving Portland Island on a full tide.*

BARRY LANGMAN

leaving until such boats were loaded. Hoping the above explanation will be considered satisfactory.[9]

Mail was a vital lifeline to the outside world, but its delivery was by no means assured. Almost from the station's inception, Portland Island keepers battled for a regular service. An early arrangement collapsed when locals proposed high prices for fewer deliveries. In 1955 (the date of the following letter) the service was still fraught with problems, of which only one was that the 'mail boat', Saucy Jean (her name so redolent of the period), later sank at her moorings.

Delivery of mail and supplies (some vital to the light so that one marvels, again, at apparent head office insouciance) could also be confounded by Portland Island's treacherous and slip-prone lighthouse road, another constant in the station's reports. Also interesting in the letter below is the role Sheary exercised and the authority vested in him as the community's government official.

<u>Carriage of Stores & Mail</u>

1. With the "Saucy Jean owned by Mr. Laurence Wairoa which is at present doing the mail contract & Ministry of Works probably going to use the "Daily Bread" owned by Mr. P[aul]. Ramsay of Waikokopu for carrying heavy stores I think it will be advisable to use the "Daily Bread" also for the mail contract as soon as possible.

At present [government personnel] are hiring the "Daily Bread" for their trips to the Island & also Keepers on the Island whenever possible going on leave will use the "Daily Bread" as the "Saucy Jean" is not seaworthy & safe enough for women and children.

2. There has been a lot of friction in the use of the jettys at Waikokopu & Portland Island between the two boats. I have spoken to Mr Ramsay & also Mr. Raureti the leasee of the Island on this matter & stated to them that it is much better for the two boats to fish from Waikokopu for the safety of both boats. They will now work in unison together & avoid petty misunderstandings.

Mr Raureti is at present running the "Saucy Jean" crayfishing at the Island. I have spoken to him about the mail contract & he is of the same opinion as myself that the "Saucy Jean" is unseaworthy for carrying of passengers & mail etc.

3. Regarding of carrying stores to the Island. I have yet had no official communication from any source regarding this matter. As I have previously stated the bulk stores fuel & coal should be worked 12 monthly through the Ministry of Works, probably using the "Daily Bread"

Other stores (Dept.). if the "Daily Bread" is used for the mail contract they come out on the normal mail trips.

4. The Fuel supply for the Diesel Engines is getting low. Stock on hand is enough for only 6 weeks. The rate of consumption is approx. 220 gallons per month.

If a further 20 drums could be sent out immediately This would last until April 1956 giving time for finalizing the carrying of bulk stores to the Island in either Jan. or Feb. 1956.

5. As the hill road is not yet cleared only one drum of fuel can be brought up on the tractor using the old sledge track which cannot be used during wet weather. This is why it is so important that the Diesel fuel should be sent over as soon as possible. There is enough Benzine Kerosene & coal on the Island to last until Jan. Feb 1956. I have mentioned in my letter dated June 30TH 1955 re Diesel Fuel & had the Ministry of Works Napier contact your office of getting more fuel out.

6. Mr Raureti has informed me that he visited your office while in Wellington & that the carrying of mail by Aeroplane was discussed . . .[10]

Percy White at Cape Saunders in 1940 waged a different war: I would be pleased if you would get the Post Office to send our mail weekly to the station by mail contractor in a locked bag as I consider the present system very unsatisfactory as I shall explain. The Assistant Keeper also does not like the present method, which is as follows: – The grocer comes here on a Thursday and delivers our mail loosely and we give him ours in the same way. There is also a box up on the hill which the Mail delivery man puts our mail in on other days of the week and if we wish to post any, well we do just the same. This box is on the side of the road and is always open to everyone, and we have to walk up for

it and wait sometimes as long as 2 hours if we wish to see the mailman and to make sure our mail is posted. The girls and the Assistants wife went up for it on Tuesday and it took there about 1½ hours ...
With the cold rainy weather coming on the conditions will be worse.[11]

Until World War ll most stations' stores and equipment were delivered by either the department's own hard-pressed steamers or by local ships. Weather, too, could upset lighthouse steamer schedules and create havoc. Not all stations were equally affected, but in June 1910 there were clearly problems at The Brothers. William Tutt: I have the honour to ask for a more regular attenttance by the Hinemoa we are now in the 9th week since she was here, and have nothing to eat this last fortnight but bread and tin meat, except a little jam and sago our butter has been done over 2 weeks ago, we have 1 tin of jam left it is usual to send over 25 lbs sometimes 30 lbs of butter each trip this time only 10 lbs was send rice and rolled oats was short, also, and this being about three weeks longer trip we are anything but satisfied with the attendance given us I asure you it is very hard to be here this time of the year with the present state of things and only 2 papers landed last trip, I also respectfully ask for a monthly mail by doing so I am only asking what other Island station has ... you will see that the S.S. Elsie will deliver mail for £15, per and stores for £15, per ton, a very moderate figure I think. My request is only reasonable for asure you that 9 weeks without any of the keepers hearing from their homes is very hard indeed.[12]

For stations dependent on local shipping, changes in shipping patterns could affect deliveries and access to and from the stations. Around 1910 at Portland Island, for instance, keepers reported ships were not passing, and again in the 1930s coastal steamer numbers began to decline markedly.

At various times Puysegur Point and Cuvier and Mokohinau stations in particular suffered communication problems not experienced by the other stations. (No letterbooks survive from Kahurangi Point, isolated by distance, tides and flood-prone rivers.)

In the late nineteenth century Cuvier Island station, marking the southern entrance to the Hauraki Gulf, was out of the path of local shipping — the Huddard Parker ships passed at night and the Northern Company boats passed some 10 or 12 miles off.[13]

Fires or raising flags, the usual means of summoning help, were no use. The southern end of the Great Barrier, some seven nautical miles away, was uninhabited, the mainland was too distant. The problems, which began in 1893, only four years after Cuvier Island light's commissioning, were not entirely resolved in 1901.

But lack of shipping meant that, towards the end of the 1890s, Mokohinau keepers fared even worse. In late July 1897 Alex Connell wrote in extraordinarily restrained tones: I have the honour to report that four months and eight days have now elapsed Since the "Hinemoa" visited this station and landed stores and consequently the keepers are now short of provisions and a few more days will See them in a state of Starvation, and if there were any chance of a Signal being seen, the Signal "Short of provisions" would now be flying.

With reference to our Memo 29th July last advising Keepers to Supply themselves with Five months Stores as the steamer cannot always be dispatched at three monthly intervals owing to being wanted for other services I beg to state that with the exception of Sugar, salt, Tea and suchlike in Tins no provisions will keep good for that length of time. Flour, if exceptionally good may keep but the chances are it wont. Matches last not longer than Lucifers that is when at their best. And it Matters not whether the Supply was Five, Ten, or Hundred Months before the end of the Second Month there would be no matches fit for use. Potatoes have been an unknown article of diet since the beginning of December, and owing to the long drought we have not had a vegetable of any kind throughout the whole Autumn.[14]

On 1 March 1898 a barque was seen off the island, but the flag "Shortage of provisions" elicited no response. On 3 April the Tutanekai *arrived. The relief was comparatively short-lived. Alex Connell's later letter, too, hints at a sense of abandonment that others would share:*
I beg to submit the following statement of affairs as existing at this station at the above date.

The twenty-first week is now entered on since provisions were landed and the consequence is that my household are reduced to a state of starvation.

All such stores as Flour, Oatmeal, Tea, Cofee, Cream, Potatoes, preserved Meat butter Rice etc are entirely exhausted, with the exception of about a pound each of Sugar and Salt and a few pounds of Tapioca I have no provisions whatever and the other Keepers are nearly as badly off. Distress Signals have been flying for several day's but as no vessel has come within signalling distance this year the hope that they will be seen by any one is a very faint one indeed …

Last December after the lapse of thee and-a-half months from the visit of the "Hinemoa" it was deemed necessary to sent the stores by a special boat, but now after a lapse of five months within a few day's it is apparently not deemed necessary to trouble about the matter. The ordinary service of the steamer is very unsatisfactory being spasmodic and without system extending from three to four and a half months and over but never in the history of the Colony has a light station been left five months without victualling. And that without a word of warning to the Keepers. This is not the first time this station has been on the verge of starvation but I refuse to believe that it meets with your Concurrance and approval, hence my appeal to you in the hope that a shorter and more regular service may be established.[15]

The above was not the only such incident. In February 1899 after having watched a barque depart on a favourable wind, their distress signals apparently unnoticed, principal keeper David

East Island station, in spite of its proximity to the mainland, suffered isolation and shortages. A Maori launch owner from Te Araroa used to carry mail over from the mainland but gave up because of the problematic landing. The local coastal steamer company, Richardson and Co., were contracted but keepers complained of very erratic deliveries, even in fine weather. The area's treacherous sea conditions, too, meant that even the government steamer often had to wait for a landing, sometimes for over a week. In 1920, with no telephone connection to the mainland and a boat with no oars or a sail for emergencies, principal keeper Conway pointed out that 'things were pretty unsatisfactory ... The food question here is rather acute that is for fresh provisions — all available goats have been killed off and we are existing of tinned foods ... The situation at East Cape under present conditions makes it purely a rock station.'

Partington wrote: I now respectfully request that you will make some changes to prevent our being left <u>nine</u> and sometimes <u>twelve</u> week's at a stretch with only a very rare chance of being able to signal to passing vessels. I can truthfully say there is not another Lighthouse in New Zealand but what have more chances of signalling to Vessels than what we have.[16]

After that such constantly erratic provisioning seems to have become a thing of the past. But children's illnesses in particular drove home the isolation, and the question of how the Mokohinau keepers got help was raised periodically until 1948 when radio and the coastguard cutter under Captain Eastmure made possible medical advice and evacuations.

Even in the 1950s and on a good day, Puysegur Point was some ten hours' sailing from Bluff; in storms it was inaccessible, and the station was facing isolation not experienced earlier. In the 1920s the once thriving mining community had gone, the fortnightly summer cruises had ended a decade before, and other regular shipping was a thing of the past. The phone line that went through in 1908 was a saga in the annals of the post office, but its construction, involving trees as posts, did not guarantee a trouble-free service. Maintenance costs grew steadily; so did the number of days it was inoperative — an average of 233 days a year in its last three years. In December 1922 communication was lost and never regained. Over the 1920s and

30s, the station's isolation was not far from the keepers' minds (see also p.186–187). J. A. Goddard's letter, July 1921, is typical: On behalf of the Keepers at this station, I beg respectfully to inform you that our telephone connection with Tuatapere has been out of repair since the 9th of April last, since which time we have held no outside communication whatever …

With this connection broken, and with no boats calling except the Government steamer on her periodical trips, we are reduced to a state of almost complete isolation, and we feel that some improvement in our communication with the outside world is an important necessity.

Our chances of communicating with passing ships are of rare occurrence, most of them passing outside of visual signal range of the station.

In view of the above, I would be very grateful if you could make some arrangement by which our mail service would be improved. A mail service to alternate with "Himenoa's" trip is not an unreasonable request, this would give us approximately six mails a year.[17]

In the mid-1950s food ran short, due to factors quite outside the department's control. Les Broom and his family were part of the drama. Les: The *Wairua* didn't arrive because the weather was bad, and they were picking up people from the Muttonbird Islands. They got back to come down and then the wharvies go on strike. They came round but there were no stores.

Jo: We had one tin of baked beans left. We saved it and saved it. Then I cooked that tin — it was a good, big tin. I dished it up at the table. I put the pot out in the scullery — and when I went back the cat had mine on the floor. And I ate it!

Les: We couldn't find a deer, we couldn't find a pigeon, we couldn't find any damn thing. We couldn't even find a paradise duck! There was no fish, it was too rough to go fishing.

Jo: Every day Les and Bill [Kemp] went hunting. Finally they did shoot a pigeon and I cooked it for Les and the two children but I wouldn't eat it! I wouldn't eat it! I thought it was sacrilege. That was the only time we were really short.

Les: We got the stores about a week later, a fishing boat brought them round for us.

Air transport in the 1950s helped reduce isolation. The Brooms were among the lighthouse families who put in the first airstrip, on Centre Island. Les: Cape Reinga was the only place where there was a district nurse. At Centre Island if you wanted any help you had to call a fishing boat in and they'd take you out to Riverton. George Hitchings arrived and he decided it was about time we had an aeroplane. In 1952 it was a big thing. We got in touch with the Southland Aero Club, they

While there was pleasure in the chase, fish were an important part of the diet everywhere. Here Mike Pilone, then assistant keeper on Tiritiri Matangi, with the day's groper. At that time, such big fish were not at all unusual.
MARITA AND PETER TAYLOR

It is 1967 and at Dog Island the flag is flying and the first aeroplane is just landing on the strip over which Alan Martin and Pip Aplin had laboured.

ALAN AND SHIRLEY MARTIN.

came out and surveyed the place and said, 'Right, we want it so big, so wide, all cleared out, and if you do that we'll come and test it.' So we marked out this strip over 200 yards long and I think about 80 or 90 feet wide. It was very flat but there was all the tussock. So the whole three families — we dug that place out. It took us just over a month to do. When we had that finished they came over in two planes, the old Tiger Moths, and tried it out and said, 'Yes, that's good as gold.' The next thing, at the southern end of the strip it was a bit boggy. We wanted some field tiles to put in, to drain it all. We got hold of the club and we said 'Can you get us some field tiles?' They said 'Yes.' So the next time the *Wairua* comes over there are all these field tiles. We said, 'How much do we owe you?' They said, 'Well, when the city council finds out they've gone, we'll have to pay for them.' And then we decided we wanted to supply the Aero Club with a big afternoon tea.

Jo: We did the landing shed up with flags and everything. We baked for days — cream sponge, chocolate éclairs, cream puffs, all sorts of things we three women baked.

Les: We had about 60 or 70 people and it got into the paper. Then the paper got to Wellington and down came all these telegrams and God knows what — 'Where's this airstrip? Is it anywhere near the lighthouse? Yayayaya. Shouldn't have done it!' They built them after that. We were the first airstrip they'd ever had.

The isolation keepers and their families faced was always worrying when anyone was ill — and such illness was not always physical. What had happened to Mrs Chalmers is unclear but William Tutt's concern, and anger at the department, comes out strongly. Pencarrow, 1917: Dr Hector has informed me that you decline to pay for his attendance on Mrs Chamers.

I beg to state that I sent for him when Mrs Chalmers would not tell me what she had taken therefore as it was impossible for me to know what do to save her life and as I did not want her to die here I did what I thought was right on the matter it was not till after I had sent for the doctor that she tould us what she had taken I knew then what to do & she was out of danger before the doctor came but then Sir she may have a relapse. Chalmers had not money to pay him as his wages were small & he had to see a doctor every week that the expense for medicine took 7/- every time he whent [?] again if it became Publicaly Known you would hardly get a keepers wife to come I respectfully ask you to think for a moment [of] the numbers of Temporary

Keepers there is now in the service & hard to get at that therefore I hope you will see your way to discharge Dr Hector account, as keepers is quite differently situated from any other Public servant.[18]

In the case of C. E. Grey and his wife at Cape Brett the department's failure to act seems almost criminally intransigent. Grey first wrote in May 1934 wanting a transfer to the Customs Department and medical attention for his wife. [My wife] is in a very nervous & run down condition ... She worries and frets over the least thing & I am sorely afraid if I keep her in this Light service much longer she will have a nervous breakdown. She has been confined to this station for fourteen months without being able to get a change away from it, as my financial position would not allow her to go for a holiday in a peaceful frame of mind. When I wish her to take the money & go out, she states she would only worry all the more, being away from the children and thinking that the money would be needed for other things. so I trust you can see your way clear to grant me this request.[19]

Grey's principal keeper Percy White, doing his best, strongly endorsed the request. May 1934: I feel it my duty to add a few remarks about her health. For some time now I've seen her getting gradually worse and I've been tempted to write to you of it long ago. She has no interest in anyone and prefers to live by herself although the wife and I have tried to drag her out of it. It's no go ... I wish the Department could do something early or I'm afraid in a few weeks or so we will be sending her out completely run down. Mr Grey likes this life as he says it suits him but his wife cannot stand it at all. We would be sorry to lose him but all the same something will have to be done very shortly.

Thanking you and I hope it is possible you will seriously consider his request.[20]

The Grey/White relationship broke down, perhaps inevitably; a doctor's recommendation to remove Mrs Grey had no effect; White himself was transferred. The Grey family finally left the station three years after the first reports of trouble.

CHAPTER 10

Illness, accidents, deaths and births

With less sophisticated medicine than is available now, relatively minor physical conditions could turn nasty — but the men kept working in conditions that today would have most of us rushing to doctors and bed. In 1915 Anders Hansen had to pay a price for a new cowl at Cape Egmont (see pp. 112–113): On 19th November Mr Davis of the Public Works Department Stratford was here to take measures for the new cowl for the lighthouse. I was in bed, not very well: but as the Assistant Keeper was away on holiday I had to go up and help get the measures: first we took measures inside, and the day was very hot, and then we were lying on the dome outside for half an hour or more to get the outside measures. It was then I caught the chill which caused congestion of the lungs and which has now turned into pleurisy of both lungs.

I saw Doctor Walker of New Plymouth on 30th November when he told me I was bad with congestion of the lungs. This morning (11th Dec) ... he said it was pleurisy now, and if I did not improve in a few days I must go into town to see him. In the meantime he is sending medicine out today which I hope I get to-night. Should I not improve I would ask your permission to go in to see him (the Doctor). I can keep my watch, but am not able to do a great deal of work. I feel sure I shall soon get well again.

Please wire me collect as soon as you can conveniently do so.[1]

Worse was to come. Eight days later: I was thrown out of my gig ... coming home from Pungarehu, where I had been for medicine for my chest trouble, and was severely injured about the head and neck and concussion of the brain, necessitating removal to New Plymouth for medical treatment and had to remain in a private hospital for four days. I am now much better and hope soon to be fully recovered.[2]

The letterbook has a marginal addition: 'The job went on.' Such stoicism was not unusual. If things got too bad, temporary keepers, usually locals such as the Quickenden family at Cape Egmont, or the Webber family at French Pass, for whom the light proved a good source of supplementary income over the years, were called in.

Cape Egmont lighthouse and station
c. 1911. HANSEN COLLECTION

One of the periodic health scares (cholera, typhoid, scarlet fever, outbreaks of smallpox in 1910, 1911 and 1912, even on one occasion the bubonic plague) meant that everyone on the Cape Egmont station was vaccinated in May 1913. All of us suffered severely & much more so than was anticipated, indeed, as regards myself, had I thought it would have affected me, as it is doing, I should have delayed having it done until Assist Keeper Johnson returned to work. I am able to take my watch, but that is all.[3]

The effects of vaccination were long-lived. Five months later, and with his eczema (see p. 182) still bothering him, Hansen reported: I have to state, with reference to Sick Return, that, there has been a considerable amount of sickness at that station, which cannot very well be classified. Mr Johnson is greatly improved, but not yet, as well as he hopes to be. Vaccination caused a lot of trouble, especially among the children, some of them not being quite clear of it yet. My daughter Annie had to go to New Plymouth to consult [the] doctor, and her arm is not yet better although it is now close on three months since she was vaccinated.[4]

Without the Hansen family's luxury of vaccination, the isolated Mokohinau keepers anxiously anticipated the annual mutton-birders' arrival: I beg to call your attention to the fact that the Maoris on the "Great Barrier" are suffering with Small Pox, & the Mutton Bird season will soon be here, & I expect the Maoris will be coming here as usual, & the Keepers have no way of being vaccinated. I think that some precaution should be taken to prevent the Maoris carrying anything like that here. Trusting that you will look into the matter.[5]

By the 1950s district nurses visited on a regular basis. But the first port of call was always the station's medical kit, though these were not always up to scratch. Even if there was an effective remedy for an ailment, there was no guarantee it would be on the station. At Cape Brett in 1957 this was not only because items were missing or bottles empty. J. Sutherland:

Report on Child's Illness and Remarks of Doctor Regarding Suppl. Medical Chests

On the night of the 11th inst. Polly Hepi, aged seven, complained of severe ear-ache and when we rang the doctor at Paihia . . .

The doctor suggested that . . . the "Ship Captain's Medical Guide" is not an adequate instructor in the use of certain drugs contained in the cabinet.

. . . He also suggests that many of these drugs are regarded as out-of-date and that the list should be revised to bring it in line with present medical practice, and that the list be submitted to a doctor with a view to making it more suitable for the particular needs of isolated lighthouse stations. He emphasises that lighthouse stations have quite different requirements to ships at sea not carrying a medical officer, particularly in that lighthouse keepers could expect quite often to have to treat children's ailments.[6]

Nurse Wharf, the district nurse in the late 1950s, was based at Tryphena on Great Barrier Island and toured the isolated Hauraki Gulf settlements. She is pictured here with Tawa Neilson on the post, her brother Richard (partly obscured), and Tim Mander. The Taylors remember she poked and prodded children and her dogmatic opinions could make her a bit of a Tartar. Nevertheless, she was a professional and a fund of mostly good advice.

MARITA AND PETER TAYLOR

On-station remedies tended to be as primitive as the medical chests — if the right equipment were to hand. 1901, Fred Cathcard, Mokohinau: With response to the Forceps for extracting Molar teeth, that I have applied for. I beg to state that Keeper Field, is suffering from toothache and if I had the proper instruments I could soon ease him of his pain as when I was at Stephens Island I extracted six teeth successfully.[7]

'Frantic with pain' Field had to keep watch. Perhaps scarred by the experience Cathcard wrote to the secretary two months later with very real concerns — what were keepers on isolated stations to do if, with one man on leave, one of the remaining two were to become incapable of doing a watch? Nor was it poor Field's only experience of agonising toothache. At Cape Egmont in 1903 Fred Erecson reported: Mr Field became so ill for want of sleep that he could not trust himself to take his watch, and I had to call in a temporary keeper, on the 4th instant and let him go to New Plymouth & have some of his teeth drawn.[8]

He was later diagnosed with severe measles.

In 2003 Bill Megennis discussed one aspect of lighthouse-keeping life that he had relished: I think I definitely enjoyed things that carried a certain element of risk. Where we are today with all the rules and regulations of OSH [Occupational Health and Safety] and you must be careful what you do in your workplace and your kids must not step out of line in case they suffer injuries – well, in that job you had to be very careful because in some circumstances you could be seriously injured through a mistake. On boat days out on The Brothers lighthouse, for example, you were working the crane that swung the jib out over into the bay and the boat came underneath. There was that element of being aware of where the boat was, getting stores or people off without causing danger or mishaps that would seriously injure anyone. But there was a sense of challenge. Coming off the boat you could jump into a rope net, you could grab hold of the hook, put one foot on it, one foot dangling off the side so that you got hooked up and were lifted, then your foot went down on the side of the island and you were there. Or like jumping out of a helicopter, just before it landed, underneath the chopper to hook up a big load of stores, or to head out in the bush on your time off. You could do these things fully aware that

Landing at The Brothers, 1960s.
GEORGE GIBBS

The Tiritiri Matangi tractor at the bottom of the cliffs, 1965. Even with taking care, everyday station life had its own excitements. On this occasion Peter Taylor was lucky he did not go down with the tractor. MARITA AND PETER TAYLOR

if you made a mistake you were going to be in trouble. So there was that challenge, and the freedom that was attached to that.

Bill was talking with the luxury of a late twentieth-century perspective, but keepers took care. Inevitably, things did not always go according to plan. In 1896 C. E. Johnson at Moeraki was finally installing the new water tanks he had requested nine months before (see p. 114). [A] heavy wooden mall which while being used flew off its handle and struck my head made a long cut on it. The consusion knocked all the Teeth in the upper jaw a drift on that side, though the wound on my head is healing up nicely my head still causes me considerable trouble particularly at night time The teeth are also troublesome.[9]

Anders Hansen, Cape Palliser, 1912: Between two and three months ago, while picking the nipple of one of the tubes, the flame lit back to the nipple, causing a small explosion, which blew the top off the mantle; a small piece of this fell on the eyelid, and in the inner corner of my right eye, burning it slightly, and causing some irritation to the eye. This slight wound has obstinately refused to heal, and now has spread to one half of face, and neck, in the form of scaly excema ... I have to keep the head and face covered with lint and the lotion during the daytime, and with lint and starch during night time, but am able to keep my watch.[10]

The Cape Palliser access road eventually claimed a victim. J. Wagg, 1949:

Cape Palliser Lighthouse — — Road Access

I advise that Mr. Todd was thrown from, and run over by one wheel of the rubber tyred vechile used by Keepers to transport Departmental stores to the Station.

The accident happened on the 1st April, while negotiating a particularly bad stretch of the road access known as Kupe's Sail.

Mr Todd has injured his left hand, right arm, and has a bruised and lacerated forehead which has swollen out half an inch. Both his thighs and knees are bruised and lacerated where the wheel passed over them.

Because Mr. Todd can still move around he makes light of his injuries and insists on continuing his duties. Any man of lesser physique would now be in hospital, or had he been alone and less lucky, the accident would have been fatal.

Part of the remains of the Portland Island tractor at the bottom of the zig-zag. Such events contributed to lighthouse life being 'the Big Adventure'. Barry Langman recalls that the tractor had originally been brought out to the station on Paul Ramsay's double-ended fishing boat, the Daily Bread, *its front wheels inside the rear cockpit and the large rear wheels straddling the coaming at the stern. Calm seas and a crane at each end helped.* BARRY LANGMAN

In the capacity of incoming Principal Keeper taking over these duties, and as witness to this accident I can only recommend that the Marine Department should take immediate action to effect improvements to this dangerous road access to the Lighthouse, to avoid the possibility of a more serious accident.[11]

Work did start on the road in August, but flood swept boulders down and the track was washed out near the Mungatoetoe. The horse had to be destroyed after a bad fall down the Sandhill. However, by the end of the year keepers were able to collect personal effects, coal, fuel and stores from the fishing village at Ngawi.

In 1957 C. A. Shepherd was grading the Portland Island station road after heavy rain. Lucky to escape with his life, he wrote off a Ferguson tractor: [W]hen starting downhill with the tractor a portion of the edge of the road gave away under the front wheel, slewing the front end of the tractor over the side, not giving me time even to reverse the tractor or even turn off the engine, and I just managed to jump off as the vehicle turned over and rolled approximately three hundred feet to the bottom of the cliff.

... I quite realize the gravity of the situation as it leaves the station without transport of any kind for transporting supplies from the landing, but I hope this statement conveys to you the state of the tractor and the damage caused to the said vehicle, and also my sincere regrets over the complete loss of the vehicle.[12]

Strains, however, were the commonest accident. T. R. Welsh had injured his back in 1950 handling drums of fuel at Puysegur Point. The problem had recurred intermittently, but at Tiritiri

Matangi five years later, the department's failure to carry out necessary repairs contributed to another flare-up — and in pre-ACC days Welsh was justifiably concerned with compensation issues: During the past five or six months we have had so much heavy work to do, such as handling coal, drums of fuel, cartage of concrete posts & shovelling etc etc that it got to the stage where I was unable to even walk or sit very long without getting pain in the small of the back ...

Recently we have had to handle all our fuel by hand because the crane on the wharf has never been fixed, we have also had to man handle our fuel 50 yards up hill from the landing shed because the road is so wet that neither horse nor tractor could get near the shed. All stores on mail trips etc have been handled the same. This has not improved my back and recently I have had to walk with a stick if going very far ...

If this treatment is to be carried out for long will I be entitled to compensation as I was at Puysegur and if so what allowances will the Dept allow me while away from home etc also seeing that this has occurred during my duties will the Dept pay my Doctor & hospital fees.[13]

'IF A BOAT HAD BEEN AVAILABLE ...': EMERGENCY ASSISTANCE

Evacuating anyone ill was no simple matter. In August 1910 J. Livingstone reported that probationary keeper Monaghan was ill before he arrived on The Brothers: [He was] continually reaching [retching] he has not been able to keep any watch with us and this morning he informed me that he was no better but getting worse all the time and wanted to get ashore to see a doctor As we do not know where the Hinemoa is I have considered it advisable to communicate to the first Boat passing to take him off hoping this will meet with your approval.[14]

Two weeks later, and with Monaghan still in considerable pain, the Hinemoa *finally managed to get him off the island.*

At Puysegur in 1906 a ship's failure to respond to signals was only one ingredient of an almost black comedy of events that Robert McIver reported over the nine days it took to evacuate a badly injured man. (Cromarty was the township built around 1892 following the discovery of Golden Site gold mine in Preservation Inlet.) I regret that I have to report to you that Assistant Keeper Kent met with a serious accident on the 22nd inst. his gun having accidentaly gone off making a Terable gash in his Leg, from the Knee towards the thigh on the inner side of the Leg. The accident happened near Coal point, where he was after Goats for fresh meat. With great difficulty we managed to carry him along to the Landing Beach, and took him home in the cart, and dressed his Wound to the best of our ability, but as the Bone was injured we decided to get the Doctor the next day. But as it was blowing too hard to go in the Boat, Assistant Keeper Dennis walked to Cromarty and got a man from there to go to Southport for the Doctor Who arrived here at midnight the same Night. The Doctor is still staying here looking after the Wounded man, but he told me that we were to get him away to the Hospital as soon as possible. One of the Cromarty men told me that there was an Oil Engine Cutter laying up at Northport that he thought he could get for to take Kent to Invercargill. But that would need a man to help him to pull across there. So I sent the Temporary Keeper over with him, if they get the cutter I will get him sent away at the first favourable opportunity, as the Doctor is very anxious to get him away to the Hospital. I may state that on Sunday the 23rd about 11 a.m. a Union Company Steamer passed by going towards the Bluff. I put up Signals that there had been an accident and that we wanted Immediate Assistance but they did not reply to the signals. Since then we have not seen any other steamer pass.[15]

On 1 January 1907 McIver wrote again: 30th signaled to the S.S. Kaipoi about the accident and asked her to send a boat. She came close in and asked if we could not send a Boat out to her. As our Boat had not come back from Northport signaled that we could not send a Boat, then she said that they had no Chart of the Harbour. But that she would report at the Bluff. asked her to report to customs and send a Steamer. Temporary Keeper came back that night and said that they could not get the Cutter from Northport he had been detained by the Weather and could not get back sooner. Doctor Fose is still attending on Assistant Kent, but he wants him away to the Hospital as soon as possible as he thinks the Leg may have to come off. During the month have been carting gravel for the Road and working on it Lenses and Lantern panes have been carefully attended to.[16]

Kent was finally evacuated on 31 December; on 2 March McIver reported that he had heard Assistant Kent was recovering in Invercargill Hospital, and his leg had been saved. By June Kent had not returned.

At Puysegur Point one grasped opportunities to get medical attention — in this case, regardless of the heavy work offloading timber for renovations to the houses (see p. 91) whatever the inconvenience to others. A. V. Pearce, 1917: I have been engaged all day from 7.15 a.m. till 6 p.m. hauling the rafts ashore with the horses leaving the keeper that put out [the light] to come down as soon he could and the keeper whose lightup it would be would go home at 4 p.m. When the steamer left this morning there were still 12 rafts to haul above high water mark and 33 rafts to be stacked ...

As Mr Wellers asked the Captain could he go out and get his tooth out Captain Bollons asked me if I had any objections I said no and let him go as it was the only chance, so Keeper Albert & myself will keep the watches ourselves as I could not get a temporary keeper until his return it came a bit hard on us after the heavy lifting work but it could not be helped.[17]

Pearce, himself not a well man at the time, was unlucky in his staff. Donnelly, whose suffering demands sympathy, was probably one of the temporary keepers that the department, facing recruitment problems at the end of World War I, was forced to appoint. He did not last his term: I have the honour to acknowledge receipt of your telegram of 19th which arrived today and in reply I wish to state Mr. Donnelly has had rheumatic fever while on active service and while he was laid up with the fever it effected his eyes that he nearly lost his sight altogether and was under an eye specialist in Invercargill for them

When he arrived here he said he could not see too well but was getting better, however during February 1 night and early in this month he was off duty 4 more nights (5 nights altogether) through his rheumatics and complained also of his eyes getting bad again, although he has medicine to drop in the eye in spite of this it has gone on him and he cant see with it; his other eye is now getting effected from the bad one and he cant see too well with it either hence my wire to you

The launch Riverton was to leave yesterday & as he was so bad and afraid he would lose his sight altogether again he thought he must go & get it seen to although he would liked to have been able to wait until the Hinemoa arrived.

He got ready to go by the launch but the weather came bad and the launch is sheltering so he is keeping his middle watches as usual while he can manage, he can't go near the glare of the light as it causes him much pain, he is going by the launch as a passenger to see the Dr. but not to work on the launch hoping my explanation is satisfactory.[18]

In 1937 the question of communications with Puysegur Point was coming to a head. Radio had been installed, but between the Matai's *(the department's steamer) three-monthly calls, the keepers were dependent on a local ship, the* Tamatea, *for their mail. Its failure to drop off or pick up what was needed or to get orders in and out, 'the very gentlemanly fashion' in which it steamed up and down the coast (to use Principal Keeper Hodge's terms) and its refusals to budge in conditions when the* Matai *would have set out, meant irregular and unnotified sailings. In short, it was unreliable – and this was worrying. If it could not be relied on in an emergency, precious time was lost summoning another ship from Bluff. Hodge's further letter, below, like Alex Connell's on p. 173, carries a telling sense of frustration at head office's apparent inability to understand the situation, disillusionment and abandonment:* Early in the month Mrs Newson was taken ill. On the night of the 9th it was plain that she was seriously ill and we suspected appendicitis. I wired the Secretary on the 10th stating the nature of the illness also where the Tamatea was. I wish respectfully to point out that we knew just what the Tamatea was doing and when she was likely to be back. My wire was sent in the hope that the Department could have thought of some other way of getting this lady, who was in agony, away from Puysegur. So far as we could tell anything was likely to happen during the 36 hrs she laid here after my wire went. If, in the case of serious illness or accident we are to rely on some little "tub" from Bluff getting here then Puysegur will not be a very nice place for women or children. The inlet would be a good landing for a seaplane and I am quite sure that this means would have been used to give aid to some adventurer. It was done not so very long ago. However, Mrs Newson got to Bluff and was admitted to Invercargill Hospital and has been operated on, successfully, for <u>appendicitis</u>

Mrs Richardson, who has not been at all well, went out at the same time and was admitted to Dunedin Hospital where she also had to undergo an operation to have some sort of tumour removed.

The Tamatea arrived here about 9.30 p.m. on the 11th. I took on the tower watch to allow the two Asst Kprs to see their wives off. Mr Newson put a mattress on a sledge for his wife but had to carry her over the worst places on the road and she was in a bad way on arrival at the landing. The Tamatea anchored for the night and we owe a lot to one of the fishermen who pulled ashore and took the patients and their husbands out to the ship. The Tamatea sailed immediately.

Today I received a telegram telling me to send in requisitions. It is just three months since the Matai brought our mail. My requisitions have been ready since 29th October but will someone please tell me how to send them out?[19]

Even on Dog Island, in sight of Bluff, prompt assistance could not be assured. S. Scholfield, 1925: I have to report that at 11.30 a.m. on the 3rd inst while changing the rollers Asst. Keeper Stringer got his hand caught in the gearing of the machine, crushing the thumb & palm of the right hand. As it was necessary that he should see a doctor as soon as possible I tried to attract the attention of Bluff signal station by hoisting flags & lighting a large fire ... A launch arrived eventually at 4 p.m., when Keeper Stringer proceeded to Bluff.

Sir this is the second accident that has happened within the last month, & as we have no flagstaff at this station it is very hard at times to communicate with Bluff Hill signal station, as the flags being so close to the tower do not open out properly.[20]

Emergencies on remote or island stations made attracting ships' attention essential but, as we have seen, the responses were not always in the best of naval tradition. E. H. Field, Portland Island, 1910: I have the honour to acknowledge the receipt of your memorandum No 172/218 asking for an explanation of the signal made from this Station to the "Shiritona" and which she made out to be — B f s e v i.

As I explained in a previous letter, the 1st assistant keeper required to get his wife away urgently, and hoisted the flats "B.G" (pay attention to signals) and u v s (when do you return) to the Shiritona when she was passing the island for Gisborne from Napier

Mr Jones informs me that the Shiritona did not answer his question but simply hoisted her answering pennant 7 …

A few minutes before signalling the "Shiritona" Mr Jones hoisted the same flags to the Napier trawler "Countess" but she took no notice of them

Probationary Keeper Conway & myself were working at the landing at the time the signals were made to the Shiritona so consequently I did not [see] all the flags that were hoisted, but it seems very improbable to me that Mr Jones should have made a mistake in simple signals

I might mention that the flags the Shiritona reports having seen (B. f s.—e v i) do not mean as stated by you that "someone has broken an arm" According to the "International Code of Signals" they mean, if there were any sense in hoisting such a signal at all, that 'there has not been an arm broken".[21]

The Countess's response was not unique. In January 1912, at a time when a dearth of local steamers passing Portland Island made attracting any passing ship all the more critical, Assistant Keeper Jones signalled to four steamers — none responded.

Even when a ship was standing by, weather could all but confound efforts to evacuate an invalid. On Portland Island in 1926 and after a serious illness necessitating evacuation, Percy White had pointed out the problems if someone fell seriously ill there — it was difficult to contact the mainland at times other than shearing, that other stations were being fitted out with "wireless", that the Tutanekai had cable-laying facilities, and a cable from the island to the mainland and a phone was the most economic alternative to radio.

Two years later another invalid had to be taken off — and if White's switch to direct speech is any indication, he was totally immersed in the drama. (Mr Nevill did the mail run, as precarious then as later. Mr Tanner was a lighthouse inspector. Note that, officially, White should have requested approval for Mrs Gausel to leave the island.) I have to report to you that yesterday at 4 p.m. Kpr Gausel informed me that his wife was very ill & he said her trouble was a threatened miscarriage as she had the symptoms of it", so I relieved him of all his light duties to render all assistance at home as Kpr Jacobs & I would carry on. She was in great pain & gradually getting worse I sent my lad to landing to see if Mr Nevill had gone to Waikokopu but he had left about 9 a.m. so we had to await a steamer passing for assistance. I went over on request to see what I could do. The wife was in & out all night until nearly midnight when he came for her & Mrs Crook as she was in awful pain and all possible done for her At 2 a.m. Mr Gausel came & woke me saying there was a boat a long way out going south Should he light 2 fires to attract attention. I got up & after calling awhile & with the 1st Assistant on telescope found he was answering so I gave him "Come closer" as we have an urgent but could not get urgent so he changed course and came straight to the lighthouse and again asked "Repeat". I gave it again but no good so we waited awhile until he asked "What is wrong Repeat". I then gave him "We have an urgent hospital case and what ship are you? Can you do anything for us? He replied Kahika [?] and we are bound for Lyttelton but will put into Napier if you wish us to do so." Well not knowing how long before we could get other help I said, "Have you a surf boat." "No." "Can you lower a boat?" "Yes". He then asked about the landing so I said Go round West side of Island and I will show a light the Tutanekai goes right up to. I said Keep the lighthouse light in clear view for safety He said "Right". He then steamed slowly around I called and told him: "Dont lower a boat until I call you as we have to take a patient about 2 miles along Island on stretcher". We then proceeded to get patient on a stretcher & proceeded to landing with the trap. I went on ahead & called steamer to go farther North until I show light & stopped him". He did so I told him "Lower a boat & come right in from ship. I guided him in best possible [word missing] by a light. He got safely ashore and as Kpr Jacob & Gausel had by this time carried her down zig zag on a stretcher we got her on board quickly & boat left for ship. Mr Gausel accompanying his wife. The children left on station with Mr Jacob & I. I called ship again & said Boat coming to you & would he telegram Sect Marine Wgtn Keeper Gausel wife taken seriously ill & taken off by you. VE & thanked him.." He replied "will do so". Then ship proceeded to Napier just about daylight 6 a.m. from landing. The wives took charge of the light from 4.15 a.m. until I returned about 6 a.m. so everything was OK. I expect the ship will have reported all this to you so now hoping my actions in calling steamer & letting Mrs Gausel go without authority meet with your approval. I am etc P White PK.

The Pukiki passing North this evening at 11 pm morsed the following message "Mrs Gausel getting on as well as can be expected "Signed Gausel".

Had we that short connecting link to Tauoupata (cable & line) we could have got Mr Browns launch as Mr Nevill holed his the day he took Mr Tanner away and he returned with the mail in a small dinghy on the 5th. Informed me that it would be a month or more before same could be repaired.[22]

Radio was installed in 1930, but when Hinemoa Bollons, schoolteacher and daughter of Captain John Bollons, became ill shortly after, it was two days before a steamer took her off.

In 1923 P. R. W. Willers' letter from East Cape shows the intimate involvement with death and its aftermath that all isolated communities faced. Perhaps, in this instance, proximity to hospital would not have made a difference; perhaps what we are seeing here is the limitations of medicine in a pre-antibiotic age — a cold, then an ear infection that turned into an abscess, and then a cerebral haemorrhage. I called in a Temporary Keeper Mr A Kahaki after dispatching a Messenger for medical aid, and that afternoon the District Nurse from Te Aroara arrived, Mrs Ager was then unconscious. The Nurse remained with her patient that night and part of the next day. By then Mrs Ager had regained consciousness but was partly paralysed and the Nurse gave little hope.

The Nurse left on Monday to get in touch with a Doctor on a phone and returned next day in company with another Nurse, and during her absence her instructions were carried out; and she was also consulted over the wire. Owing to their being called elsewhere the Nurses left that afternoon, and Mrs Ager passed away a few hours afterwards, or to be exact at 5.30 p.m. on May 22nd.

I have to say that everything was done that could possibly be done to Save Mrs Ager.

To have taken her to a Doctor over such a track was out of the question whilst in her condition. Neither was it possible to call in a Steamer after her case became serious enough to warrant it.

After her death, my Wife, aided by the Wife of the Horoera School Teacher, made the necessary preparations for burial, and the next day, I made all arrangements for the coffin etc and after receiving your permit, I attended to the grave digging etc

The following morning the 24th the funeral took place and everything was in order, and the Deceased was laid to rest at 2.30 p.m., the Service being conducted by the Rev P Kohere of Rangitukia

I advised you from time to time by wire of progress, and have noted your instructions re cemeteries act etc.[23]

For women, pregnant and worried about possible complications, the isolation was frightening. Robert H. Lloyd, Centre Island 1893: I have the honour to inform you that my wife, after visiting the main-land last March, told me she could not venture on the water again, either by boat or steamer, before her confinement for fear of mishap, which occurred to her at this station in April '92 where a doctor had to be sent over. This occasioned her to engage the services of a competent woman to come to the Island to confine her, but as she made no appearance in the last 10 days, we were much alarmed. My wife declared she would risk the journey across, rather than remain here without the slightest hope of attendance.

I consulted the Principal Keeper, but he was not in favour of my wife returning on this water; yet as she entreated so earnestly, I had no alternative but to comply with her wishes. The weather being favourable I took her over to Colac Bay immediately, where she got every attendance, but the seasickness caused her to be taken ill shortly after. A fisherman came out the next day to say she was safe; also the child.

I beg to mention that my wife has never entirely recovered from her illness here in April '92. The unusual severity of last winter was not conducive to improvement. I would humbly ask that you will kindly consider removing me to another station. I think the change would be beneficial to her. Trusting I have not incurred any displeasure by this letter.[24]

At Dog Island in 1928 Mrs Haven went into labour and at 11 a.m. the station flags were signalling for a doctor. After an hour, and with no response from Bluff Hill, the keepers at-tracted a fishing boat, which ran into Bluff to get assistance. R. Haven: Sir, this is just such an occasion when a telephone on these places would be much appreciated by the keepers, and would also lessen the worry and anxiety at such times In this case I was very fortunate in getting the fishing launch Brandy and I don't know what would have happened if the weather had been rough, as Bluff Hill Signal Station had not seen or answered my signals which were flying until 3.20 p.m. when the doctor arrived. I am glad to say both mother and child are well.[25]

By the time the Kroenings had joined the Service, pregnant women were supposed to leave remote stations three months before their due date. Weather conditions sometimes made it impossible to leave. The requirement placed financial hardship on the families, women without family or friends boarded nearby alone, and babies were often weeks old before their fathers saw them. For Jean Kroening at Akaroa (which qualified as an 'island' station), unreassured by the doctor's promise to come out if she went into labour with their second child, the trip from Akaroa Heads was arduous. The Marine Department would not take any responsibil-ity for pregnant women after six months. I had to go home to my parents 'cause you had no money. Don't know what people who didn't have parents' homes to go to did – the wages you were paid, you just didn't have enough to live on. At Akaroa I was nearly seven months by the time the road was free enough from snow and dry enough to come out. The stores truck came out but it couldn't get back up. It kept sliding. So George put rope and wire round the wheels of our Model A and drove halfway into Akaroa, up the grass slopes, backwards and forwards, zig-zagging. I had to get out to open the gates and we met another vehicle belonging to Cooks part way down hill to Akaroa. He was bringing chains out for the truck. Well, I had to go the rest of the way in the ute, catch the bus into Christchurch with my wee girl who didn't know what was happening, and I stayed the night with a cousin in Christchurch; caught the express from Christchurch to Greymouth which was a seven-hour journey.

Getting out from Akaroa pregnant was fraught; getting back on to Mokohinau with their first-born was hardly straightforward. Lynne Kroening was far from being the only new baby thrown from ship to shore. When I came ashore for Lynne she was a fortnight old

The first baby born at Cape Brett.

HANSEN COLLECTION

before George saw her. He came from Moko to Auckland. We used to wait at the Admiralty steps at the base of Queen Street in our old clothes because you never had good clothes at any of the islands. The first thing I did on one trip from Moko was – the fashions had changed and the ladies were wearing long skirts – the first thing I did was buy a long skirt and a long coat.

We left Auckland at midnight with a new baby, our month-old baby, and the weather had been rough. When we got to Moko they couldn't launch the tug's dinghy or take the tug to the wharf. So they had to launch the station dinghy and row out to pick us up. Which meant Lynne, wee Lynne, month old, tucked up in her carry cot. As the boat rose, the dinghy came in, and Lynne was dropped down into the boat and then they rowed out so they didn't get caught under the bulwarks. The next time when the boat rolled I jumped into the dinghy and they rowed. Not being able to get to the landing, we went into a crevasse in the rocks and I jumped ashore and they rowed back out with that wave, and rowed back in again, literally threw the carry cot with the baby in to me, and I had to walk all through the scrub round to where I could get down onto the landing. And then George had to do the same to get ashore. I'll never forget that. I jumped off in the first pair of nylon stockings I ever had and they got torn to ribbons. But I couldn't care less because I was ashore and no way would you get me back out on the boat.

By the time the Martins joined the Service, regulations had loosened somewhat. Alan had been to a 'Big Party' at the principal keeper's house to celebrate meeting an old mate. Shirley Martin: It was late in the evening Alan arrived home bit the worse for drink and next thing we know, just after midnight or so, Ronnie Sears is coming into the house saying, 'Alan, Alan, Maria's having her baby!' And Alan says, 'You don't want me, you want Shirley.' By this time I'm sort of dressed and gathering up things because we're 70 miles from Kaitaia. The only sober male on station was the second assistant so they woke him up to drive the car and Maria down. And Maria says, 'No panic, I always have a long labour.' This was her sixth child – always have a long labour. And it's foggy and the lights on the car were playing up – they were starting to dip, we didn't have a torch, and the pains are getting closer together and she says, 'I'm not going to make it to Kaitaia!' And I'm, 'What are we going to do!' Anyway we ended up at the Te Kao store, bashed on the door there and by this time it's about three o'clock in the morning. Ossie Kitchen who owned the store comes to the door and I say, 'Maria's having a baby!' 'Oh, you want some petrol,' he says. I say, 'No, we want a bed!' That threw him by the ears. He sort of managed to retreat into the furthest corner of the store and his wife came out – Maisie – and we got Maria into a bed, and she's getting pretty close to delivering, and Maisie's starting to panic and I'm boiling up a bit of string and some scissors – and

then she says, 'Would you like me to fetch May?' And I say, 'Who's May?' And she says, 'Oh, she's the lady that delivers all the babies round here.' I say, 'Yes, fetch May!' And May arrived and gave me a hand to deliver the baby. They sent an ambulance up from Kaitaia to get her — well, the baby was delivered at Te Kao store before it arrived. And had it been a girl it was going to be called after May and myself but it turned out to be a boy so they called it Peter Oswold, cause Ossie was the name of the storekeeper, as a memento.

CHAPTER 11

Lighthouse stations and their communities

In 1917 P. W. Grenfell at Cape Egmont seemed worried about the flighty station horse 'placing the keepers in a very undignified position' and 'jeopardising their safety'.[1] But in their small communities lighthouse keepers had standing. They were doing a job universally recognised as important, they were seen as government representatives, they were on school boards, they supported local dances and fund-raising efforts. If, as at Puysegur Point, the lighthouse station was the logical place to take a sick person, neighbourly transactions were by no means one-way. In the following letters we see keepers playing their part in the network of community interdependence so essential to isolated settlements.

In 1909 Sam Hart at Cape Egmont sought permission to lend the station horse to a settler called Gray for a couple of weeks. [He had] a hundred-acre farm two miles distant ... to help plough 12 acres of his land. Another farmer named Symonds also living two miles from here tells me he had the use of him for ploughing last year, and that the horse was the better for it. He is very fat and some steady work for about three weeks would do him good. We can spare him for that time, but while not anxious to lend him, if the Department sanctions it I will let him go.[2]

Conversely, in 1909 Anders Hansen at Cape Palliser was grateful for the help from neighbours: Re Assistant Keepers accident. I beg to draw your attention to the readiness to help Keepers, shown by Mr Donald Ross, Manager of "White Rock" sheep station. He sent, without being asked, a man to act as temporary Keeper, and rode, during the night, a long distance to meet Dr Palmer and show him the way to Mr Berry's Place. The man sent by Mr Ross is a good reliable one.[3]

Peterson, a miner on Coal Island, was one of those hopefuls who occasionally washed up at Puysegur Point. The keepers had already been supplying him with provisions (although they'd told him he was not to come to them again for food) and were keeping an eye on him. In November 1917 they faced a new and more dramatic crisis involving all the Puysegur community, and we see, again, A. V. Pearce's humanity: I have the honour to inform you that on the 14th inst Messers Powell & Longuet came for me to go over & see Peterson as he was so bad. I at once went over & ... I examined his leg & I regret to state it has gone too far to be saved ... I told [Peterson] he must [be] got over without delay to the station where I could look after him & after arranging that Powell & Longuet bring him down to their landing & that I would take two men & boat him over I departed.

He has not had any food only what Mr Longuet has given him so I took him some milk & eggs ... I have brought him over where I can do all I can for him to make him comfortable & placed him in the linesman's hut. I will visit him frequently & feed him on soft diet until relief comes but he is worse today probably being exhausted in getting him over, however I think I will make him as comfortable as I can & feed him little & often, I am taking the responsibility of making him abide by my orders alone & trust I am not doing anything wrong considering the urgency of the case ...

I have instructed Mr. Powell to send a wire for a steamer to get him out at once before he dies & to go as far as Mussell beach, also telling him to wait there & get the steamer that is coming out to call there & pick him up & save him the long walk back, I also told him that I expect the Govt. would meet his expenses for going out trusting my explanation is satisfactory & that I have done the right & only thing.

I do not myself intend to ask compensation in this case for the food & attention I am giving him but should the Department consider I deserve anything I will accept it with thanks.

Nov 18th Since writing the above I have the honour to state I have found Peterson's left leg & foot going in the same way & he is so weak that he can't walk at all or even bath his leg. I bath his legs twice a day for him & have a bandage round the blackened parts ...

I have been with him from 9 a.m. till 7 p.m. today & did not care to leave him alone as his mind seems to ramble at times.[4]

Five days later there were new crises, and again Pearce made himself unstintingly available — while the other keepers, presumably, shouldered his lighthouse duties: I am with him all day and at any time at night as he can do nothing for himself ...[5]

On the 30th, 15 days after the accident, Pearce reported the Rita *had taken Peterson out. Powell claimed £7 10s for the journey to get medical assistance. Pearce told the department in a letter supporting Powell's claim:* [The journey] had not been an easy one: He had a very rough time of it and his clothes were torn from his legs and arms he also being badly cut about the hand struggling over logs trees Etc.[6]

The subsequent outwards correspondence makes no reference to any reimbursement.

At French Pass in 1926 Ray G. Stanley's fulsome tribute again indicates just how valuable such good neighbours could be: I beg to acknowledge receipt of your memo M18LL/1908 of the 9th inst In which you ask for particulars of the nature of the services rendered by Mr G[eorge]. Webber since I have been at this Station also the dates of such services if any have been rendered In reply I beg to state that the services done by Mr Webber are assisting in the boat to change the beacon light daily or whenever required that is to say in the event of the light going out or smoking through the night he is always available. If the weather is too bad to launch the station boat from the skids he uses his motor launch and we do the light from that It would be a very difficult job for one man in the boat at times to do the light as it really requires two men in the boat always as at times there is a nasty sea running through the pass and one man on his own would have no chance of changing the light.

I might state here that Mr Webber or his man are always on hand to assist me at all times.[7]

At Castlepoint in 1954 M. Armstrong was not just a search-and-rescue man, but someone alive to local problems and, like Sheary on Portland Island (see pp.170-71), able, as an outsider, to arbitrate over local bickering.

Monthly Letter – November 1954

This has been a very worrying month the Temp Keepers hut was burnt down on the 5th on the 7th a fishing launch Sea-Witch was missing in a northerly gale all night with the Principal Keeper keeping a watch all night & keeping in touch with Police Engines broke down on the 9th Store-keeper went broke on the 15th & I lost the two keepers I had trained, a party attempted to salvage the David on the 29th & I was up all night keeping a watch for it. The boat engines broke down some two miles out at sea & I arranged for the police to have the crew taken ashore.

The third member of the salvaging party arrived at Castlepoint in the early hours of the morning, smashing into another car on the way, rounded up our drive & smashed down the picket fence & finally smashed up his car completely returning over Castlepoint Hill. Arbitrating in many fishermen's disputes etc etc.[8]

At more northern stations, the local communities were largely Maori. In spite of some different notions of land use (see pp.77-78) keepers' relations with Maori generally seem to have been conducted on the same sort of basis as with Pakeha. As with E. H. Field on Portland Island in 1911, this might entail coming terms with quite new concepts: I have to acknowledge receipt of your memorandum No 599/229, of the 2nd inst. enclosing a copy of a letter from the Hon. Mr Ngata to the Minister of Marine, in which Mr Ngata accuses me of desecrating some burial grounds on this island & taking therefrom some fish-hooks etc

In explaining the matter as requested by you I have to state that Mr Ngata has been misinformed, and that I have never disturbed any burial ground, nor was I aware that there was one on the Island

The hooks that I have found have been taken from among shells, fishbones, & other refuse from old Maori camps

While scratching about these old middens I have often come across human bones, but in almost every case they have been more or less charred and broken, and quite obviously the remains of cannibalistic feasts. All bones that I have unearthed & many that have been exposed by the action of the wind & the natives sheep I have carefully buried

As the Mahia Natives have known for at least two years that I have been in the habit of scratching about the old camping places in search of curios, and in fact have often stood by & talked to me while doing so, it seems most strange to me that they did not ask me to desist if they thought I was disturbing a burial ground

It is very evident that the Maoris themselves do not look upon any part of Portland Island as a "Wahi Tapu" or sacred burial ground as they graze sheep on all parts of the island and eat the sheep so grazed. They have erected sheep yards and a sheep dip, and have sunk holes in search of water among the middens from which I took the hooks

These acts go to prove that they do not regard the ground as "Tapu" or else they too, are guilty according to "Maori law", of the crime of desecration or sacrilege

Mr Ngata, in his letter to the Minister of Marine says, "the facts", as he states them, have not been disputed – but I may say that hitherto I have not been given an opportunity to dispute them

In another part of his letter Mr Ngata suggests that the fish-hooks I have found be "returned" to the Chairman of the Maori Council, but as they have never been in possession of the Chairman of the Maori Council it is impossible to return them to him. Probably Mr Ngata means that the Maori Council would like to have them

I attribute the whole trouble to the machinations of a rather notorious halfcast with whom I have had some trouble over sheep

Now that I know the natives object to me looking for curios needless to say no further search will be made by me for them; and if instructed by you to do so I will send those now in my possession to the Chairman of the Maori Council.[9]

The evidence suggests that keepers knew they needed to get on with whoever lived near them, and appreciated their Maori neighbours. However, in spite of Percy White's efforts at East Cape in 1938 (below), head office subsequently again employed one of the (Pakeha) Goldsmiths as temporary keeper until 1944, and he was the coastwatcher over the war years. In reference to your Memo of 29th July … concerning employment of the present temporary keeper. You have been correctly informed, as Mr Goldsmith is certainly, I should say the best well to do farmer here having a big farm, plenty of sheep & cattle and seems to be the only go ahead one here. We, on arrival here often wondered why he held down the temporary keeper job.

We, after coming to know the people around and the conditions, reckoned that Mrs Kahaki's son (the late temporary keepers stepson) this Mr Albert, who is married and lives with Mrs Kahaki (his mother) ought to be engaged, but as we do not want to fall out with our Maori people residents and the Dept, as the present man is so reliable, let things go on as they were, but on every hand we hear "Poor Taha and his wife." Why don't we let him have the temporary keeping to help his mother carry on with her small pension. Of course we are helpless [to make the change] unless our temporary keeper is unreliable. As far as I could say I think Mr Albert would be quite suitable but to save trouble with the Maoris here & us it would be best for you to let Mr Goldsmith know that you have heard of a deserving case and I'm sure he would be satisfied, and us keepers need not come into the matter at all as we do not want to get into their bad books being such a small community and they are all so friendly with us all.[10]

On Mokohinau, Norm Miller firmly supported local muttonbirders against the department. Two days after the following letter, he equally firmly reiterated his views and recommendation, pointed out that the Maoris' stay had been prolonged by a week of unfavourable weather, and that they they were intending to go through appropriate bureaucratic channels.

Maoris – Mutton Birding

In consultation with the above and with reference to my telegram and your reply of the 24th November 1947, I have to advise that a party of fourteen Maoris arrived from the "Great Barrier Is." on the 23rd November, and remained on the Island for fourteen days, while engaged in securing Mutton Birds from this and neighbouring Islands.

This is the same party of Maoris who have visited these Islands for the same purpose for many years past, and they claim the traditional right, dating back to tribal times, to "occupy" these Islands for a short period at this time of year.

With due respect to your telegraphed advice that the Maoris have not hitherto been allowed to camp on the lighthouse Island, I venture to suggest that they have unofficially been allowed that priviledge on many occasions.

Certainly this was the case in the two previous years when the station was in charge of a caretaker, or the Public Works Dept. and on these occasions they were also permitted the use of the landing shed.

Consequently there was a well established precedent for the request made on this occasion.

On their recent stay, I carefully observed these people, and found them to be polite and agreeable, and willing to agree to and abide by any restriction or request made of them.

They appear to be a superior type of Maori, sober and industrious, and respected residents of Great Barrier Island.

These people live in the settlement of Motairehu, which is the closest settlement to these Islands, and being in possession of a number of launches could conceivably be of assistance in an emergency. I would prefer to have their goodwill rather than the reverse, and from my observation on them on this occasion, would suggest that there may be no objection to their yearly visits on future occasions.[11]

George Kroening has (slightly conflicting) memories of that incident. We had the Maoris come over from Great Barrier and get the mutton birds. They were there for about three and a half weeks. It happened while infantile paralysis epidemic was going on. We didn't keep a watch on the light, we only did the midnight weather there, and we woke up with the dogs barking, the cows going mad round the place and there were about 22 Maoris and about 29 dogs. Livened the place up a bit. Hadn't been warned. So straight away there was an urgent telegram sent to the Minister of Marine and it came back that they had the sole rights and could come whenever they liked so we had to sort of retreat into our shells again! We saw quite a bit of them and they were a good crowd, really good. They did all their plucking of the birds and preserving them in their own fat down at the landing. While they were there we had a New Year's Eve party, we held it in the workshop up by the lighthouse tower and we decked the place out the international code flags, they had their own music, accordions and guitars. It was really good. It was Ladies a Plate.

Alan Wright, arriving on the East Cape as relieving keeper in the late 1950s, acted immediately to resolve differences that had developed between the keeper there and the local community: First thing I did on the Sunday I went to the marae because I gathered from the village there'd been some problems between the local Maoris and the lighthouse keeper. I decided, well, I'd better look into this. I'd lived at Wairoa in Hawke's Bay where there's eight Maoris to every Pakeha, I knew all the right things to do and not do. So I went to church on Sunday morning at the marae, went up to the chief, shook his hand, rubbed noses, said the right things, and from then on, for the period I was there, I was well in with them.

When I left at the station in town to catch the bus out, half the town was there to see me off.

For the Martins at Cape Reinga from 1964 to 1966, Maori were part of the local network.
Shirley: When you're off duty you got to know the Maori because if you're driving up and down the road they'd say, 'Oh, call in and see us and have a cup of tea.' And you couldn't go past without offending them. So going down to Kaitaia, which we were allowed to do once every six weeks (in between the truck would come up once a fortnight) and you'd start off at say eight o'clock in the morning and it would be dark by the time you got back because you had to stop here and have tea with this one and have stop and say hullo to this one. It was quite a major operation. And we were often invited to their social do's and things and we used to go as long as there was someone on duty.

By the time Bill Megennis was at the Cape in the late 1980s, societal understandings had moved again: The people at Cape Reinga, the people in the district whom I'd met — it was just nice to communicate with them. They were the farmers. There was Te Paki station, the Conservation station. Te Hapua which was 15 kilometres down the road, there were people in that area who'd come to the Cape, who'd lived thereabouts. Often they would meet once a month at Te Paki settlement and they'd have a party at the woolshed. And they'd say, 'Oh good, on Sunday come down to my house.' So I met all these people who were extremely hard-working rural folk … you had a connection with the rural life of New Zealand. What stood out at Cape Reinga was that it was all about areas of spiritual significance. It had an impact on me and this was through Cis Mitgardt [the wife of the principal keeper] who's East Coast Maori from Tikitiki who took me round the area. This is not her spiritual area, it's not part of her turangawaewae — and she said, Look, there's the maunga [mountain or mound], up there, this has no meaning to me but I respect it. And Spirits Bay — I remember standing on the beach down there and looking around and she was telling me about the history. I'm not one for spiritual significance, but I think what Cis was saying is that there is a Maori presence here, she's not part of and it was just the atmosphere of the place.

Proximity to communities and accessibility also occasioned some unique problems. The situation that David Partington at Nugget Point in 1910 describes below is explicable; what led to the other situations at East Cape is now lost in time. I have the honour to inform you that when Keeper Smith went to light up last night he met a welldressed man near the Tower showing peculiar conduct but he did not suspect the real condition of the man's mind till entering the Oil Store with the man following and shutting the door behind him. Seeing the Telephone he took off the Receiver and bashing it about in a most violant way so Keeper Smith closed with him and eventually removed him out of the Building when he promised to return later on and do for Smith. Keeper Smith then rang me up to watch the man's movements as he was making his way back. I at once collected the women and children in my house and armed with a stick went out to see what he might do. Meeting him near the stone Dwelling I bounced him to move on as far as the stable, when he returned to the stone house so I warned Keeper Smith by telephone and stayed near my house in case he should come by way of the Track leading up to the flag-staff. At this time Keeper Edmonds was returning from the Bay with the mail & in company with two Dustings, so they met the man between the stable and stone house with two guns, one loaded, and the funnel of a Graphopone which he had taken out of the house after smashing and upsetting Keeper Edmonds property. These guns & the funnel were thrown over the cliff by this man and he picked up a palling hammer in the Quarry and threatened to do for anyone who dared to molest him Nevertheless, Keeper Edmonds and the Dustings managed to down him when I arrived, we found and moved him back to the lighthouse as the most suitable place to keep him till he could be taken away with safety. I took the liberty of engaging the two Dustings to assist Keepers to guard this active and apparently dangerous lunatic.

I then tried to trace him through the local Telephone Stations and within a couple of hours Temporary Keeper Dabineth came and identified him as one Scott of Port Molyneaux; so I rang up the Port Telephonist and he sent Scott's brother who stayed with us till daylight; then he, with the assistance of Mr C Arthur who seemed to control the man and who stayed with us most of the night, took him away on the understanding that he would be sent to a Mental Hospital without delay It was a great relief to all of us to see the last of this active and dangerous man, who, they say could roughly handle four or five men in his most insane moments. Had he tackled me in the Oil Store instead of Keeper Smith, I might have been killed and the valuable Lighthouse property seriously if not hopelessly distroyed Keeper Edmonds has suffered considerable loss and should be compensated. The Station D.B.B.L. Gun is much damaged and the Telephone Receiver, though workable, is fractured. Trusting you will consider that we and those who kindly rendered assistance did our best under the sudden and peculiar circumstances Enclosed please find two Vouchers for payment to the two Dustings.[12]

Partington subsequently wrote repeatedly to Scott's brother asking for some financial recompense for what had been destroyed, but his last letter has him approaching the Public Trustee in case he was dealing with Scott's property and could make some reimbursement.

The issues round the next two reports from East Cape are lost. (Members of the Kahaki family were long employed as temporary keepers.) P. R. W. Wilson, 1923: I herewith forward to you a letter from Keeper Simmonds as to a threatening note which was placed under the store room window of the Assistant dwelling on the night of the 11th of April The note reading, <u>Mr Simmonds & Willers better Look out tomorrow night and Wifes,</u>

Sir I have to state that keeper Simmonds inform me also give me the note about 1 p.m. of the 12 inst I therefor informed the Police at Te Araroa of this matter the Police Officer informed me he could not get out to East Cape that night as he was 16 miles from Te Araroa and the best thing to do was to get some one to watch the North and South sides of the keepers dwellings so therefore I got Mr Goldsmith and Mr Kahaki myself and Mr Kahaki doing the watches in the Tower Assistant Keeper Simmonds and Mr Goldsmith watching the keeper dwellings Sir during the night all was well as this matter his in the hands of the Police I will report Later of this matter [13]

E. G. Foster, 1952: On my appointment from Baring Head Lighthouse to East Cape Lighthouse, I understand I was instructed to keep the Surrounding Settlers from entrance to the Lighthouse Reserve, particularly to coming inside of keepers dwellings, unless on Lighthouse business only. I believe you understand from past keepers what "<u>Friction</u>" it occurs when the Surrounding Settlers are allowed entrance on the Station and inside of the keepers dwellings. Needless to say I am referring to the women folk of the Settlers, During the past year and recently I have had to tell two persons ('Ladies') to stay away from the Station as their entrance on the station dwellings was causing Friction between Keepers Famileys The surrounding Settlers themselves admit it is not advisable to keep running backwards and forwards to the Keepers Dwellings, As they Admit from past experience that it has cause a lot of "Friction" and trouble between the Keepers Famileys and themselves. If keepers and their Famileys wish to see the surrounding Settlers, I suggest 'Sir' that they should go and visit the Persons, they want to see, not to invite them on the Station, and inside of the Dwellings. Would you please advise and give a strict ruling, as regards to the admittance of the Surrounding Settlers to the Lighthouse Reserves etc. [14]

As the population got more mobile, casual visitors, far from being a welcome link to the outside world, were a nuisance. At Waipapa Point, as early as 1907, G. Gwynne had to explain why he had denied entry to a tourist party: I have the honour to acknowledge receipt of the above [memo asking for the explanation] and state in reply that, Mr McKenzie & party were refused admission to the Lighthouse on Sunday 11TH inst; so have <u>all</u> Sunday visitors since that date. In doing so I have only complied with sub-section 3 of section 4 Chapter XII Instructions to Lightkeepers.

As we are working 76 to 80 hours per week (including night watches) to overtake the work on the station it is necessary that this regulation be enforced to allow us a little recreation

At least one of the party knew before they came that the Lighthouse was closed to Sunday visitors.[15]

As visitors increased, so did the problems they presented. In 1938 at Moeraki A. H. Saunders was faced with the unenviable task of attempting to enforce unnotified regulations amongst those whom he probably knew or fraternised with. I would like to be advised what authority I have to stop motor cars entering the reserve This is a very popular place for fishing & picnic parties during the week end & anything up to a dozen car loads visit here all and wish to go through to the landing, you can imagine the litter they make and even the stones from under the landing store are taken to build fire places a fire place was recently made within three feet of the landing store, and keepers can not be watching all these people all the time. I don't wish to be a spoil sport, & prevent people from fishing at the landing, but until I locked the gate at the entrance to the reserve some time ago these cars used to be brought into the reserve at all hours even during the night. My action in locking the gate is very much questioned, even in some cases insultingly resented ... there is no objection to sober people going down fishing if they leave their cars outside the reserve, & its quite safe for them to light fires for boiling their tea water providing they do so on the beach or rocks, but I suggest that a notice board be sent this trip with the Matai definitely stating the position as regards motor cars.[16]

In the 1950s visitors at Baring Head were such a nuisance that Frank Shepherd reported: ... the present [trespass] notice is of no value, in fact it is misleading because when trespassers are questioned they maintain that they have a right to be on the road, and when they are informed that they have no right to be on the road, they then say they can trespass off the road.[17]

Shepherd and Mr Aitken of the adjourning Orongorongo station drafted a new trespass notice for the road end.

On the other hand, keepers and their families could build quite strong ties with their local communities. Between 1970 and to the end of 1973 the Martins were at Baring Head. Shirley: For the first time in my life since we'd joined the Light Service we were within reach of me being able to do some occupation. I had learnt to drive, the children were going to school and I'd joined a group, and was painting and learning to spin; we had friends up and down the road between us and Wainui; the DSIR [Department of Scientific and Industrial Research] had set up a station near the lighthouse that was sniffing the air to find out how many parts carbon there were, what was happening with the pollution around

The Martins leaving Dog Island on the first stage of the journey to Baring Head. Sometimes transfers affected more than the outgoing family. The children remaining on the station could be farewelling significant friends. ALAN AND SHIRLEY MARTIN

and where it was coming from, and I actually had a part-time job with the DSIR going through all these sheets and working out air pollution. I had the rug pulled out from under my feet when they phoned up and said, 'Oh, look, you're going to Cuvier.' I really didn't want to go there. We could have left the Light Service there, but we had a family conference and three of the family voted for Cuvier so I had to go along too. If you didn't want to go, you left, and that's all there was to it.

On The Brothers, as elsewhere, radio was important, in reaching out into the wider lighthouse community or beyond, bringing in the outside world and forestalling boredom. Chris Staley: The radio was quite important to most remote lighthouses. Most of the traffic — messages, things like that — was done by telegrams over the radio. Six o'clock at night was the main time when messages were being sent out to all the lighthouses and so everybody used to be into this 'earwigging' as they called it, listening. It was rather a small community of lighthouse keepers, rather tight knit, and naturally this produced a lot of gossip. I remember

married keepers in particular were very much interested who was where and who was going to be shifted to another station. One of the blokes off The Brothers decided to play a joke by sending a telegram to The Brothers saying he was going to get married in two month's time and he had been posted to Baring Head, which was a plum station – everybody wanted it. This created an uproar: 'Why the hell should he get Baring Head?' Phil Gamby [a lighthouse inspector] went to Puysegur Point after that and he was immediately attacked, 'Why has that bloody Greg been posted to Baring Head?'

One keeper, he'd never had radio work before. He said to me, 'You better get in touch with the Marine Department, it's too much for me, too complicated.' I said, 'Don't worry about it. What are you scared of?' He said, 'I don't fancy talking to Wellington Radio on a regular basis.' I said, 'Oh, bull shit, tell them it's the Voice of Cook Strait calling.' And that stuck with him. Even to this day he remembers the Voice of Cook Strait.

Those single side bands you just sat up there and twiddled with them and you could listen to all sorts of things. I've even heard Russian whalers. They used to overpower us, speaking in Russian of course, and at one stage I complained to the blokes at Wellington Radio – I was late in getting the weather through – 'Can't you stop those bloody guys? They were going right through the silence period.' This bloke says. 'How?'

Oddly enough people say, 'Weren't you bored', or 'Weren't you lonely?' You can't be because there's always something happening – I dunno, May Days – you can't help but hear them. I clearly remember a fishing boat

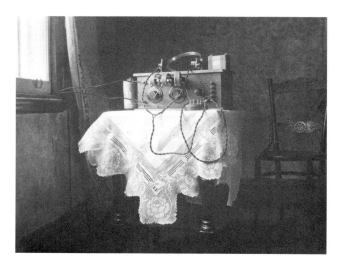 

ABOVE LEFT *Fred Hansen sent to his family these two photos of the wireless at Cape Brett and inscribed them: 'Mr Pearces Wireless set like it was when I came here he has had it added to very considerably.'*

HANSEN COLLECTION

ABOVE RIGHT *'The Wireless Set Without loudspeaker. Mr Pearce, Inez [Hansen], Mrs Shearwood (right), Cape Brett Lighthouse'. Radio did not only bring in the outside community; listening was a communal activity in itself.*

HANSEN COLLECTION

sinking out there one day and the bloke was telling Wellington Radio what was happening. First of all the water was coming in. 'It's up round my bloody ankles now', he said. And then it was up to his waist, and next minute the boat was gone!

STATION HIERARCHIES AND GETTING ON TOGETHER

One of the remarkable things about the Lighthouse Service over its 150 years was how relatively rarely keepers and families fell out badly. Forbearance, tolerance and transfers helped dissipate station tensions, and while irritations within the small, isolated lighthouse stations could arise from often seemingly trivial incidents, remarkably few escalated sufficiently for keepers to complain to head office.

When, in 1867, Balfour established the structure and rules for the Lighthouse Service he set out three ranks, with the two lower obliged 'in all things connected with the Lighthouse Service' to 'implicitly obey' the principal keeper. Shirley Martin attested to the hierarchy's longevity: There was a definite pecking order, a definite hierarchy — the principal keeper and the first assistant, and the second assistant.

These pervaded all official aspects of a keeper's life. [Chris Staley] I think hierarchies have always annoyed me. We were supposed to have an egalitarian society in those days and yet going through Picton for instance, as a principal keeper I could stay at the Terminus Hotel and an assistant keeper had to stay in Oxley's Hotel, a lower grade hotel.

Not everyone could stomach the hierarchies: D. Meister resigned from Tiritiri Matangi in 1955: Reasons for resigning being as follows:

(a) I object to the archaic Victorian Regimental policy of the Lighthouse service. However I agree that such a policy is apparently necessary to satisfactorily supervise control –

(b) intellectually stunted types who have been attracted to the past and subsequently have risen to the dizzy heights of Principal Keeper. Their lack of necessary powers and consequent inconsistence in conduct of such types made life on this Lighthouse station more intolerable than that of the less quiet and solitary atmosphere of a city.[18]

The hierarchies also affected the women's relationships. Barry Langman: The women paid a certain obeisance to the principal keeper's wife and they were afraid of upsetting the wife of the principal keeper in case it rebounded on the rest of the family.

Shirley: On Mokohinau, it being our first station, I was very aware that I was the junior woman and you didn't address the other two by their Christian names unless you were invited to. It was Mrs Jones and Mrs Johnson. I think, too, it was what you did then. Some of the stations perhaps were more relaxed.

Yet the structure was not entirely unreasonable and effective principal keepers, contributing positively to training and how the station was run, helped keep good people in the Service. Shirley: I'm pleased that the Johnsons were our first principal keeper because your principal keeper can make or break you, they really can. We started off under a really good couple, and so we knew what it could be like so that we weren't going to be put off.

On Stephens Island in the mid-1950s principal keeper Roger Blanshard organised the work to help minimise friction. Barry: The men got on well. We followed the instructions of the principal keeper. He was a very informative person and we liked working with him. The shifts rotated so we all did the same work in equal proportions. When there was a job to be done we worked together, whether it was putting a fence up or shearing. We took our turn at operating the winches where one operated the crane and the other was having to walk up the cliff to the top winch house. The work was always equally shared, without rank or anything.

Principal keepers initiated station socialising. Barry: On Stephens Island in particular we had a regular weekly function where we moved around from house to house. We would play games, we would have a nice supper – the ladies competed with each other to put on the best supper – and we would play Monopoly, Fun Worder, canasta, and some other card games. Not gambling games. It was one evening a week which we looked forward to and the children could intermingle in the early part of the evening before going off to bed. Roger would have arranged that.

Picnicking was a favourite activity, whatever decade you belonged to. This photo is inscribed: 'This is a picnic held on the top of the real Cape Saunders [the lighthouse was on a lower headland] about a mile or a little more NE of the lighthouse and hundreds of feet higher From there we look towards Tairoa Heads the entrance to Dunedin Harbour'. HANSEN COLLECTION

Keepers in the 1950s on Centre Island, where for some unfathomable reason the horses went blind, had picnics that included all the community. Jo Broom: If we had a picnic, the Big Pig and the horse came with us, and Big Pig led the horse. He'd be in front of Prince and he'd grunt and Prince couldn't see him but he would plod along, the pig leading way down the beach or down the rocks. We had a lot of fun. We had more fun in the Light Service than we ever had in town.

The extent of socialising differed from station to station. Shirley: At Christmas time we might get together — we were invited over to the principal keeper's place for dinner at night, have a buffet or something like that, or a social get-together.

Especially on The Brothers, where the men all lived in the Big House, a change of personnel could make a huge difference. Alan Wright: Whenever the boat came in the first thing two keepers did, each went to his room with his box. That was the last you saw of them until the crate of whisky had gone. They were alcoholics, both of them and virtually nothing got done during that period. They'd go into their room on a night when you'd had your meals. I had to do the cooking. I'd been forewarned about this, whereas when Chris came on, we got together, we kicked up hell with Skiffington, ripped the kitchen out, relined it all and made it presentable.

On that station it was particularly important to eliminate possible causes of friction. Too many bosses and opportunities to feel that everyone was not pulling their weight could easily become bones of contention. Despite his view of hierarchies, Chris did not hesitate to pull rank if necessary: I had an ex-policeman on The Brothers and he was determined to do things his way. I had to point out to him that there was only one boss out there and it was me. Another guy – I remember I had him cleaning the engine room one day, and he was polishing the brass on the diesel engine, and grumbling all the time, 'Why do the Marine Department want this bloody lot cleaned like this?' I said, 'It's not the Marine Department that want it clean.' 'Well, who is it then,' he said. I said, 'It's me.' I suppose I was rather forceful in those days. Military training gets you that way, y'know. Most guys that I met had service in the military or the Navy or something like that, and you've got to have a certain amount of discipline to run a place in isolation like that. But that's not to say you can't be very friendly with people. I made tremendous friends with people out there.

It was my job to make sure they knew what my house-keeping standards were and that was it. And we had a very, very rigid roster. Every little job that needed to be done was covered by that roster. Whose turn was it to fill the coal bucket for instance, or whose job it was to do this or that and immediately I could see who had not done something and I would make sure they did it. Everything had to be done, and when the weather is bad and you're cooped up indoors, that's when friction can build. But if there is a rigid structure of who does what it cuts out any arguments.

Well used, authority could be constructive. Chris: This assistant keeper had been a relieving keeper on two stations, had got two bad reports from the principal keeper. I found out afterwards that they [Wellington] decided they would send him out to Chris on The Brothers and he could sort him out. Anyway, in retrospect I guess maybe I did speak sharply to him at one stage and after that he turned out to be one of the best assistant keepers I ever had out there. Fantastic guy, so talented, particularly with metal work. He'd served part of his time as an apprentice in the metal business, and things like soldering he was really, really good at. He was good at everything from mixing concrete to moving boats. He stayed with me for quite some time – only left to get

TOP *Socialising: different decades, different patterns and different fashions of photography. Here the Hansen family (Elizabeth is holding the baby in a bonnet on her knee, Anders is sitting beside her) gather with the other keepers and hangers-on for their somewhat formal 1883 Christmas photo.* HANSEN COLLECTION

BOTTOM *Christmas 1963 at Mokohinau, From left: Cliff 'Spike' Jones, Thelma Jones, Shirley Martin, R Eagleton.*

ALAN AND SHIRLEY MARTIN

Families and friends, always welcome, were new faces in the little lighthouse communities. Here, on Portland Island in 1946 are Jean Kroening's mother and her sister and children.
JEAN AND GEORGE KROENING

married. He respected me and because of his talent I respected him. It was mutual respect and maybe on the other places he never got a chance.

Inevitably, irritations could arise and fester, sometimes because of the way that principal keepers used their authority. Appointed basically on length of service and put into positions for which they had no training and little experience in people management, they did not always act wisely. Shirley: Principal keepers could be very picky, nit-pick at you for various little things, very petty at times. There was one principal keeper we had, my husband was digging a hole for something. 'Why was he digging this, why hadn't he got permission?' He almost wanted it in triplicate! I think a little bit of power went to their heads. And others could be very lax and let standards drop considerably.

The informal information networks that operated forewarned and forearmed keepers on transfer. Alan Martin: Practically everybody knew everybody else and if you said you were going to a certain station, 'Oh yes so and so's there', and they'd say they're either OK or they're not OK or they like this or they don't like that. So basically you knew what you're going to get before you arrived. You formed your own opinion, your own ideas once you got there but at least you got a basic idea of what you were going into.

Both principals and assistants could report to head office on personnel matters but they were mostly resolved without such recourse. Some temperaments helped. George Kroening: You got used to people's peculiar ways, you went with the tide. I think being brought up to do what you were told at home was the mainstay of it, and then doing what you're told at sea. I was fortunate there that I was with mainly older men and I got taught the right way. Only one way to do things and that's the right way. Do it once, do it right.

Shirley: I think for Alan there were times when it got quite stressful, and it would get stressful for me because he'd be coming home and telling me about it and he'd be all wound up. But you got on with it. You wanted to live that way of life, you knew you were going to be moved before too long and if things got really, really bad you could always request a transfer to somewhere else and if they could transfer you, they would. But we never struck any violence. The men might have had the odd word now and then but for the most part, we've always been able to get on with people fairly well. I suppose I've always been fairly laid back.

Getting away to let off steam was a common way of defusing a situation: Chris: The Brothers was not all that confined. You can get away from people when you want to so. You can't actually walk around the island, you can only go up or down so if you wish to go round the island, which I have done, you've got to do a little mountaineering. You cling to the cliff, work your way around. It's not advisable because if you drop off, you're into the sea. But most people try it.

Sometimes you do have to walk away. I never had any problem. I was a pretty robust sort of a guy, y'know, I could look after myself. I'd knocked about a bit, ships and barrack rooms and what have you.

Alan Wright: We had a dog on The Brothers that acted as a buffer. If you felt you were getting scratchy with somebody you'd take the dog for a walk and talk to the dog. You got no sense out of him, but you'd talk to him, and at least you'd let off steam.

Shirley also felt that talking things over helped. A bit like crying, makes you feel better when you've stopped. You'd have a little grizzle about whatever it was that was annoying you — the state of the stores because the boat was late — and you'd get over it.

A 1950s aerial shot of The Brothers, with its clear potential for rock-climbing.

ANZ (WGTN) ABPL 8848 W5221 ALBUM D, P.13

Alan Martin, at the oars, and his son Peter, getting away from it all on Mokohinau in 1963.

ALAN AND SHIRLEY MARTIN

Alan Martin, like many others, found: A lot of the problems we had on the stations was because of the children. If the children didn't get on there could be a lot of tensions between the families.

Shirley: You could have trouble with the children, bullying, and you couldn't keep complaining to the parents because you'd end up having an argument about it so you had to put up with it. I'm not confrontational and so if there's something going wrong I tend to deal with it myself and try to explain to the children, if it was involving them, to avoid those situations. I'd have a quiet word with the parents. For the most part it worked.

Three's an awkward number. You'd find that two would be more friendly. I think in a way the women didn't get too close to one another. That way it wasn't going to cause any problems. If we got on well with somebody then we would meet socially, we'd have evenings where we'd play cards or something like that, or have them down for a meal. There'd be other times where you'd socialise at morning tea, but that would be it.

I think the most time that we would meet and socialise would be on stores day when we went down to the landing to watch the stores being unloaded. We'd stand and chat then. You saw more of the men folk because they'd be working round and you would take it in turns to give them a cup of tea, morning tea time.

Barry: The women were left to their own devices, basically. The men were constantly in each other's company during the day but the women were at home — a certain amount of isolation.

Lack of company did not worry Shirley: You had your husband there for all his meals, you'd go and do things such as swimming together, you'd go out fishing, and you did things as a family, it's excellent for that sort of thing, family building. I suppose Alan and I have always been very self-sufficient as regards to being able to entertain ourselves and cope with just being together. Alan was there all the time, for all the meals, and you did things together. It was — it was wonderful. You end up best friends or worst enemies, one of the two.

The men on The Brothers faced another possible tension. Chris: This is quite important for single men on a monastic place like that — sex. I learned — I was in my early thirties, so rather a horny goat shall we say — I found out you would think that rather like tobacco [craving] you'd get desperate. You don't. There was one guy out there used to get *Playboy* delivered all the time, but if you don't look for any stimulus, if you don't look at things like that and you don't see women around, it's surprising — I don't know whether this is how Catholic priests do it — but you forget all about it. It's quite amazing. And yet the moment you get off and have a few beers you go like a randy old goat again.

Lighthouse inspections were initially carried out by head office staff, then by the captains of the lighthouse steamers, most famously Captain Bollons. With the demise of the steamers, PWD or MOW staff on periodic visits filed reports on the equipment and station, not on the staff. About the time the Martins joined the Service a new inspectorate had been developed that was to address pastoral as well as station care. Alan Martin: Bill Kemp took over from Phil Gamby — and there was a third. One would come on station, he and the principal keeper would get together, discuss the work that was to be done on the station for the year and from there the principal keeper would write off for paint and things like that. Then he would come to each of the families to see what our reactions were and how we were getting on. [If the tensions weren't resolved] these things were generally referred to head office and they'd assess the situation. Bill Kemp had to be called in and he would try to sort things out, listen to both sides, go back to head office and put in his report and recommendations and it would be taken from there. You could write direct to the department if you were not a principal keeper, but generally what you wrote had to go through the principal keeper so he could add his comments. It was quite possible that one or other of the keepers would be moved on to another station.

There are occasional reports of Captain Bollons being sent to investigate station tensions, but whether he played any sort of mediating role or simply backed up authority, as the letter below does, I was unable to determine.

The letter below, copied into the Portland Island letterbook in 1888, has no prefacing material to give it context.

A Reply
to the Principal Keeper
Portland Island Lighthouse

With reference to your and Assistant Keeper Edgar's letters of the 28TH ultimo, I have to state that Keeper Edgar was greatly to blame for fixing anything to the spouting of his house, and still more so for using the language he did to his superior officer; but as he has previously borne a good character, I will not take any further steps in the matter. He should however be warned that any further misconduct will be severely dealt with. Assistant Keepers must remember that they have to comply with the Instructions to Lightkeepers and if they cannot or will not do so they will have to leave the service.[19]

Mostly keepers wrote about disagreements that had escalated beyond resolution at station level. These reports constituted a formal complaint that could result in disciplinary proceedings. Men, often unused to writing, had to document charges knowing that the other party had a right of reply; the reports were serious business. What head office made of them is not recorded. But they were not common — perhaps because it cannot have been pleasant to acknowledge such breakdowns in relations, most keepers did not resort to such a measure lightly. When they did, the accusations and counter-accusations could drag on over weeks, they would often throw little light on who was at fault and at this distance do not make terribly edifying reading.

Richard Tregurtha's letter from Nugget Point in 1881 is typical: I beg to call your attention to the last monthly letter that was forwarded to you by the Principal Keeper from this Station. In the last paragraph he states that "<u>We</u> have forwarded 17 messages and received 8 since the telephone" etc. I presume the personal pronoun <u>we</u> implies himself and myself. Now the fact is, I had nothing whatever to do in the matter, and I must respectfully object to being associated with the telegraph any way until it is conducted in a more business-like and satisfactory manner.

From the time the "Morse' instruments were set up here to the present, the Principal has manifested a most childish and selfish disposition, in endeavouring to get everything in connection with the telegraph, into his own private keeping. I maintain he has <u>no right</u> to offer the telegraph officials one of his private rooms, wherein to erect the instruments until he had the sanction of the then Secretary of the Marine Department. By that act he knew I should be excluded from all practice, for prior to that event he had <u>falsely</u> accused me of the most outrageous and immoral conduct, for which he had not foundation whatever. I was then compelled, for my honor, to inform him that I should not visit his house again.

As you are aware sir, the instruments referred to have been replaced by telephones, and the line opened for public business.

What arrangements Mr. Logan made with Mr. Cunningham I know not as I have not received a syllable of information from either. I cannot believe, however, that it is intended to use the line <u>only</u> when it suits the Principal's convenience and to close the office in his absence. As a matter of fact, yesterday the telegraph was closed to the public till after 4 p.m. (Mr. Cunningham having to take his family to meet the Balclutha coach). On each alternate night also, he has to be at the Lighthouse before the telegraph hours are expired. I have reason to believe that he is receiving payment for his services, and I respectfully submit that he has not acted honourably to the Public or myself either, in undertaking a service he must have known he could not perform.

I beg to request that you will (in conjunction with the telegraph department) give this matter the attention it demands.

Since the telegraph was opened here, our outdoor work has been entirely neglected, and road work, fencing etc (which, if done at the proper time – i.e. before winter commenced – would have been a pleasant pastime) will now – if done at all – be an irksome and disagreeable labour.

There is another matter which demands you interfere, viz: – the overstocking of the Reserve with cattle by the Principal. I have suffered from this for a long time.[20]

William Cunningham replied immediately, Tregurtha counter-claimed. His literary skills were superior to Cunningham's, as his final words show: In apportioning the number of cattle, I respectfully inform you that there are only about five acres of clear, but inferior land; and you know, Sir, that timber will not produce good milk or butter.[21]

On Portland Island Charles Robson had twice previously reported Skill unwilling to do his share of the station work, and becoming abusive. The situation then further deteriorated. (Bartlet was a local, Komene Te Ito the principal chief, Jeffares the other keeper. Robson had been demoted for some unascertained reasons – see pp. 223–224) In March 1882 Robson wrote again: I have the honor to report that Mr. Skill in his desire to be revenged on me for having brought his misconduct under your notice, he's lately been trying by means of slanderous letters to create a disturbance of the friendly relations hitherto existing between the native owners of this Island and the Lightkeepers ... he tries to induce these people to believe that I am killing or procuring others to kill the native's sheep with the intent to steal them, he tells Bartlet that I have a feeling of enmity to him because he is a favourite at head quarters, whereas I am not, but have been sent from a large station to a smaller one, here, and my pay reduced ... that I have got Mr Jeffares to join in a conspiracy against him but he will see us both out of this, he states that he could not expect any thing else from us as we are both Irish ... fortunately for me neither W. Bendall nor Komeme believed a word of Mr. Skill's statements, but we do not at present know what mischief they may have done with the other natives who are part owners of the sheep. Mr. Skill still continues in this same line of conduct as I before reported to you, he comes out to work when it suits him, and absents himself when it does not. As Mr Skill has by the letters quoted made a libellous attack upon my private character, and so placed himself within reach of the law, I shall be glad if you will inform me, whether you will protect me in the discharge of my duty, or leave me to seek my remedy in a court of justice.[22]

Some months later, Skill was transferred – about the time he would have been due for a rotation.

The situations in which such tensions rose were never simple. William Tutt, on The Brothers in 1911, was apparently suffering from bad insomnia. He was principal keeper when Powell

(Len Lye's step-father) went mad at Cape Campbell and was very worried (apparently without reason) that the public might blame him for what had happened: I have the honour to report Probationary Keeper Mr Kane for his ill temper and insulting remarks to myself during his short stay here, I wrote a letter reporting him on November 30 but withdrew it at his request, in which he said that I was afraid to put the flags up when Randle was here althou we were starving (not a nice thing to throw in my face) he has done that more than once, I may state that he is the worse tempered man and the laziest man I have ever come acrosses if I after cleaning the lenses ask him to paint if the weather is a bit rough he begins to complain like this that's it rush the thing through and we shall have nothing to do and if I speak to him at all he answers thus I am not frightened of you I will soon put your pot on us I have a member of parliament that will fix you alright he makes the station very wretched with his discontented ways last night at 7.45 p.m. I whent to bed he at once began to walk back and forward in front of my window making all the noise he could on my asking him to stop as I had been painting the afternoon while he was in bead [bed] he answered come and hit me I waited a while and then got up and saw that Mr Livingstone was on the balcony so I called out to him as a witness Mr Kane than came round and said that I was a liar but that he was walking at the end of the house after that he kept walking in and out of his room making all the row he could I had the watch from midnight to sun rise his conduct is getting unbearable and I request that you will remove him from this station as soon as possible, as I could not recommend him as a keeper.[23]

Kane wrote a very lengthy justification / counter accusation; Tutt wrote again on 13 February raising different accusations; there was an inquiry in which Livingstone was called as witness; on 2 May Kane wrote again with fresh accusations. There the matter rested. But alongside the letterbook copy of that last letter Tutt made one final thrust — Exercable orthography. The letter of an illiterate.

CHAPTER 12

Pay and employment conditions

Lighthouse keeping often took men and their families into remote places and uncongenial surroundings, to make do with primitive conditions, be bombarded with nit-picking regulations, face frequent upheavals, and work long and broken hours in a job where requests for equipment, materials or an understanding of their situation must have seemed like dead letters. Did the pay or the employment conditions compensate?

Establishing how well jobs were remunerated is always difficult historically because it depends on relativities with other jobs, costs, inflation, attitudes to money and saving and so on. Although later keepers were more forthcoming, few early keepers wrote about the pay, so whether those that did voiced a common complaint is impossible to ascertain. Richard Tregurtha, for instance, was unusual both in responding to the 1880 cut to public servants' salaries (see letter p. 157) and in complaining about the lack of opportunities to increase his salary of £99 a year: As I have just received an intention that my salary has been reduced by ten per cent, I beg most respectfully to request you to reconsider my case. I have always felt that the present "Scale of Salaries" has placed your assistant keepers at a great disadvantage, as compared with those who have been several years in the Service. According to that Scale, I find, that I have to serve <u>at least Seventeen years</u>, before I can receive £160 per annum, whereas on the other hand, those who are not paid according to that Scale have drawn much larger Salaries than the sum mentioned many years past. This, Sir, has a very degrading effect, as it makes two distinct classes of men, and to make it worse, the Second class cannot possibly qualify themselves for the first-class, (that is as regards salary).

Now, Sir, I would respectfully ask, are those men better educated, better workers, or better watchers, than the young assistants? I am convinced they are not. When I first made application for an appointment, I discovered that I could not be a lightkeeper without (among other things) having an intimate knowledge of arithmetic. Now I find, Sir, that the first-class men (at any rate those under whom I have served) have little or no knowledge of that branch of education, and could not therefore comply with the "conditions" now in force.

[In] April 1878 ... I had a really good chance of getting an appointment as lightkeeper from the Oamaru Harbour Board, with a salary of £140 a year, holding as I do first-class certificates from the chairman and the Secretary of that body.[1]

In 1912 P. I. Henaghan at Nugget Point pulled no punches with his view of the salaries. I have the honour to state that in my opinion the Maximum Salary for Lighthouse Keepers has been fixed too low. The cost of living is much higher now than formerly when the limit of pay was £200 a year. It should also be taken into consideration that Lightkeepers duties are for every day of the year, which includes Sundays and public holidays, besides Keeping a responsible watch every night. They have also to act as Signal men and attend to fog Signals at Some of the stations for no extra pay.

I therefore trust the Board will carefully reconsider the claim set out above and allow for a more liberal remuneration.[2]

From 1913 keepers' salaries were adjusted in line with other public service sector salaries but keepers continued to feel they were underpaid for the hours of work, wrote G. Ager on Dog Island in 1938 to Peter Fraser, the Minister of Marine, and backed it up with more facts than had Henaghan: [I]n the first place, lightstations are either two, or three handed. The duties are identical which of course means that on a two Keeper station, two Keepers have between them to do exactly the same amount of work as that done by three Keepers on a three Keeper station. During the winter months the light is going practically 16 hours of the 24, <u>seven days a week</u>. Added to this, keepers are obliged to work on the general upkeep of the premises two hours daily for five days each week ... If you care to go into the matter, you will find that there is somewhere in the vicinity of five hundred hours per year for which we get no remuneration whatsoever. It is the custom during the long winter nights to work the watches four hours on, and four hours off. On two handed stations, Keepers have nothing but broken sleep throughout the greater part of the year. The majority of us after a year or two, are unable to enjoy good restful sleep during daylight hours, and the broken rest at night almost invariably interferes with our health, makes us very irritable, and in other ways affects our well being.[3]

The recruitment problems in the 1950s saw not only additional increases and salary restructuring but the range of work that attracted allowances (previously largely limited to the post office work, weather reporting and, on Stephens Island, the lizard allowances) considerably increased. By then individual appeals to head office were channelled through the PSA, the public service union. However, George Kroening, who started in 1945 on £278 a year, considered the pay contributed to keeper dissatisfaction: Now that was for 365 days work on end without holidays, without weekends, no penal rates, no overtime, or anything like that. If you did weather reporting you did get an allowance but it didn't amount to very much. Also there was what they called a station allowance, depending on the isolation of a station – about £28 a year, good money in those days; the weather reporting was about £14 or £16 a year and a lot of the places you did weather reporting every three hours, day and night, midnight, three o'clock in the morning, rain hail or shine, blowing a gale, when most of the weather equipment was up round the lighthouses! We paid £50 rent a year [the equivalent of a state house rent then]. Coal was supplied but not in abundance. We had to consciously ration the coal and gather driftwood, anything that could be burnt we'd burn it because they were all coal ranges in those days, even on the electric stations they were still coal ranges. The salary increase just after we left went up to £520 a year. Looking back we were underpaid at that time, compared to other people, definitely.

Les Broom started in 1949: The first month pay was about £24 a month – we thought it was good money. We saved, we always went on holidays. The kids always wanted to go home. We were quite happy. It seems funny now, we used to love going to Auckland. I wouldn't go to Auckland now if you paid me. First thing in Auckland was you got there, next day was Farmers. The top of Farmers and the canteen. George Courts. Watching all these women walking up and down Queen Street in fashion dresses.

Barry Langman joined six years after the Brooms. (His records showing he paid no rent were atypical): My salary payment says I was on a salary of £609 5s 0d which gave me £21 8s 10d a fortnight, less £2 18s 5d. for the social security and super[annuation], which brought me back to £18 10s 5d. No rent was charged for the house and no cost was involved in the heavy furniture, like the beds and dressers and wardrobes, that was all supplied. I don't recall seeing any allowance taken off for the house on Portland Island either. We were able to accumulate small savings to buy such things as sewing machines, a radio, a washing machine, a knitting machine. These were pricey items within a household, but we were able to buy them and pay them off. We didn't accumulate any great savings. Probably the holidays we had between stations we spent any surplus. When I left the service I had a bit in the bank account, but I couldn't have gone out and bought a car.

Alan Wright, who joined in 1958 as a single man, had a different approach to money: I don't think it worried me because I'd been in the Navy. And when I first joined the

Navy in 1945 we used to get ten shillings a fortnight. But you were clothed and fed. Till I joined the Lighthouse Service I didn't even have a cheque book. I went in to see Skiffington [the departmental officer in charge of relieving keepers] when I came from Portland Island and he said, 'We've got to sort your salaries out. As you're a relieving keeper, it's got to go into a bank account.' I said, 'I haven't even got one.' So I had to go round to the bank and organise a bank account and a cheque book. I'd never bothered before because in the Navy you went up once a fortnight, quoted your number, and got your pay in your hands. And you spent it.

In 1962 the Martins worked out the finances before committing themselves. Alan: Well, by joining the Light Service I actually dropped in salary because I was on a fairly good wage at that time. But we worked it out that by only paying peppercorn rent — only about, I don't know, a pound a fortnight — with that, not having to pay for power, no rates, telephone bills, growing our own food, having cattle beasts, the coal was a certain tonnage a year — I can't recall, three tons per house, you wouldn't pay for more, it was worked out so you knew how much you could burn — it was no problem. We worked out that we could save for our retirement.

From early on, many keepers found ways of supplementing their income. Some sold surplus farm produce — an activity that posed a considerable dilemma for head office. To ensure that not too much time went into farming and enough into lighthouse work it set limits on how much keepers could sell. The keepers themselves had other headaches. Barry Langman on Stephens Island: We always had a surplus of butter which we used to sent back up to Picton to relations or the local grocer. Having 50 sheep each we had a surplus of meat, we didn't have a requirement to keep the old sheep. We kept the skins when the sheep were slaughtered and sold them to the local farmers. The wool we also sold off to the local wool place in Picton. Generally we could get about four or five bales of wool. It was a supplement to our wages. When the Korean war was on and wool was reportedly selling at one pound per pound weight, keepers apparently earned more from their wool than from their salaries. Some of the stations we regarded as 'perk' stations because they brought in extra revenue — it was frowned on by the department but was a fact of life. Castlepoint used to provide milk to the local campers during the summer; Cape Egmont, because the tanker pick-up actually came to the door, sent the milk into the local factory.

Because we had seven cows producing seven calves on Stephens Island, we couldn't eat all the meat. I thought it was worthwhile getting a 18-month old heifer, worth about £180 at the time, off the island to the freezing works. As my father worked for the freezing works, I arranged with him to come down with the *Enterprise* to offload the beast. Brian Pickering said if we could tie it up and swing it down with the crane on to the deck, he'd leave it roped for the six-hour trip back and take it up to the freezing yard's wharf and Dad could take it from there. The day came, we went to catch the beast, but couldn't get anywhere near it. We devised a trick of walking the cows through an area where we could lasso the beast we wanted. Unfortunately the silly thing jumped over the edge of the track and took the full length of the rope and strangled itself!

The Brooms on Centre Island: [We] used to supply all Bluff with curly kale — it's like silverbeet with a curly leaf. It was a new garden we built. We built a whole new fence right the way down, cane, hit and miss, six feet, seven feet high. If you build an ordinary fence the wind just goes over the top and sucks down inside. If you build one with all the holes in, the wind disperses.

Income-generating measures were not limited to farm and garden produce. Shooting rabbits and possums, gathering agar off the rocks or the activities Alan Wright remembers do not feature in official correspondence. At Farewell Spit you had the old Army truck tour buses coming out and we'd be out in the surf surf-casting for snapper and selling them to the tourists.

We all had hobbies in the Lighthouse Service. We had one chap, he used to do this crochet work. This was a common practice among naval men at sea. They'd make these crochet frames up for something to do. Some did wood-work, the bulk of them were all keen on fishing, one chap did leatherwork. They'd sell it on shore when they went on leave.

Another trick we had. You talk about enterprising. The publican at Hohora, he had this big sign up on the door. It says, Last Pub in New Zealand Heading North. Somebody'd come in and buy a dozen beer to take with them for a picnic, going camping, and he'd always say, 'Oh, don't forget the lighthouse keepers!' So these tourists would come up and we'd chat to them and, 'Oh, here's half a dozen beer for you.' We'd stack that in the shed. Then when the tourist season started at Christmas tourists would come up, 'You wouldn't have a dozen beer you could sell, would you?' 'Oh, um, might be able to manage it. Stores came in the other day.' And you'd go in the shed and there'd be thirty-four dozen beer in there, and you'd flog it for a bit extra. These were the little things you got up to.

If you were a nineteenth-century keeper, biology had a profitable side. Charles Hepburn Robson (the father, not the diarist son) has left a number of engaging letters on his collecting of specimens for the noted men of science of the day (an activity that would impact badly on the very species in which the scientists were interested).

Robson had earlier corresponded with Bishop Williams on relations with local Maori; we first make our acquaintance with him when, in his late forties and something of a naturalist manqué, he was principal keeper at Moeraki. His correspondents read like a roll call of the great contributors to science and exploration in New Zealand. Johann Franz Julius von Haast, Fellow of the Royal Society, was a geologist, explorer, collector and museum founder; Dr James Hector, also a geologist and explorer, played a critical role in the colony's geological survey and establishing and administrating the Colonial Museum in Wellington; ornithologist Buller hardly needs introduction; Dr. Albrecht Günter, who had proposed Buller for a RFS, was director of zoology at the British Museum of Natural History; Captain Hutton, Otago's provincial geologist and a university teacher, made outstanding contributions to the advancement of biology and zoology in New Zealand; Walter Mantell, responsible for extinguishing native title to huge areas of land, was associated with Richard Owen, superintendent of the British Museum. Robson wrote as a knowledgeable equal to his important correspondents on whom he did not hesitate to call for assistance in lesser, or greater, matters. September 1878 to Haast: As I know no business[?] people in Christchurch I take the liberty of asking for your kind attention to a matter personal to myself and shall feel obliged if you will drop ... a line in reply. I find that we can get a quantity of crawfish quite close to my house and I wish to know if any respectable Fishmonger in your city would take a quantity weekly and at what price per dozen. I could forward them alive by rail in boxes purchased ... paying freight. Trusting that you pardon the liberty I take.[4]

He was in a good position to ask for favours. In what 'the colonial relationship that then existed in science'[5] the New Zealand naturalists amassed specimens, often forwarded to them by others, that they then sent on to London. Robson, in isolated and out-of-the-way places, was valuable, knowledgeable and painstaking. In October 1878 he wrote to Haast about bird skins: They are all good specimens in fine plumage, & were some of which I intended to have set up for myself but I have no room for the cases and cant stand the expense so I shall be glad to sell them for £16 or thereabouts if you do not want them for the Museum you may know of some one who would like such a collection they are cheap enough.[6]

A few days later: As I am in want of all the money I can get just now, I will take £8 for the skins and will forward them as soon as I receive your instructions to do so ... he [the gentleman purchaser] may depend on all skins from me being well cured I use a rather expensive mixture for that purpose (which no insect will go near) as well as carbolic powder and Alum, which last mixture is the only thing used in the Colonial Museum.[7]

In May 1880 he wrote to 'My dear Dr. Buller', an indication of the familiarity between the two men. The Prion Turtur, the fairy prion or Turtur pachytila, still exists. But the other, almost fabulous birds? Colin Miskelly[8] mentions the Hapagornis — an eagle, said to live in the top of the mountains and known only from fossil bones (that give it an estimated weight of up to 13 kg). Might stories of it, handed down over generations and on to the Europeans, account for the large white savage bird? He has also suggested that birds said to have a startling call that rose to a roar and increased until the air vibrated and birds with disproportionately large wing spreads and seven joints in the wing, were the hakawai (hokioi was another of the various spellings) or Steward Island snipe. (The distribution of the snipe, however, did not extend to the Auckland Islands.)

But to return to Robson: I am sorry not to have been able to procure more specimens for you from the Auckland islands but it was not possible to manage it An expedition of one or two persons next season to go in one of the sailing schooners and remain till her return collecting specimens of all sorts would well repay the expense, my son would be willing to go, amongst other things he heard of a large white bird with a straight beak like a very large tern larger than our largest gull it is very savage living in the highest peaks of Adams island living chiefly on the young of the white albatross it is so fierce that the sealers are afraid to lie out of doors & sleep in the sun for fear of losing their eyes it will also attack their hands when moving about if there is any blood on them. There is also a very large bird larger than the big Albatross which is only seen at nights giving a peculiar scream it is said to have 9 joints in the wing. A Petrel also inhabits Adams island of a buff colour with a yellow breast it is not quite so large as the mutton bird and makes holes in the ground like Prion Turtur & other Petrels, there are also a number of very large bones on the Campbell islands and various kinds of metal All the above information was given to my son by W Murray owner of the Sealing schooner Friendship seems to be person of some education he had never seen the Rail and said that the snipe which my son got is very rare on the islands. It has been blowing very hard all day and I have been away in the Stella all day trying to land stores at Pencarrow head but without success it was blowing too hard it is now ½ past six & have no time for a word more, hoping to hear from you soon.[9]

By then matters other than specimen-related were consuming a lot of Robson's energies, and he did not hesitate to call on his powerful friends. The same month as he was writing about the Auckland Island birds he was telling Buller of perceived skulduggery to drive him out of the service, fuming at the promotion of younger men over him and asking Buller to intercede for him with the powers that be before, again, returning to the subject in which both men delighted — new discoveries of birds.

Some ten days after that initial cry for help, Robson reported to Haast from Wellington: You will no doubt be rather astonished to hear from me from this wet and windy city but not more so than I am a finding myself here greatly against my will. I thought when last I had the pleasure of seeing you that fortune had for once smiled and that I was safe at Godley head for years but to my great astonishment on the 11th Inst. Mr Gregory received a telegram to say that he was not to be moved but that I was to proceed to Wellington per Stella and go thence as Asst Keeper to Cape Maria Van Dieman when I got here I tried to induce Capt Johnson [then Marine Department secretary] to alter this and send me to Pencarrow head as Principal Keeper this he refused and as I knew that going to Cape Maria 70 Miles from a town, on an Island which I was not permitted to leave even for a few hours & as assistant to a man who had been unduly favoured was as nearly penal servitude as they could make it, I wrote to Doctor Buller asking him to telegraph Major Atkinson to see me, he did see me & there has been I believe a grand row[?] and I believe I shall get Pencarrow head indeed I have just been told so but not in an official way or in what capacity. I have written to the man (Mr Manson) at Moeraki, who has your tank & the fishes desiring him to forward same to you but I find that the last jar of spirit did not go into the tank so I will collect for you and forward it by Steamer to Lyttelton. I will write again as soon as we are settled somewhere With many thanks for all your kindness

PS please address C/- Marine Department Wellington.[10]

Robson did not get Pencarrow. Instead he was transferred to Portland Island, then to Cape Egmont where he was demoted. After three more postings he resigned from Cape Maria van Diemen on the grounds of ill-health and died in 1893.

Although there is little correspondence about promotions, Robson's sensitivities, doubtless exacerbated by his contretemps with head office, were not unique. We have already seen how the issue exercised Chris Staley's mates on The Brothers (see p. 204); in 1913 the two assistant keepers on Cuvier Island, H. Harvey and G. McPherson, were equally outraged. Their letter is typical of the issues that would be raised through the decades. We, the undersigned Assistant Keepers at this Station, desire to enter our protest against what we hear rumoured & what we consider a grave injustice to us & to all assistant keepers in the service. It is said that C Reisap[?] signalman at Manukau is shortly to take the place of Mr W. C Champion at Portland Island as Principal Keeper, we have reason to believe that this is correct & if so kindly permit us to point out how decidedly unfair it is. There are at present Assistant Keepers with as much as 10 to 12 years service to their credit & to think that a man who knows nothing about the work of keeping a light & station & who has not served a day in the service is to be put on the list ahead of them as Principal Keeper and draw a considerable higher salary is anything but pleasing & sufficient to cause a great deal of dissatisfaction, should such a thing come to pass, it may mean years of waiting & delay to some, when promotion should be near & directly or indirectly it effects every Assistant, whether a new hand or otherwise. Trusting that the matter will be looked into in a proper light & that all other assistants will inter a protest.[11]

Keepers were equally vociferous about a raft of other HR matters. P. I. Henaghan was on Stephens Island in 1897 when the department proposed there be only two keepers there over the winter months. I beg to state that in my opinion the Small Saving effected by this arrangement do not in any way compensate for the risk incurred to the Safety of navigation. I presume the Department has based its decision on Chap. X clause 11th of the Instructions to Lightkeepers, where it is stated, but when there are three Keepers on a station, So long as two are fit for duty, no temporary assistant shall be allowed.

Now Sir, it is quite obvious that the above lines quoted were never intended to apply to Stephens Island or indeed to any Island at all, but to mainland stations where three Keepers are located. If by any possible means they can be made to apply to Island stations, it can be only to those having Telegraphic communication with the mainland …

If by any mishap or illness one of us became incapacitated during our recent experience of six months at this station, I maintain the other man could not possibly keep the Light going with perfect safety to navigation. It will be observed he would have at least 15 hours constant watch to Keep, and during all this time he could not indulge in even five minutes sleep. If the Department places any reliance on the assistance that could be rendered by the Women in an emergency Such as I am discussing, I am afraid they would be greatly disappointed for the women know nothing about it at all.

On the other hand if it was thought safe enough to entrust a Revolving Light of the first order, and one of the latest type at that, to two men on an Island for a period of Six months in the middle of winter, and that it was found that the duties of the Lighthouse were performed well & Satisfactorily, it would be only reasonable to assume these duties could be carried out indefinitely by the Same number of persons, and thus a great Saving effected. I hardly think however that the Department would entertain the idea of making Such a radical change in this direction.[12]

For a long time The Brothers was manned by three keepers on the station and one on shore, with the shore-time rotated amongst them. On shore they were at the department's beck and call. William Tutt, 1912: I have the honour to respectfully ask you for more consideration for the keeper on this station, when we arrive in Wellington Mr Pottinger after being on this Station over 4 months arrived at Noon on a Saturday was met by Mr Mitchell who tould him he had to tallie coal at once he worked til after 5 p.m then carried his box to the Marine store then got his tea, after that had to look for lodgings the result being he had to go to the Marine Store for his box and carrie it to the top of Murphy Street it was then nearly 9 p.m being Saturday night he could not get any conveyance to carrie his box no matter what time we get to Wellington we have to be at the Store at 8 a.m next morning therefore we ask for a reasonable time when landing so as to alow time to get lodgings, and we also ask that we leave the Marine Store not later than noon the day before coming here so as to enable us to inspect the vegetables get our boxes on board or do a little privat business we may hav to do.[13]

A least one lightkeeper's memoir suggests that leave was more of an issue than the number of letters on it suggest. R. S. Wilson, at Mokohinau in 1922, spelt out some of the reasons why it was impossible to give keepers public service holiday and annual leave provisions. 1st that the nature of our Duties & the regulations in the book of instructions strictly bind us to perform our work in the maintainance of the light, and other necessary Duties connected thereto, such as signalling, & telephoning etc. When you consider the time spend on this work, and the night watches that are done, very little is left which constitutes a holiday ...

A keeper situated at some of the remote stations throughout the Service, has very little of his annual leave left, when ever he gets into civilisation, for a week or more, is often spent on travel, to get there.

For my own case Sir, I was six days coming, to and fro, from Moko Hinou Lighthouse, to Auckland, this is six Days out of annual leave ...

It must also be recognised Sir, that whilst in town, a Keeper's time, is very often, for the greater part taken up in calls upon a Dentist of, which services he is deprived of, these privaliges, of course, other Branches of the Service may obtain at anytime. Whereas a Lightkeeper has to cram them all into his annual leave. Therefore I am sure that Keepers one and all, would appreciate your kindness if you could arrange to have these special Holidays added to annual leave.[14]

Many keepers also worked their passage to and from their stations. D. D. McFarlane, assistant keeper in 1928, had left Farewell Spit for Wellington: I was ... landing coal, oil, stores and painting at French Pass, painting and cleaning panes at the Ninepins Light, painting, cleaning lenses and helping with cylinders at Karori Rk. and I was away in the boat to land Captain Bollons at the Brothers for inspection ... You say in your letter that ... Keepers at this station are allowed one day coming and going Well Sir that is news to me ... [15]

Captain Bollons was not the only one to make use of an extra hand: Alan Wright was due off The Brothers: We'd heard on the radio that all the Cook Strait ferries had stopped running, the weather was that bad. I said to Chris, 'I won't be going off today in this weather.' Chris says, 'I bet you you are.' Then Brian [Pickering on the *Endeavour*] called up from Stephens, 'Right, I'll be at the south landing at such and such a time. Get ready to embark.' So I got my gear all ready and went down to the south landing. It was reasonably calm once you got round the corner, I hopped on board — the boat would come in, you'd stand on the block and jump across, there was no crane or anything there — it was one of these places where you had to rely on the tide a lot. And I said to Brian, 'What time are we getting to Picton? I haven't made my bookings for the plane yet.' He says, 'We're not going to Picton.' 'Where are we going?' He says, 'Wellington.' I said, 'But the ferries have stopped running!' He says, 'We're going to Wellington.' Karori Rock light was out and the reason they picked me up was because they wanted an extra hand. So we got to Karori Rock, managed to land. When it was time to come off the tide was all rip and he came across with his bows — he'd run across with his bow and you jumped as he went past. Well, the first time I missed. He put his head out the window, 'If you don't jump the next time you'll be staying the night. I'll pick you up in the morning.' I jumped!

As noted earlier, wives were expected to board and feed visiting workmen and departmental officials. The department did pay allowances — to the husbands — to compensate, and while some reckoned they did quite well out of them, others considered the reimbursement inadequate. Either way, it meant a lot of extra work for the women. Jo Broom: We had a new secretary of Marine and he went round the lights with his wife while we were at Cape Reinga. They stayed with us for three days. When I had workmen I used to give them all tea in bed every morning and then I used to give them a cooked breakfast and if they were up round the powerhouse or that doing work I'd give them morning tea, and then I'd give them lunch and if they were round I'd give them afternoon tea. Then they used to have a cooked meal at night. Then there was supper. I spent a lot of time cooking!

But some time before the Brooms joined the Service, keepers were beginning to refuse to assist. V. G. Whiteman, Stephens Island, 1939: In reply to your memorandum of the 13TH instant re stores supplied by the "Matai" . . .

Had I received sufficient notice that the painters were arriving, there would have been no necessity to requisition stores from the "Matai" at all. Mrs Whiteman was good enough to supply meals to men working here, when their meals did not come ashore from the "Matai", & no claim was made for this. Also, meals & board have been supplied by us out of consideration for the men, & at considerable inconvenience to ourselves, especially Mrs Whiteman, who had all the extra work to do, & supplying meals at 1/- each, with morning & afternoon tea thrown in , we were doing it at a financial loss to ourselves, as 1/- a meal does not cover the actual expense. In most cases I have been put to the trouble of claiming the amounts from the Department, & now I have all this correspondence over a few stores supplied by the "Matai". Under the circumstances Mrs Whiteman & I cannot be blamed, if we do not feel disposed to supply meals or board on any future occasion. Up to the present we have supplied all meals & board required, as the Asst Keepers & their wives declined to do so.[16]

In 1948 Tom Smith and his Portland Island assistants, J. A. Pullen and S. J. Luton, were equally polite and equally adamant. [We do] not wish to provide board for Temporary Keepers or visiting workmen making a prolonged stay on the station. Their wives were already fully occupied with their own domestic routines, the children and their lessons. Why not equip the bach on the station where the workmen could do for themselves?[17]

The suggestion was not adopted. Two years later Smith's tone was more militant. His wife, without the modern conveniences available to her city counterparts and supervising correspondence, was already stretched; there was no comparison between board on a station and board in town. [It is] not the keepers who are inconvenienced by supplying board, but their wives, whom, after all, are not employed by the Department ... I will not ... agree to board workmen and others remaining for indefinite periods on the station. Under the conditions if the Public Service Commission and the Department insist on making this a condition of our employment, I will have no alternative but to leave the service.[18]

Smith resigned from French Pass a few years later over the costs of secondary schooling.

CHAPTER 13

Relations with head office

'Employing men but treating them like schoolboys' is a paraphrase of Tom Smith's in a letter suggesting that principal keepers should no longer have to read the Instructions to Lightkeepers to the other keepers every week. After World War II attitudes to rules and regulations were changing, and the keepers, often returning from the front, were part of that change. But if challenging head office edicts was particularly apparent then, it was by no means limited to that period.

In the early days of the Lighthouse Service and with their jobs potentially on the line, some keepers were almost effusively apologetic over any perceived transgression. Others, like Andreas Sandager and Anders Hansen, were not.

In 1902 Sandager, still at Puysegur Point and smarting over being accused of being drunk while principal keeper on Centre Island, relieved some of his feelings about his demotion and transfer to Puysegur Point by putting a fluent pen to paper — although a large cross marking the letter may have meant it was not sent: As we have a precedent in this country for letting a convicted murderer off after a couple of years imprisonment it might fairly be expected that a seven or eight year sentence (coupled with what is practically a fine of several hundred pounds) might be deemed sufficient in the case of even a Lightkeeper charged with a somewhat less offence — a charge moreover not justified one whit beyond what was admitted in my statement sent in at the time.[1]

Anders Hansen was prepared to admit his system of watches (easier for the men on a two-man station) was not the officially sanctioned system, but obviously had no intention of changing it. October 1913, Cape Egmont: With reference to your Circular No. 196/258. I have to report that I have regularly sanctioned two (2) night watches to be kept in the Lighthouses during the summer months, and have done so without any authority from the Secretary of the Marine Department.

In sanctioning the keeping of only two (2) Nightwatches during the summer months I have carried on a practice which I believe has been common ever since I entered the Lighthouse service, and I think, I am right in stating, ever since the beginning of the Lighthouse service in New Zealand.

I frankly admit that I have acted contrary to the Instructions to Lightkeepers in regard to the keeping of Night watches in the Lighthouse during the summer months.[2]

In August 1915, still at Cape Egmont, he was interested in what was practical, not what head office may lay down. Here, too, we glimpse again (and was this part of a wider, necessary mindset?) the almost stoic acceptance of, and working within, the Heath Robinson lighthouse world in which rusty tins leaked vital fuel and when critical spare parts for equally critical equipment did not arrive for months: I have to state in reply to your memorandum No 8/6/22, [about using shipments of kerosene in their proper rotations], that I always empty the worst tins first, irrespective of their arrival at the station; for it sometimes happens that we get shipments in which all the tins are new and not a drop of leakage, and the following that we may get all bad tins, in such a case as this it is, I think, advisable to use the last shipment first. We make it a rule to put all bad and rusty tins to one side, so that we may use them as soon as possible; and we have little or no leakage after receiving the oil. I may also state that we weigh all the tins, using 35 lbs as a standard or full tin; every pound less than that is counted as one pint lost, in that way we quickly and correctly get at the amount of leakage. In the case of this station a good deal of leakage seems to take place in the transit from New Plymouth by the waggons, in which the cases get a good bumping about.

Trusting that my way of dealing with the oil will meet with approval.[3]

In March 1917 J. Duthie at Pencarrow, on whose professionalism the department had cast aspersions, did not hesitate to lay his version of events: I have the honour to acknowledge receipt of Memo No 80/301 re fog signal being watched on the morning of the "Maroroa" mishap & My statement by telephone was :—"That we commenced working the fog signal a few minutes before 9 a.m. but owing to the weakness of the battery the machine did not get going properly until 9.10 a.m." I see no reason to alter my statement. As the gentleman residing on the hill at Lyal Bay says the fog was <u>nearly</u> up to the lighthouse <u>by about</u> 7.30, it took 1½ hours to fill in the <u>nearly</u> & make it necessary for the fog signal to be started so that his guesswork is useless. I was in front of my house at 8.40 a.m. as was also the temporary keeper, watching the broken fog coming in off the sea, & we were discussing how soon we would have to go down the hill. Very often the hills on both sides of the harbour are fog hidden, but down on the water it keeps quite clear & in foggy weather the keepers are busy climbing up & down the hill all night on watch & get soaking wet Mr Mclaren not having seen the fog signal working, we both went down together, therefore he can bear witness that the time given was correct.[4]

In 1941 Kenneth Webby's explanation for why the light at Cape Brett stopped while he was on watch carried none of the contrition of some earlier letters on such matters: On the morning of the 3rd Aug. I wound up the machine at 0525 and then made out and sent the weather report at 0545. From then till 0605 I was occupied with various lightroom duties & before sitting down I omitted to wind up the machine. I went to sleep almost immediately. At 0610 the machine stopped & the light became stationary. The Principal Keeper woke me when winding up the machine at 0630. The light was stationary for 20 minutes & the clock on the machine was 20 minutes slow by the light-room clock after the machine had been put in motion. I was recovering from an attack of influenza at the time & my only comment is, that a keeper does not go to sleep purposely. I shall be obliged if you will advise me of your decision as soon as possible.[5]

Webby resigned two months later.

The change in keepers' relationships with head office was partly because men coming back from World War II were less prepared to put up with the conditions in the Service, and there was no shortage of other employment. The department considered that when the Matai, the last of the lighthouse steamers, was withdrawn in 1949, they lost touch with their keepers, and men like George Kroening thought the way the department operated had changed. There was a big changeover. Lots of things had an effect on the Service in those days. Radar was just coming in, echo sounders, all modern technology, and lighthouses became less important to what they had been previously. Also the fact that it was getting too expensive to run the steamer round all the time servicing the lights. They let out contracts to launch owners for the island stations and the more remote mainland stations, and road transport to the other stations, which fragmented it. Instead of being under one big umbrella there were little bits here, little bits there, and so on. Also the administration changed hands in Wellington. Bill Smith retired and a chap Turner came and he was from the Prison Department. Well, maybe he had the clerical experience but he didn't have the background experience of lighthouses and he was entirely different kettle of fish to what Bill Smith was. I don't know if the prison administration reflected on his character, but he was very adamant in his ideas and very strict, do this, do that style of thing. We lost that fatherly touch that we had with Bill Smith, caring about the people. Also when we went to Mokohinau Island Captain Davies was the Marine Superintendent in Auckland, an old sea captain and he had hands-on experience of lighthouses and there again he had a personal interest in all the keepers round the Hauraki Gulf and to the north of Auckland and down as far as East Cape. He administered that area

Henry Philips (right) talking to keepers at the lighthouse keepers' school. Peter Taylor remembers that the school, which ran for a few years from 1964, brought keepers together and helped create a sense of community that many felt had been lost when the Matai, the last of the lighthouse ships, was withdrawn from the Service at the end of the Second World War. Tom Clark, who later wrote a book on his experiences in the Service, is on the far left; the Eastbourne wharf is in the background.

MARITA AND PETER TAYLOR

and he did take a fatherly interest in it. When he retired they did a special trip out to Mokohinau on the tender and he came out and he shook hands with everyone before he retired. That's the sort of thing you didn't see in government departments. When those two gentlemen retired, we were put under Wellington. And I think that was also reflected in the attitudes of keepers from there on. Looking back I can see that myself. If you were in the service say before 1950 or 1955, it was a different aspect to what it was after 1955.

Increasingly keepers voiced their frustration, wanting a working environment less bound by red tape, and some recognition for what they did. In 1947 Frank Shepherd, attempting to get Cape Brett station into working order after the war, penned an indignant letter: I have to advise you that all I was asking for was the Dept. to put the station in good order for us, to give us something solid to work on ... it is all very well for these inspectors to pay a flying visit to the station & tell one that this wants painting & that wants chipping we are grown men & can see for ourselves the necessity of the work ... our req. [requisitions] are held up at Opua for nearly four months, as far as outside painting, it has been absolutely impossible since I have taken over here, with the rain & storms we have had as our records show. Keeper Jennings & Myself are both tradesmen having served our time in the Woodworking trades ... Gilliland has spent most of his life at sea, so we should know something about painting etc. but there is not much encouragement in it when these casual inspections take place to be told like a lot of kids what to do, I know myself the hours Keeper Ager & I spent at Nuggets often 12 hours a day relining the houses with Pinex pulling down & rebuilding tumble down unsightly outhouses, & coal bunkers made out of 400 gal tanks & rebuilding permanent brick & concrete & wooden ones I don't regret it & would do it again as long as I am given a free hand & the material, with no outside interference.[6]

In 1949 H. B. Jamieson arrived at Farewell Spit station and was prepared to take the department on over its penny-pinching: Replying to your memo 21/2/25, and your suggestion of mowing the poison ivy [1.8 to 2.4 metre high] & blackberry with a scythe. It is quite evident that you have no idea of the conditions here … As to your enquiry for what purpose a sack of grass seed is required, I did not think it necessary to explain that, as anyone knows, that when you burn off an extensive area of land you must sow it with grass unless you want the land to be overrun with noxious weeds … if you can provide a really efficient flame-thrower I have hopes of clearing up the whole place, but if the flame thrower is not a really good one, it will be useless sending it here.[7]

Three months later he became even terser in his efforts to make head office understand why he needed the seed, and why he couldn't identify precisely how much land he would need it for: I could not give you the precise area of land we wished to sow, else I would have done it in the first place. I have tried to make it clear, and can only conclude my letters have been disregarded.

In June 1950 C. T. Bowles at East Cape wrote interminably about the access road and the difficulties of getting in stores, increasingly inclined to set out his letters as if he were writing to simpletons: Is there any point in letting you have a report regarding the delivery of stores? Suggest you <u>read</u> my memorandum dated 28th March 1950; 118/60/11 14th April 1950; 118/60/11 of 15th May 1950.

Here again, for your information, or to file without reading as the case may be, are answers to your queries

1   There is no method of receiving stores from Te Araroa unless by the good nature of the neighbouring farmers.
2   The farmers have been prevailed upon too much in the past & are now reluctant
3   During the summer months Wards Transport may make two or three trips out to the Cape (Summer months September or October to March)
4   The mail is delivered once a week by horse-back, by special contract with the contractor and the Post and Telegraph Department
5   The day of delivery is Saturday
6   Light stores could be carried by the same method as the mail delivery – if you can find anybody to do the job

7. There is quite a possibility that the mail service will be cut out before long due to the decreasing population in this area, the Postmaster at Te Araroa informs me.

8 The additional cost would be phenomenal if the experiences of the Assistant Keeper are to be taken into account, one example 1 loaf of bread & 1 pound of butter, the freight charge 2/6 (two shillings and sixpence) or more recently, 3 lbs sausages, 2/-

9 There is obvious reluctance on the part of anyone to cart stores or to have anything to do with the Marine Department due as far as I can make out to former employees & the Department itself in their laxness & length of time between services rendered and payment received

10 Ward's Transport will not venture off the road if there is any sign of rain or if the rivers have more than 10 inches of water in them

11 There are three unbridged rivers between Te Araroa and the Lighthouse and a long stretch of beach to travel and tides to contend with.[8]

Three months later, Bowles resigned; the letterbooks end eight years later, the problem still unresolved.

In 1945 Norman H. White on Dog Island saw no reason to continue to put up with head office incompetence: It has been my experience in the past that co-operation between various departments has been conspicuous by its absence. On the 8/3/45, Mr Tanner [lighthouse inspector who the following year would become assistant secretary] visited the station and during a conversation he told me to expect a shift shortly and to get packed up ready … That is just six months ago and to the time of writing neither hint or reason has been given for the delay. As I did as Directed and packed all but the bare necessities the position is that we have been very much inconvenienced & the articles as packed for a promised quick shift do not improved by being packed up in this damp atmosphere. You've touched on the difficult days ahead, well I wish to remove one obstacle from the road of progress and do hereby submit my resignation to take effect as soon as possible.[9]

Les Broom was among the growing number of keepers who were willing to withdraw the goodwill that for so long had underlain the services on which the department relied. Below is an excerpt from Broom's longish justification authorising a special trip to bring a keeper's cow to Cape Reinga station in 1956: [T]hat is the only way of getting milking cows to the station besides driving them 74 miles. *That, he pointed out would mean no milk and a keeper absent for a week. He then went on to justify the cost:*

2 On the day which the cow was carried was a special trip but a full load was carted beside for the dept in the way of diesel fuel, and as the dept implies very unfairly that the keepers are working the special trips for their own

use the trip before which was a mail trip a full load was also carried in 2 tons of fuel 8 jars of distilled water 2 cases of paint and keepers stores well over the contracted 2½ ton. The trip the cow was carried also 2 ton of fuel was carried besides The following mail trip the load w as 2½ ton coal, Cape Maria batteries & stores

If required I can quote the loads right up to yesterday just to show that [without] this special trip, either coal or diesel would still be sitting on the wharf [at Hohora] unprotected, where any one can help themselves …
And finally as the dept does not seem to have any faith and place any relibility on my judgement when special trips are required, I will refrain from requesting any in the future and fuel etc can be lifted by the mail trips every 2 weeks and if any backlog piles up it will have to remain on the wharf untill it can be brought to the station.[10]

Perceptions of departmental stinginess carried over into other walks of life. During their time in the Service, Jean Kroening remembered, we didn't have the Country Library as regularly and we weren't allowed as many books, and when we were at Akaroa we didn't get the library service, they cut out the *Auckland Weekly,* they cut us down on coal. Talking of pettiness – at Mokohinau I got an ear infection and the *Ikatere,* the fishery protection vessel, came. I was ashore six weeks before the ear infection cleared. When I called the Marine Department in Auckland saying I was allowed to go back, I was given a bill ten shillings for the ambulance that was sent to take me to hospital. The doctor took me to hospital, and didn't use the ambulance. But I had to pay that ten shillings.

Bill Megennis saw head office administration as irrelevant, with 'no contact, no concept, totally out of their depth' – a view many shared. Chris Staley: The Administration staff wouldn't have a clue. Most of them had never been on a lighthouse. One guy, he'd been appointed as the administrator of lighthouses and I was quite blunt and said, 'Some of you guys want to go out there and have a look and see what it looks like.' And he was on the next boat going out with me. Stayed just for the day – a couple of hours. We did have another English administrator. He was a lower rank than this guy I've just mentioned. He came out and stayed overnight. That really intrigued me. The day he came out, there would be three blokes on there, one would be coming out, I'd be going on, and this English chap from the head office said to Brian Pickering, 'Oh, tell them I shall require lunch, too.' I looked at him and I said, 'You must be bloody joking, mate. Lunch? Who's going to cook it?' I said. 'Those guys will be flat out on the block loading and unloading this boat, who's going to get lunch ready?' I said, 'You might get a bottle of beer and that'll be about your luck.' That gives you an idea of how those people thought. We didn't have a resident cook!

Alan and Shirley Martin check the Nugget Point weather station for the last time yesterday.

Martins say goodbye to Nugget Point lighthouse

BALCLUTHA

The last manned lighthouse on the mainland officially lost its man yesterday.

Nugget Point lighthouse keeper Alan Martin and his wife, Shirley, have lived and worked in some of the remotest parts of New Zealand during Alan's 27-year career — from Cape Reinga to Dog Island.

When they are gone from the South Otago lighthouse, it will stand empty for the first time in 119 years.

The Martins fought the decision last year to de-man the lighthouse — their attempts included a pet-

ition signed by many supportive locals — but have now resigned themselves to life without a light.

They have bought a house in Balclutha, where they have made many friends, and hope to move in shortly.

Mr Martin said he had been "pretty choked up" to learn of his redundancy but the few months left at work had given him time to adjust to the change.

Wrapping blankets around

wrecked seafarers and making them cups of tea while radioing for help was only one of their duties as lighthouse keepers.

They also monitored the Nugget Point outdoor weather station, where information has been collected for the Meterological Service since 1930. Alan Martin was given a gift in recognition of his work there.

The station will now be monitored from Invercargill and the light tended from Wellington.

The demanning of Nugget Point marked the end of Alan Martin's 27-year career in the Lighthouse Service. 'We were done out of a job by a microchip,' he said. Lighthouse keepers' jobs were inevitable casualties in the march of technological progress, but the Martin's departure marked the first time in 119 years that Nugget Point was without a keeper. ALAN AND SHIRLEY MARTIN

The uneasy relations between keepers and head office would, from the late 1970s, over the final stages of the coastal lighthouses' demanning, have a insidious effect. Technology had made the process inevitable, but head office handled the inevitable redundancies badly and apparently lacked imaginative sympathy for the keepers' situation. The Martins, at Nugget Point in 1989, believed the job there would be disestablished when Alan retired. Shirley described what happened:

I suppose not having had any background in lighthouse keeping Brian Rees [in charge of implementing those end stages] wasn't sentimental about it, and that he saw it as a job he had to do. But I do feel we could have been told a little more softly than we were. We didn't know at the time we were going to be demanned, and if it had been left to Brian Rees he would have appeared out of the blue and told us we were going to be demanned, just like that. We were very grateful to the administrative office down in Invercargill because they phoned us up the day before. We were both terribly upset. I remember feeling sick to my stomach and bursting into tears wondering what on earth was going to happen to us. I was pleased that he had done that because we were able to react very stoically when Brian Rees appeared. 'I'm here to tell you the demanning plan', and that was it. It was like being hit, it really was, we felt as though someone had died, as if there had been a death in the family.

CHAPTER 14

What kept people there

Reading the letterbooks it is easy to wonder how the Service retained its keepers. In many instances it did not, and its periodic difficulties with recruitment and retention reached new heights in the 1950s when different expectations, perceptions of better prospects elsewhere and frustration with the department forced out many who might otherwise have preferred to stay. But others remained until health or other changing circumstances precipitated reluctant resignations, while men like Anders Hansen retired from the Service at the end of their working lives.

Indications of job satisfactions have already surfaced in previous sections, but I want now to look behind the accounts to discover what it was that allowed some men and women to look back on their time so vividly and warmly. The few written specific comments on why keep-ers remained in the Service tend towards broad general statements. T. R. Welsh, on Tiritiri Matangi in 1955, reckoned that [although I could] find a more congenial job with as good if not better conditions ... this sort of life with good conditions and homes is better than any city job ...[1] *More interestingly, in his vitriolic letter of resignation (pp. 206–207) D. Meister distinguished between* ... the solitude and quiet way of life [the Lighthouse Service] appeared to offer and the less quiet and solitary atmosphere of a city.[2]

Anders Hansen, after he retired, with his wife Elizabeth at their home in Northland, Wellington. HANSEN COLLECTION

The oral accounts, traversing topics that the official nature of the written records precluded, provide clues — though, as noted, these recollections, recalled well after the event, are coloured by time and memory. How far those accounts reflect earlier keepers' responses is impossible to tell. One keeper, for instance, reckoned the lights' electrification in the 1950s turned the job into a picnic — technical and medical advances and changes in social attitudes meant later generations of men were less tied by shift work and tough physical labour, the women less constrained by the demands of children and the drudgery of housework than their earlier counterparts. On the other hand, Robson's diary note on the founding of the Portland Island Rifle Club is indicative of the simple satisfactions and pleasures my respondents found and which allowed them to look back on their time fondly.

Perhaps temperament more than anything else dictated how much the life appealed and, all things being equal, how long you stayed. Chris Staley: One guy while I was on The Brothers wasn't there many days and he was definitely not suited to the job – you could see, he was more or less like a town guy, he didn't want to be stuck on a rock in the middle of the ocean. So one day there was some yachts sailing around The Brothers. He went down the block and called one, the boat came over and he hopped aboard and was gone. Deserted his post! Quite strange. What can you say? What can you do? He's gone!

Alan Wright: The ones that couldn't develop a hobby were the ones that didn't stay very long.

The stolid pragmatism that enabled the men to plod on with uncongenial work was useful. Alan Martin found the job fun: But there were times when it wasn't quite so enjoyable – unloading boats, surfboats, up to your neck in water – things like that. Dog Island I used to have two sets of army gear, trousers and jackets. Half way through I'd get out of the wet gear and put on some dry gear. Handling bags of coal that were all wet and soggy wasn't too pleasant, but that's in most jobs.

Jean Kroening reckoned, 'It was what you made of it.' So what sort of temperament was needed to find the satisfactions and opportunities the job offered?

Young fit men made their own versions of extreme sport. Chris: We used to swim [at The Brothers] most of the year round out there. Of course it can be quite dangerous. There was one time – afterwards I realised how dangerous it was. We used to bolt a small piece of timber on the edge like a diving board to get over the rocks and we had a wooden ladder with heavy weights on the bottom and a couple of ropes. We used to throw that down to climb back up over the rocks because they're very sharp and jagged. This particular day two of us went down there and the seas were really crashing in, big seas. I guess it was a bit of bravado on my part – Oh, I'm going in – and I dived in. But the seas were crashing so heavily that they would pick the ladder up and throw it up on to the rocks. Each time I swam towards it the swell would throw the ladder so I couldn't get out. I think it was Alan Wright who was on the ledge and would throw it down and then run for his life because another wave would be coming in. And of course, you can only stick that cold water for a few minutes, y'know. Eventually I managed to grab the ladder and climb out. That's why I'm here.

Bill Megennis enjoyed swimming for its own sake: I swam several times at The Brothers. I was very careful. I was fully aware of the tide movement, very fast, and I would swim underneath the block where the crane is on the north

Lena Hansen and her sister Ann on horseback at Cape Palliser c. 1912. For a number of women, being on the light station offered opportunities to do things they would not have done in other environments. Certainly, when this photo was taken most women rode side-saddle, and few went off with guns. JIM HANSEN AND DENNISE COOK

Skinny dipping off The Brothers, 1960s.
CHRIS STALEY

side at slack water. Gosh it was cold! It is cold water. But it was so refreshing. I still remember on very hot days in January and February when there was no wind, beautiful days, and I would go down underneath the block at slack water.

Fishing had its own intrinsic pleasures as well as being a way of varying the diet. At Portland Island George and Jean Kroening had fairly primitive equipment. George: We just had handlines. We used to launch the station dinghy and row out to the edge of the papa shelf. That's where you'd get the best fish, but they were really temperamental, and we couldn't go far away having just oars to power the boat, clinker-build wooden boat, heavy to handle, took three or four people to launch it, three or four people to get it.

Jean: We spent a lot of time fishing, did enjoy it. I learned to eat fish eventually because when it was too hot and we didn't have any meat. I got tired of tinned corned beef.

Alice Langman with a crayfish, Portland Island. BARRY LANGMAN

There was pleasure in the chase. Barry Langman: At Stephens I could go down and get a sugar bag of cod in 20 minutes which I could take back and then smoke for the three families. And on Portland Island there were millions of kinas.

Crayfish were there for however you chose to take them. George's method of catching them on Portland Island was one of a number of ways: It was very, very easy to catch a crayfish, provided the sea was smooth enough to get down on to the rocks at low water. We had to start off from the top of the island 300 feet up, go down the sheep tracks down the side of the island, strip off a blade of flax on the way down, on to the rocks, turn a stone over, get a paua off and thread it on to the flax

and walk out on to the rocks and dangle it down in a bit of a gap in the rocks and soon crayfish come out from underneath like a lot of spiders and we would gradually pull the bait up towards the surface, grab their feelers and go home!

Barry on Portland Island: [I] would go down with a spear and come back with a sugar bag of crayfish by going round and take them out of the rock pools when the tide went out. Though it was illegal, if you happened to strike a female, well, you had to take it back and eat it.

Exploring, too, had intrinsic satisfactions as well as the excitement of unexpected finds. Jean remembered walking all over Mokohinau. George always carried a gaff. We were walking around the rocks at Moko and I said to George, 'Oh, look at that pretty fish.' All I saw was the head and the colours like a goldfish. And George still doesn't know to this day why he didn't put his hand in, why he put the gaff in.

CLOCKWISE FROM LEFT *On a number of stations you had to be dedicated to want to fish. At Cape Saunders the heavy, clinker-built station boats were 'hauled straight out of the sea as you see her, & swung in on to the trolley when hoisted high enough'.*
HANSEN COLLECTION

Boat launching tackle at Cape Brett — one of the other stations where the crane had to be called into service to launch the station boat. ALAN AND SHIRLEY MARTIN

At Centre Island in the early 1950s, Prince helped drag the boat down the beach.
LES AND JO BROOM

The Hansens crayfishing from the cliffs below the lighthouse, Cape Saunders.
HANSEN COLLECTION

It was a sea snake. And after one of the storms, we went down to the landing and there were sea snakes washed up dead on the rocks, and George opened the mouth and put a stick in — and rows and rows of teeth! We mentioned it to one of the fishermen, and they said they were known to bite through the wire of their craypots.

The Martins: We had an old roof rack, tubular metal. We turned it upside down and put a deck on it, a couple of handles, bicycle wheel on each side and went camping down Ninety Mile Beach. We were taken down in the station wagon down to Te Kao. We walked into the beach from there and then gradually worked our way up to Te Paki station. I think it took about seven days, pulling the cart. We worked from one stream to another. We were looking for Maori artefacts and things like that. We didn't find much, but it was a marvellous trip, camping on the beach.

Bill Megennis: I wasn't into shooting at Puysegur but I spent a lot of time in the bush. After my first visit to Puysegur, I'd talked to a lot of fishermen who'd been there for a long time. So on the next trip out I went to the Hocken Library and got some of the old original maps and information on the miners who were there. On the miners' maps was where shafts went in and where they dropped down. I went into the bush and found them – just indications of the old mines. The races – one that I found was at a place called Sealers Creek, it's on a track that goes off from the landing to the lighthouse at Puysegur. You walk round the coast and you come across a ridge and after about three kilometres on the top of this ridge there's this water race. It's cut I'd say in places nearly two metres tall and it's wide enough for a person to stand in. And it's dead straight. It's obviously weathered by the rain and conditions, but some people had spent – I don't know how long it took them to do it!

I read a book on the region, got right into the historical significance of the place, loved it. Because there were two keepers on the station I could go away for a couple of days, three nights at a time. Bill Black – he worked for Alpine Helicopters, they had a contract to bring in supplies – brought in a canoe for me, funny little canoe but big enough to use. So I would say to the keeper on the station, 'I'll do all this work, I'll paint, do this, do that, but I want a few days off.' We'd compromise and off I'd go in my canoe. It was such a wild place, you could sense all these hard-working people that lived in Port Preservation and I'm thinking, 'You're here in the 1980s but those people – it was so hard.'

Bill Megennis and the sweep of dunes at Cape Reinga. Many keepers spent time in the sandhills, looking for Maori artefacts. Alan Martin found a greenstone adze; Alan Wright would 'never forget this young couple that asked me the way to the beach. So I showed them the way to go down, and they came back and they had this beautiful pair of greenstone earrings they'd just found on the beach. The number that was found there! After every storm we'd go down there looking.'

BILL MEGENNIS

Other keepers, and those named below are not an exhaustive list, made the most of opportunities to become involved in scientific work they may never have done in normal life. We have already seen Charles Robson's contributions; at about the same time, keeper Andreas Sandager whom Alexander Parks described as 'an ardent Entomologist and Botanist [3], *'filled kerosene cases with beautifully prepared ferns, named correctly with Latin names, ready to send away.' He had birds and insects named after him, wrote articles for* The Royal Society's Transactions and Proceedings, *collected for Buller and furnished him and others with observations on plants, insects and birds, which they used in their papers to the learned societies of the day.* [4]

Anders Hansen, when principal keeper at the Tiritiri Matangi station between 1906 and 1909, sent specimens to T. F. Cheeseman, the botanist who from 1874 ran the Auckland Museum for nearly 50 years. The correspondence, which carries no mention of payment, is perhaps a little more prosaic than Robson's; but the letter below, typical of the communications, are indicative of Hansen's intelligent, articulate interest and his careful observations and deductions, while his wry humour about the fly and his contemporary sensibility towards conservation issues are endearing: Last Sunday, while looking for plants on a steep, clayey face, I found a plant which was quite new to me. After searching through your book "Manual of the New Zealand Flora", I came to the conclusion that it must be Drosera auriculata. However, before looking it up in the Flora, I knew I had found one of those curious plants that partly subsist on a flesh diet, if I

An unidentified group at Tiritiri Matangi station, about 1911. The origin of the ghostly finger on the right is unknown.

ATL: F32650½

may call it so; this I knew because I had seen a plant on the pakahi, or iron sandstone heathy lands at Addisons, near Westport. This plant, although quite different in appearance from the present specimen, had characteristics which at once suggested a similarity between the two. The West coast plant, if not exactly like or identical with the "Venus flytrap", or catcher, is very much like pictures I have seen of the latter. I potted one [of] the D. Auriculata and planted one in the garden, both were on the point of flowering. The one in flowerbed has opened its flowers, but the one in the house has not, perhaps because of being shut up in the house. I gave the plant in the house three small pieces of boiled white of egg, which it nearly[?] consumed in 24 hours. I had this plant in the parlour, near window curtain and a spider (small black one) started to make a webb from curtains to cluster of flower buds at top of plant, and had he stopped there things would have been alright for the spider, but he put a stay to the nearest leaf, and that ended his career, for he is now snugly in the centre of the leaf with all the "feelers" tugged round him ...

The work of collecting is getting very interesting to me, and I look forward to your letters with the greatest interest, always hoping something interesting may have been among the plants sent up, but even without that I like to know the names of even the commonest plants. I am very sorry I didn't begin years and years ago.

I am getting more familiar with the Manual of the New Zealand Flora now. At first it appeared too advanced for a new beginner.

I have just received Dr Cockayne's Report of the botanical survey of Kapiti. I am surprised at the paucity of species of plants on such a big island, too, one with great diversity in localities. It is very interesting to read that the species on Kapiti are more akin to those of the northern part of the South Island than to those on the neighbouring mainland, only a few miles away.

Very few birds strike this tower and are hardly ever killed. I shall keep a note, in future, of all birds striking. The pied fantail sometimes comes on summer nights to collect moths on the lantern panes, of which they reap a fine harvest on still, dark nights.

The little black shag of which I sent some eggs, is, I think, a new arrival here. I feel shure they did not nest here last year. It appears that the tree shags can only have been building on the island the last few years as only one or two trees were occupied. This year new trees have been built in, and it is on these new trees that the small shag has built its nests. The trees in which the shags build are very soon killed by the acrid nature of the excrement.

I think the reason of the recent appearance of tree-building shags here is due to the fact that the rabbits which at one time overran the island are now all died out.

When rabbits were plentyful parties of shooters came down here and the shags offered admirable targets for their abominable pea-rifles. Only a short time ago some young man came here to shoot shags, telling me that he would get sixpence per pair of legs, or some such sum. I told him that even if it was desirable to shoot the shags, I thought it would be very inhuman to do so with the helpless young chicks in the nests to be left to die of starvation, and further, pointed out to him that the shags building here, so far as I knew, lived exclusively on seafish of which there were an abundance for all. Any how so long as I am in charge of Tiri there will be no shooting of birds except that they be wanted for scientific purposes.

Wild cats are on the increase, and I hardly know how to deal with them.

Will you kindly inform me if plants are packed well enough. Am sending 19 specimens. Hope there may be some rare ones among them.[5]

In the twentieth century, keepers also got happily involved with the work being carried out by scientists visiting the stations and developing new interests and skills. Barry: When I

got up to Portland Island Jock Morland, the ichthyologist at the Dominion Museum, got on to me and said, 'There's a lot of paper nautilus come ashore up there, would you like to save me some?' Dudley Neilson showed me one shell he'd recovered from the sand spit. It was 10¼ inches across the opening, one of the biggest ones I'd ever seen. I never had any hope of finding any decent ones because whenever there was a storm that used to wash them up on the sand spit, the seagulls had got out before any of us got down there, and they'd smashed the shells to get the little squid that live inside these things. So I was not able to help out. But the scientists were after information on the sea snakes that used to come across from Australia and whether we'd sighted any of these damn things, anything else unusual.

[On Stephens Island] Bill Dawbin [a scientist from Victoria University] said 'If you ever find any dead tuataras, let me know.' So one day in a big clump of stinging nettle I found some bones. In true archaeological style I got a paintbrush out and I brushed the dirt away and I recovered these bones and two jaw bones with teeth stuck in — it was crushed up a bit — but I put them all together and I put them in little separate wraps of newspaper, and I sent them off to the university on the next boat. I got a letter back. They were the remains of somebody's fish dinner!

Barry Langman festooned with tuatara, Stephens Island. BARRY LANGMAN

Barry's father and brother had previously helped Dawbin and Kinsky, ('the national ornithologist, an international birdman' said Alan Wright) with their work on whales and the rare shags at Perano Heads. When Dawbin found out I was at Stephens Island he said to me, 'You're quite interested in this, would you like to do some field work for me 'cause I can't come out that often.' So he supplied me with all the weighing instruments and so on and I had his code. He used to mark the tuatara by clipping the joints of the claws and when the combinations from the 20 claws had run out I used gentian violet to mark the tuas on the back — it used to last for several months. I was plotting their grazing areas, whether they migrated, their weights at various times to show how they were feeding, whether I'd ever seen any of the mating, egg-laying, and any unusual things. At the end he said 'You've done a lot here, it'll figure well in the history of the tuatara.'

The stations offered children, too, a close view of nature. Here David Taylor is surrounded by seagull chicks, hungry because two nestings that year meant food shortages. 'The birds would come waltzing into the kitchen after crumbs', Marita Taylor remembers, 'and skid on the highly polished floor.' MARITA AND PETER TAYLOR

It was thanks to the Lighthouse Service that Alan Wright became a keen ornithologist. It started with Brian Bell, the supervisor of protected species in the New Zealand Wildlife Service, and Fred Kinsky. The first job was banding red-billed gulls on The Brothers. We had another colony at Kaikoura and another colony at Nelson and we were trying to find out the distribution, where these birds were going. We put coloured bands on each one. As a result of this Brian got us mist nets for trapping. I virtually had it going all the time. You look through my diaries. 'Cooking, housework, cleaning drain sumps. Let out today three house sparrows, a gold finch. Two repeats head sparrows, house sparrows, albatross. Finished boxing on hen house. Poured concrete. Northwest winds twenty knots all day.' That's all I did with my diaries. 'Light building, Chris crook in bed all day, called the doc, suspected malaria. Nest up on the path. House sparrows, gold finches. Chris a bit better today.' Brian Bell and I developed a competition between us. We eventually became known in the Wildlife Service as Ring and Sling. On The Brothers quite a lot of stuff that had never been recorded before would come in at night, hit the lighthouse and drop down.

But being on the fringes of the scientific world could carry its own disappointments. Charles Hepburn Robson had sent, with Dr. Hector as emissary, some specimens he had collected for Dr Günther F.R.S. in London: [S]ome of [these] I felt sure were new to science, through some mistake however, the Doctor it seems got them mixed up with the others and presented them in his own name so that I have never heard a word about them till I received Vol IX Trans NZ Inst where at pages 471 & 472 I found my little fishes Crepiaogaster[?] and Leopilus Hectoris etc at the time I felt very sore about it, but as Dr. Hector wrote saying he was very sorry there had been a mistake I let the matter drop ... Situated as I nearly always am from the nature of my occupation, in out of the way places, I have very good opportunities for collecting ... I have to depend upon others to describe and name what I find. [incomplete] [6]

Robson had one satisfaction — a marine spider he had discovered was acknowledged to be a new species and Powell got it named after its discoverer — Desisrobsoni.[7] *Barry Langman, suffering a similar disappointment, had no such consolation:* The lizard I had found was pictured in the Forest and Bird magazine which laid the discovery down to another. He [the scientist to whom Barry Langman had sent the specimen] also mentioned about this lovely tank half buried in the lawn at No. 2 house – 'It makes an ideal terrarium,' he said. That's what I built it for, that's where the eggs hatched out! Well – it's the sort of thing I got the thrill out of finding it and it was indeed a new discovery and it has now been recognised in one form or another.

George studied while watching, and there were also opportunities to read and expand horizons. James Nelson, The Brothers, 1878: We have a small collection of books here that was presented to the Brothers by Mr Mirfin [an artificer] and the present Keepers and I beg to ask you if they could be exchanged for some other books at some other Lighthouse or in Wellington as we are very badly off for something to read.[8]

C. T. Bowles, East Cape, 1950: It is the opinion of the lightkeepers on this station that copies of "Weather" provide some interesting reading matter, but is inclined to be too technical and hard to follow unless the reader has had some previous knowledge of meteorology ...

A magazine dealing with the formation of fronts, depressions, troughs of low pressure etc, and the formation of cloud types would be of more and informative interest to the majority of lightkeepers

For instance if the keepers knew that certain clouds are the forerunners of a front or depression (I am fairly safe in saying that 90% of the keepers do not know anything about weather or cloud types other than that provided by the wall sheets and MO233 Cloud Forms), they would show more interest

If such a publication, preferably written in humerous style, is available it would be more widely read, to the <u>benefit of both the keepers</u> and the Meteorological Office in that more accurate reports would be forwarded. It would also give a more standard type of report and form a basis for Principal Keepers to train new keepers in the method of reporting or, for that matter, the training of anybody for weather reporting.[9]

The Country Library Service was enormously appreciated and its books were treated with all due care. Chris: You don't need to take books to The Brothers. Plenty of books out there. Marvellous service from the Country Library Service. They used to send us a couple of boxes plus all the ones you'd ordered. I used to be the librarian, that was another of my jobs. I used to have to fill in request cards, send them in. It was a wonderful service. I remember one bloke out there he was interested in the artillery. Anyway he requested a book about the history of the Royal Artillery. And there was only one book in New Zealand, an enormous tome, highly insured, and they sent it and told us to look after it. And we sent it back.

Barry: The Country Library Service used to give us first preference on all the books that came into the library. I read books in those days I'd never think of reading, autobiographies of famous women, explorers. I'd have never normally gone for them — they were across-the-board subjects that could interest a whole range of people. I read everything. Books always brand new. Came to us first and then back into general circulation. A hamper would come and there might be about 30 books in it.

The life also offered less tangible pleasures whose enjoyment may well have transcended generations and centuries. In Wind in the Willows, *Rat dreamily and lovingly rhapsodises about 'simply mucking about in boats'. Charles Hepburn Robson's ability to quietly and unhurriedly observe and lovingly record his specimens, perhaps the qualities he needed in the Lighthouse Service, also made him a good scientist. In 1880, in a letter in which he used the word 'gnathopodii' two years before the OED cites the first usage of gnathopodite — ' one of those limbs which, in crustaceans, have been modified into accessory organs of mastication' — Robson wrote to Dr. Günther with loving detail of a crustacean he found:* [Moving] his cask from place to place he used to come out take hold of one end with the first pair of gnathopodii and swim behind pushing it before him just like a nurse with a Perambulator . . .[10]

One hundred and twenty-four years later, George Kroening remembered the pleasures he got from simple things that had happened almost fifty years before. Perhaps more than anything else the ability to find and accumulate pleasure from unsophisticated, unremarkable things marked out those who enjoyed the life from those who did not. George: There was the entry in the log book every day, 'routine duties two hours', 'routine duties two hours'. But there was variety of work. And as long as you got permission from the principal keeper you could do practically anything you wanted to. If you wanted to go off the station and go wandering down round the beach, go fishing, use the boat — it was quite free and easy. And Portland Island especially with no ties with the children, we used to spend a lot of time wandering round the beaches and this and that. We'd even be honoured to take the truck sometimes and

Before the advent of mass entertainment, and like others in the backblocks, keepers made their own fun, making do with what they had. Christmas Day 1947 on Mokohinau, and Father Christmas George Kroening, dressed in code flag 'B' (the red danger flag) makes his way towards the houses. JEAN AND GEORGE KROENING

go down and spend a couple of hours on the road cutting coming up from the landing, chucking the loose papa over the side to make it a little more accessible, and at the same time we'd go down round the spit at the northern end and look at nautilus shells and things like that, and come back to the station in time to milk the cows.

Chris: For a couple of years, three of us had two rifles and we used to save up all the old bean cans and I set up some shelves across a gully on a bank. On a nice day somebody would go across with a sack of empty cans, arrange them carefully on these shelves and then we'd all step back and blast away at them. It was quite entertaining. We used to drop the bottles to bob along in the tide and then when we'd got a string running out to sea then we'd start shooting at them too.

Jean got satisfaction out of being competent: making a meal out of nothing and making your pennies stretch. Even today, if I won Lotto, I'd never be extravagant, I couldn't. The shortage of money, you only had carrots, parsnips, silverbeet, cabbage not the exotic fruits and vegetables you can get today and just take for granted. Nancy Miller's people came from Whakatane and we always had cases of grapefruit, lemons, that sort of thing. I even learnt to make peel and it was so much better than what you buy in the shops.

She found pleasure, too, in the quiet patterns of the day: If the tug came early in the morning Nancy Miller and I'd milk the cows, talk away, think nothing of it, just shift one cow out and bring another in. Perhaps we were lucky with the keepers, the children — Nancy Miller's children used to come over and play with Lynne, pick her up and take her out.

We played cards at night but during the day we'd row across to this little bay to what we called the Arches. But there was always a man watching out at the point for the sharks, so that the children would be all right. We'd picnic there. My mother and sister and her husband and her two children — they came up. There was so much. The men went fishing, the women — we just seemed to have, I don't know what we did, but we enjoyed it. To come back to mainland, it's more of a humdrum existence.

Bill Megennis: [The life offered me] a sense of freedom, which is a hard thing to define if you're on a little island. I liked the freedom of often being on your own — well, with other people but you were in charge of your own destiny in a lot of ways. And you couldn't really muck up too much because you could be seriously hurt. You had to be aware of your own limitations.

I think different people had different concepts of freedom. My one was having all this space out here, it's all yours, you can do what you like with it, you can hate it and it can make you angry because it's raining and the weather's

getting you down and it's a mind thing. There was just this sense of open space round you and you had the freedom let your mind go where you wanted to go. I think for me that was the main thing.

Chris Staley: The kind of life I've lived here for many years is humdrum. But on a lighthouse every day is different. There's always something happening, there's always the wind blowing, always the sea running, the sea birds, you're never away from the sound of the sea.

Endnotes

ABBREVIATIONS

AJHR: Appendices to the Journals of the House of Representatives

ANZ: Archives New Zealand Te Whare Tohu Tuhituhinga o Aotearoa. Regional branches in Auckland, Wellington, and Dunedin are designated ANZ (Ak), ANZ (Wgtn), and ANZ (Dn).

ATL: Alexander Turnbull Library, National Library of New Zealand Te Puna Matauranga o Aotearoa, Wellington

HL: Hocken Library Uare Taoka o Hakena, University of Otago, Dunedin

Prologue

1   MS–Papers–6271–1 Copy of transcription of Charles Hepburn Orlando diary, ATL.

Chapter 1

1   AJHR 1865, Report of the Marine Board Department of New Zealand by the Postmaster General, D–No. 1C, p. 4
2   AJHR 1867, Third Report on the Marine Department E–No. 6, p. 3.

Chapter 2

1   DAAL/D28/7a Nugget Point Outwards correspondence 1896–1913, 2 June 1875, ANZ (Dn).
2   DAAL/D28/14b Waipapa Point Outwards correspondence 1906–1919, 6 October 1913, p. 136, ANZ (Dn).
3   DAAL/D28/3e Centre Island Outwards correspondence 1912–26, 14 February 1923, p. 205, AN(Dn).

Chapter 3

1   DAAL/D28/10b Puysegur Point Outwards correspondence 1878–92, 28 February 1879, ANZ (Dn).
2   ZAAP 15125/1a Cuvier Island Outwards correspondence 1889–1914, 31 January 1901, ANZ (Ak).
3   ML–Cape Palliser 3/2 Outwards correspondence 1912–24, 4 August 1921, pp. 183–5, ANZ (Wgtn).
4   DAAL/D28/3d Centre Island Outwards correspondence 1888–1912, 31 May 1901, ANZ (Dn).
5   ML–Stephens Isl 3/1 Folder 2 Section 9 Outwards correspondence 1894–1910, 17 May 1901, p. 169, ANZ (Wgtn).
6   ML–Cape Egmont 3/2 Outwards correspondence 1895–[95] 1915, 30 April 1901, p. 81, ANZ (Wgtn).
7   ML-Castlepoint 3/5 Outwards letterbook 1941–42, 1 May 1941, ANZ (Wgtn).
8   ML–Baring Head 3/1 Baring Head Outwards correspondence 1935–36, 2 December 1936, ANZ (Wgtn).

Chapter 4

1   ML–Pencarrow 3/1 Outwards correspondence 1898–1920, 20 September 1899, ANZ (Wgtn).

2   ZAAP 15125 Ia Cuvier Island Outwards letterbook 1889–1914, 31 March 1909, ANZ (Ak).

3   DAAL/D28/7a Nugget Point Outwards correspondence 1896–1913, 14 May 1900, p. 58, ANZ (Dn). The earlier letter is ibid., 28 March 1899, p. 36. The first letter referring to three men being employed is ibid., 21 March 1904, p. 142.

4   DAAL/D28/7a Nugget Point Lighthouse Outwards correspondence 1896–1913, July 18, 1911, p. 387, ANZ (Dn).

5   ML–Cape Egmont 3/2 Outwards correspondence 1895–[95] 1915, 23 February 1900, ANZ (Wgtn).

6   DAAL/D28/14b Waipapa Point Outwards correspondence 1906–1919, 12 October 1914, p. 170, ANZ (Dn).

7   ML–Stephens Island 3/3 Outwards correspondence 1918–21, 15 July 1921, pp. 234–8, ANZ (Wgtn).

8   ZAAP 15120 Ic Cape Brett Outwards letterbook 1932–41, 26 April, 1938, p. 205, ANZ (Ak).

9   ZAAP 15120 Ic Cape Brett Outwards letterbook 1932–41, 26 September 1939, ANZ (Ak).

10 ML–Pencarrow 3/1 Outwards correspondence 1898–1926, ANZ (Wgtn), 1 September 1913, pp. 247–9, ANZ (Wgtn).

11 ML–Pencarrow 3/1 Outwards correspondence 1898–1926, 10 October 1910, p. 206, ANZ (Wgtn).

12 DAAL/D28/3d Centre Island Outwards correspondence 1888–1912, 31 May 1899, p. 209, ANZ (Dn).

13 QAAW 15130 2a Mokohinau Outwards letters 1896–1914, 16 September 1900, p. 40, ANZ (Ak).

14 Hart, Samuel, 'Lighthouse-keepers' experiences The Flying Scotchman, 'The Public Service Journal, 20 December 1919, Hart family papers.

15 ML–Cape Egmont 3/2 Outwards correspondence 1895–[95] 1915, 16 March 1904, p. 137, ANZ (Wgtn).

16 ML–Cape Palliser 3/6 Outwards correspondence 1941–47, 2 October 1945, ANZ (Wgtn).

17 ML –Brothers 3/1 Outwards correspondence 1877–1882, 30 September 1877, ANZ (Wgtn).

18 DAAL/D28/14b Waipapa Point Outwards correspondence 1906–19, 30 June 1917, p. 271, ANZ (Dn).

19 DAAL/D28/10b Puysegur Point Outwards correspondence 1878–92, 30 November 1885, ANZ (Dn).

20 P Taylor, *As Darker Grows the Light*, p. 24.

21 ML–Cape Palliser 3/1 Outwards correspondence 31 August 1910, ANZ (Wgtn).

22 ML–Cape Palliser 3/1 Outwards correspondence 27 February 1912, ANZ (Wgtn).

23 ML–Farewell Spit 3/5 Outwards correspondence 1947–51, 10 February 1948, ANZ (Wgtn).

Chapter 5

1   ZAAP 15120 Ib Cape Brett Outwards letterbook 1927–32, 1 July 1927, ANZ (Ak).

2   DAAL/D28/2B Cape Saunders Lighthouse Outwards correspondence, 1 September 1940, ANZ (Dn).

3   ML–Cape Egmont 3/1 Outwards correspondence 1881–95, 31 August 1883, ANZ)Wgtn).

4   Ibid., 1 November 1889, ANZ (Wgtn).

5   ML–Cape Egmont 3/2 Outwards correspondence 1895–[95] 1915, 1 May 1897, p. 2, ANZ (Wgtn).

6 Ibid., 2 August 1907, p. 235, ANZ (Wgtn).

7 ML–Portland Island 3/1 Outwards correspondence 1878–89, June 1881, ANZ (Wgtn).

8 ML–Baring Head 3/1 Outwards correspondence 1935–44, 12 November 1936, ANZ (Wgtn).

9 ML–Cape Palliser 3/1 Outwards correspondence 1897–1912, 1 December 1898, ANZ (Wgtn).

10 ML–Farewell Spit 3/3 Outwards correspondence 1934–39, 27 December 1935, p. 44, ANZ (Wgtn).

11 Letter 18 August 1894, Benjamin family papers.

12 ML–Stephens Isl 3/1 Outwards correspondence 1894–1910 Folder 1 Section 2, 18 April 1895, p. 6, ANZ (Wgtn).

13 ML–Portland Island 3/1 Outwards correspondence 1878–89, 20 March 1880, ANZ (Wgtn).

14 ZAAP 15125 Ia Cuvier Island Outwards letterbook 1889–1914, 8 June 1893, ANZ (Ak).

15 ML–Cape Palliser 3/1 Outwards correspondence 1897–1912, 31 December 1910, ANZ (Wgtn).

16 DAAL/D28/10b Puyseur Point Outwards correspondence 1878–92, 14 May 1878 ANZ (Dn).

17 Ibid., 28 February 1879, ANZ (Dn).

18 Ibid., May 1880, ANZ (Dn).

19 Parks to Secretary of Marine, 2 September 1895, Benjamin Papers. Also in DAAL/D28/10c Puysegur Point Outwards correspondence 1892–1907, p. 30, ANZ (Dn).

20 Parks to Secretary of Marine, 15 February 1895, Benjamin Papers.

21 DAAL/D28/10c Puysegur Point Outwards correspondence 1892–1907, 1 December 1896, p, 54, ANZ (Dn)

22 DAAL/D28/10d Puysegur Point Outwards correspondence 1907–23, 9 May 1917, p. 228, ANZ (Dn).

23 DAAL/D28/7a Nugget Point Outwards correspondence 1896–1913, 2 July 1898, p. 18, ANZ (Dn).

24 DAAL/D28/14d Waipapa Point Outwards correspondence 1925–35, 1 November 1928, p. 197, ANZ (Dn).

25 ML–-Brothers 3/1 Outwards correspondence 1877–1882, 31 August 1881, ANZ (Wgtn).

26 Ibid., 31 July 1882, ANZ (Wgtn).

27 DAAL/D28/10c Puysegur Point Outwards correspondence 1892–1907, 12 June 1895, p. 21, ANZ (Dn).

28 DAAL/D28/4b Dog Island Outwards correspondence 1923–29, 1 May 1927, ANZ (Dn).

29 DAAL/D28/10d Puysegur Point Outwards correspondence 1907–23, 2 August 1917, p. 240, ANZ (Dn).

30 ML–Stephens Isl 3/1 Outwards correspondence 1894–1910, Folder 2 Section 6, pp. 97–101, 27 August 1898, ANZ (Wgtn). The earlier correspondence referred to is in Ibid., p. 90.

31 ML–French Pass 3/7 Outwards correspondence 1957–59, 30 September 1957, ANZ (Wgtn).

32 ML–Stephens Isl 3/1 Outwards correspondence 1889–1910, Folder 2 Section 9, 30 April 1901, pp. 166–67; ibid., p. 168, 4 May 1901, ANZ (Wgtn).

33 Ibid., 17 May 1901, p. 169, ANZ (Wgtn).

34 Ibid., Folder 2 section 15, 1 June 1907, p. 321, ANZ (Wgtn).

35 ML–Stephens Island 3/4 Outwards correspondence 1921–37, 23 November 1923, ANZ (Wgtn).

36 ML–French Pass 3/1 Outwards correspondence 1884–97, 21 January 1885, ANZ (Wgtn).

37 ML–French Pass 3/7 Outwards correspondence 1957–59, 30 September 1957, ANZ (Wgtn).

38 ML–French Pass 3/2 Outwards correspondence 1897–1926, 1 March 1910, p. 151, ANZ (Wgtn).

39 ZAAP 15137 Ia Cape Reinga Monthly reports & letters 1943–45, 12 April 1944, ANZ (Ak).

40 Undated letter [early 1892], Letters of A. E. Parks, Benjamin papers.

41 DAAL/D28/13h Waipapa Point Outwards correspondence, 4 July 1888, p. 114, ANZ (Dn).

42 DAAL D28 3d Centre Island Outwards correspondence 1888—1912, 1 September 1888, p. 6, ANZ (Dn).

43 ML–Cape Egmont 3/2 Outwards correspondence 1895–95 [1915], 21 July 1914, p. 459, ANZ (Wgtn).

44 ZAAP 15120 2g Cape Brett Outwards correspondence 1956–57, 5 June 1956, ANZ (Ak).

45 ML–Portland Island 3/9, Outwards corresponcence, 12 January 1949, ANZ (Wgtn).

Chapter 6

1 ZAAP 15125 2a Cape Brett Outwards letterbook 1946–52, 2 July 1947, ANZ (Ak).

2 ML–Cape Palliser 3/1 Outwards correspondence 1897–1912, 1 November 1897, ANZ (Wgtn).

3 Ibid., 23 October 1906, ANZ (Wgtn).

4 ZAAP 15120 1b Cape Brett Outwards letterbook 1927–32, 6 February 1931, p. 104; 10 March 1931, p. 109, ANZ (Ak).

5 ML–Farewell Spit 3/5 Outwards correspondence 1947–51, 2 July 1951, ANZ (Wgtn).

6 ML–Pencarrow 3/1 Outwards correspondence 1898–1920, 31 October 1904, p. 78, ANZ (Wgtn).

7 ML–Cape Egmont 3/3 Outwards correspondence 1915–31, 28 February 1917, p. 133, ANZ (Wgtn).

8 ML–Cape Palliser 3/7 Outwards correspondence 1947–57, 10 November 1947, ANZ (Wgtn).

9 ML–Pencarrow 3/3 Outwards correspondence 1946–52, 6 October 1947, ANZ (Wgtn).

10 DAAL/D28/10b Puyseur Point Outwards correspondence 1878–92, 14 September 1878, ANZ (Dn).

11 DAAL/D28/4a Dog Island Outwards correspondence 1903–18, 18 June 1915, p. 286, ANZ (Dn).

12 ML–Cape Egmont 3/3 Outwards correspondence 31 July 1915–31, 31 July 1915, p. 35, ANZ (Wgtn).

13 DAAI/D28/14e Waipapa Point Outwards correspondence 1935–43, 8 February 1938, ANZ (Dn).

14 DAAL/D28/2B Cape Saunders Outwards correspondence, 1 September 1940, ANZ (Dn).

15 ZAAP 15120 1d Cape Brett Outwards letterbook 1941–46, 15 May 1943, ANZ (Ak).

16 ML–Cape Egmont 3/2 Outwards correspondence 1895–95 [1915], 1 August 1897; 2 September 1897; 1 January 1898, ANZ (Wgtn).

17 ZAAP 15125 1a Cuvier Island Outwards correspondence 1889–1914, 31 January 1901, ANZ (Ak).

18 DAAL/D28/5b Moeraki Outwards correspondence, p. 14, ANZ (Dn).

19 ZAAP 15140 1c Tiritiri Matangi Outwards letterbook 1955–56, 2 June 1955, ANZ (Ak).

20 ML–Manukau Heads 4 Letterbook 1917–1944, pp. 139–40, 6 February 1927, pp. 150-151, ANZ (Wgtn).

21 ML–Cape Egmont 3/4 Outwards correspondence 1931–53, 1 September 1945, p. 180, ANZ (Wgtn).

22 Ibid., 24 September 1945, p. 192, ANZ (Wgtn).

23 ML–Portland Island 3/8 Outwards correspondence 1947–48, 25 May 1947, ANZ (Wgtn).

24 ZAAP 15125 2a Cape Brett Outwards letterbook 1946–52, 2 July 1947, ANZ (Ak).

25 ML–Cape Palliser 3/1 Outwards correspondence 1897–1912, 31 May 1911, ANZ (Wgtn).

26 ML–East Cape 3/1 Outwards correspondence 1921–23, 1 September 1923, p. 70, ANZ (Wgtn).

27 Ibid., pp. 64-66

28 Ibid., 4 May 1924, p. 98, ANZ (Wgtn).

29 ML–Farewell Spit 3/2 Outwards correspondence 1924–30, 22 June 1929, pp. 108–11, ANZ (Wgtn)

30 ML–Castlepoint 3/5 Outwards letterbook 1941–42, 25 June 1942, ANZ (Wgtn).

31 Ibid., 2 August, 1942, ANZ (Wgtn).

32 ML–Castlepoint 3/6 Outwards correspondence 1942–45, 8 September 1943, ANZ (Wgtn).

33 ML–Cape Egmont 3/3 Outwards correspondence 1915–31, 25 May 1915, p. 19, ANZ (Wgtn).

34 Ibid., 31 May 1915, p. 22, ANZ (Wgtn).

35 ML–Pencarrow 3/1 Outwards correspondence 1898–1926, 30 November 1918, p. 383, ANZ (Wgtn).

36 DAAL/D28/5e Moeraki Outwards correspondence 1938–42, 17 October 1940, ANZ (Dn).

37 ZAAP 15137 1a Cape Reinga monthly reports and letters 1943–45, February 1944, ANZ (Ak).

38 ML–Castlepoint 3/4 Outwards correspondence 1933–41, 1 October 1939, p. 190, ANZ (Wgtn).

39 ML–Castlepoint 3/6 Outwards letterbook 1942–45, 6 August 1943, ANZ (Wgtn).

40 ML–Castlepoint 3/5 Outwards letterbook 1941–42, 11 June 1942, ANZ (Wgtn).

41 Ibid., 12 October 1942, ANZ (Wgtn).

42 ML–Stephens Isl 3/5 Outwards correspondence 1937–44, 16 May 1944, ANZ (Wgtn).

43 ML–Stephens Isl 3/6 Outwards correspondence 1944–47, 31 October 1944, ANZ (Wgtn)

44 ZAAP 15120 1d Cape Brett Outwards correspondence 1941–46, 5 November 1945, ANZ (Ak).

45 ZAAP 15140 1a Tiritiri Matangi Outwards letterbook 1947–53, 15 July 1947, ANZ (Ak).

46 Ibid., 25 May 1950, ANZ (Ak).

47 ZAAP 15130 1d Mokohinau Outwards correspondence 1935–47, 2 February 1947, ANZ (Ak).

48 Ibid., memo, February 1947, ANZ (Ak).

49 ZAAP 15130 1e Mokohinau Outwards letterbook 1947–48, Report, July 1947, ANZ (Ak).

Chapter 7

1   Hannah Parks diary, Benjamin papers. I have used a transcribed version.

2   ML–Brothers 3/1 Outwards correspondence 1877–1882, 24 November 1879, ANZ (Wgtn).

3   Ibid., 31 March 1882, ANZ (Wgtn).

4   Ibid., 31 July 1882, ANZ (Wgtn).

5   ML–Brothers 3/2 Outwards correspondence 1910–1919, 29 February 1912, p. 42, ANZ (Wgtn).

6   ML–Portland Island 3/1 Outwards correspondence 1878–89, 31 May 1881, ANZ (Wgtn).

7   DAAL D28 3d Centre Island Outwards correspondence 1888–1912, p. 6, ANZ (Dn).

8   ML–Cape Egmont 3/2 Outwards correspondence 1895–[95] 1915, 1 December 1896, ANZ (Wgtn).

9   ML–Castlepoint 3/2 Outwards correspondence 1921-24, 23 January 1923, ANZ (Wgtn).

10 DAAL/D28/4b Dog Island Outwards correspondence 1923–29, 29 September 1926, ANZ (Dn).

11 DAAL/D28/5c Moeraki Outwards correspondence 1923–32, 11 January 1928, p. 101. ANZ (Dn).

12 ZAAP 15136 2a Cape Reinga Outwards correspondence 1954–55, 24 September 1954, ANZ (Ak.)

13 ZAAP 15136 2f Cape Reinga Outwards correspondence 1955–56, 25 May 1956, ANZ (Ak).

14 DAAL/D28/3f Centre Island Outwards correspondence 1927–40, p. 168, ANZ (Dn).

15 ZAAP 15120 1d Cape Brett Outwards correspondence 1941–46, 13 October 1944, ANZ (Ak).

16 ML–Stephens Island 3/4 Outwards correspondence 1921–24, 5 April 1922, ANZ (Wgtn).

17 ZAAP 15120 2b Cape Brett Outwards correspondence 1952–53, 7 January 1953, ANZ (Ak).

18 ZAAP 15140 2a Tiritiri Matangi Outwards letterbook 1956–57, 6 September 1957, ANZ (Ak).

19 ML-Castlepoint 3/1 Outwards correspondence 1912–21, 15 December 1920, p. 149, ANZ (Wgtn).

20 ML–Cape Egmont 3/2 Outwards correspondence 1895–[95] 1915, 1 October 1909, p. 289, ANZ (Wgtn).

21 ML–Stephens Island Outwards correspondence 1918–21, 20 May 1921, p. 222, ANZ (Wgtn).

22 ZAAP 15120 1d Cape Brett Outwards correspondence 1941–46, 13 October 1944, ANZ (Ak).

23 ML–Castlepoint 3/2 Outwards letterbook 1921–24, 31 May 1923, ANZ (Wgtn).

24 ML–3/3 Stephens Island Outwards correspondence 1918–21, 6 June 1921, (inserted between pp. 221–2), ANZ (Wgtn).

25 ML–Stephens Island 3/3 Outwards correspondence 1918–21, 2 July 1920, p. 266, ANZ (Wgtn). (Lovell dated this letter 1920, wrongly if the sequence of letters is to be believed.)

26 ML–Stephens Island 3/3, Outwards correspondence 1918–21, 6 August 1921, p. 244, ANZ (Wgtn).

Chapter 8

1 DAAL/D28/6h Nugget Point Outwards correspondence 1871–81, 26 August 1880, ANZ (Dn).

2 ML–Castlepoint 3/1 Outwards correspondence 1912–21, 29 September 1921, p. 185, ANZ (Wgtn).

3 ZAAP 15130 1a Mokohinau Outwards letterbook 1915–23, 1 December 1922, p. 193, ANZ (Ak).

4 Ibid., 8 January 1923, p. 201, ANZ (Ak).

5 ML–Stephens Island 3/1 Outwards correspondence 1894–1910, 15 February 1909, ANZ (Wgtn).

6 DAAL/D28/3d Centre Island Outwards correspondence 1888–1912, 30 June, 1896, p. 162, ANZ (Dn).

7 ML–Stephens Island 3/2 Outwards correspondence, 24 November 1916, pp. 293–4, ANZ (Wgtn).

8 DAAL/D28/5b Moeraki Outwards correspondence 1895–1917, 20 June 1895, p. 11, ANZ (Dn).

Chapter 9

1 DAAL D28 3d Centre Island Outwards correspondence 1888–1912, p. 62, ANZ (Dn).

2 DAAL/D28/10c Puysegur Point Outwards correspondence 1892–1907, p. 30. ANZ (Dn).

3 Ibid., 3 July 1896, p. 45, ANZ (Dn).

4 ML–Cape Egmont 3/2 Outwards correspondence 1895–[95] 1915, 7 October 1914, p. 481, ANZ (Wgtn).

5 ML– Cape Egmont 3/1 Outwards correspondence 1881–95, 30 June 1885, ANZ (Wgtn).

6 ML Cape Palliser 3/6 Outwards correspondence 1941–47, 20 July 1945, ANZ (Wgtn).

7 ML–East Cape 3/2 Outwards correspondence 1933–43, copy of letter from Mr W. Walker, 30 June 1935, p. 31, ANZ (Wgtn).

8 ML–East Cape 3/3 Outwards correspondence 1943–48, August 1947, ANZ (Wgtn).

9 ML– Portland Island 3/2 Outwards correspondence, 25 March 1905, p. 54, ANZ (Wgtn).

10 ML–Portland Island Outwards correspondence 3/12 1955–56, 27 September 1955, ANZ (Wgtn).

11 DAAL D28 2bCape Saunders Outwards Correspondence 1936-43, 5 December 1940, ANZ (Dn).

12 ML–Brothers 3/2 Outwards correspondence 1910–1919, 17 June 1910, ANZ (Wgtn).

13 ZAAP 15125 1a Cuvier Island Outwards letter book 1889–1914, 1 April 1905, ANZ (Ak)

14 QAAW 15130 2a Mokohinau Outwards letterbook 1896–1914, 23 July 1897, ANZ (Ak).

15 Ibid., 18 May 1898, ANZ (Ak).

16 Ibid., 1 February 1899, ANZ (Ak).

17 DAAL D28 10d Puysegur Point Outwards correspondence 1918–22, 15 July 1921, ANZ (Dn).

18 ML–Pencarrow 3/1 Outwards correspondence 1898–1926, 24 October 1917, p. 353, ANZ (Wgtn).

19 ZAAP 15120 1c Cape Brett Outwards letterbook 1932–41, 14 May 1943, pp. 55–56, ANZ(AK)

20 Ibid., 15 May 1943

Chapter 10

1 ML–Cape Egmont 3/3 Outwards correspondence 1915–31, 11 December 1915, p. 67, ANZ (Wgtn).

2 Ibid., 31 December 1915, p. 69, ANZ (Wgtn).

3 ML–Cape Egmont 3/2 Outwards correspondence 1895–95 [1915], 31 July 1913, p. 374, ANZ (Wgtn).

4 Ibid., 30 September 1913, p, 397, ANZ (Wgtn). See also Ibid., 31 May 1913.

5 QAAW 15130 2a Mokohinau Outwards letterbook 1896–1914, 13 August 1913, ANZ (Ak).

6 ZAAP 15120 2g Cape Brett Outwards correspondence 1957–58, 12 October 1957, ANZ (Ak).

7 QAAW 15130 2b Mokohinau Outwards letterbook 1896–1914, 1 November 1901, ANZ (Ak).

8 ML–Cape Egmont 3/2 Outwards correspondence 1895–[95] 1915, 18 August 1903, p. 125, ANZ (Wgtn).

9 DAAL D28 5b Moeraki Outwards correspondence, 30 April 1896, p. 27, ANZ (Dn).

10 ML–Cape Palliser 3/2 Outwards correspondence 1912–24, 30 November 1912, ANZ (Wgtn).

11 ML Cape Palliser 3/7 Outwards correspondence 1947–57, 2 April 1949, ANZ (Wgtn).

12 ML–Portland Island 3/14 Outwards correspondence 1957–59, 29 June 1957, ANZ (Wgtn).

13 ZAAP 15140 1d Tiritiri Matangi Outwards letterbook 1956–56, 25 June 1956, ANZ (Ak).

14 ML–Brothers 3/2 Outwards correspondence 1910–1919, 12 March 1910, ANZ (Wgtn).

15 DAAL/D28/10c Puysegur Point Outwards correspondence 1892–1907, 21 December 1906, pp. 278–9, ANZ (Dn).

16 Ibid., 1 January 1907, p. 280, ANZ (Dn).

17 DAAL/D28/10d Puysegur Point Outwards correspondence 1907–23, 9 May 1917, p. 228, ANZ (Dn).

18 Ibid., 20 March 1918, p. 276, ANZ (Dn).

19 DAAL/D28/10e Puysegur Point Outwards correspondence 1932–43, 1 December 1937, pp. 87–8, ANZ (Dn).

20 DAAL/D28/4b Dog Island Outwards correspondence 1923–29, 3 February 1925, ANZ (Dn).

21 ML–Portland 3/2 Outwards correspondence 1903–15, 29 December 1910, pp. 158-9, ANZ (Wgtn).

22 ML–Portland Island 3/4 Outwards correspondence 1928–31, 10 May 1928, ANZ (Wgtn).

23 ML–East Cape 3/1 Outwards correspondence 1921–23, 25 May 1923, pp. 52–3, ANZ (Wgtn).

24 DAAL/D28/3d Centre Island Outwards correspondence 1881–1912, October 14 1893, p. 103, ANZ (Dn).

25 DAAL/D28/4b Dog Island Outwards correspondence 1923–29, 16 March 1928, ANZ (Dn).

Chapter 11
1   ML–Cape Egmont 3/3 Outwards correspondence 1915–31, 28 February 1917, p. 133, ANZ (Wgtn).
2   ML–Cape Egmont 3/2 Outwards correspondence 1895–95 [1915], 1 August 1909, p. 283, ANZ (Wgtn).
3   ML–Cape Palliser 3/1 Outwards correspondence 1897–1912, 31 December 1909, ANZ (Wgtn).
4   DAAL/D28/10d Puysegur Point Outwards correspondence 1918–22, 15 November 1917, pp. 252–4, ANZ (Dn).
5   Ibid., 20 November 1917, p. 255, ANZ (Dn).
6   Ibid., 1 Dec 1917, p. 258. ANZ (Dn).
7. ML–French Pass 3/2 Outwards correspondence 1897–1926, 15 March 1926, p. 437, ANZ (Wgtn).
8   ML–Castlepoint 3/9 Outwards correspondence 1954–55, 1 December 1954, ANZ (Wgtn).
9   ML–Portland Island 3/2 Outwards correspondence 1903–15, 10 November 1911, pp. 182–3, ANZ (Wgtn).
10 ML–East Cape 3/2 Outwards correspondence 1933–43, 4 August 1938, p. 81, ANZ (Wgtn).
11 ZAAP 15130 1e Mokohinau Outwards letterbook 1947–48, 8 December 1947, ANZ (Ak).
12 DAAL/D28 7a Nugget Point Lighthouse Outwards correspondence 1896–1913, 15 September 1910, p. 366, ANZ (Dn).
13 ML–East Cape 3/1 Outwards correspondence 1921–26, 13 April 1923, p. 45, ANZ (Wgtn).
14 ML–East Cape 3/7 Outwards correspondence 1951–52, 1 May 1952, ANZ (Wgtn).
15 DAAL/D28 14 Waipapa Point Outwards correspondence 1906–1919, 31 August 1907, ANZ (Dn).
16 DAAL/D28 5d Moeraki Outwards correspondence 1932–38, 2 January 1938, p. 216, ANZ (Dn).
17 ML–Baring Head 3/3 Outwards correspondence 1954–56, undated, ANZ (Wgtn). 18
18 ZAAP 15140 1c Tiritiri Matangi Outwards letterbook 1955–56, 26 July 1955, ANZ (Ak).
19 ML–Portland Island 3/1 Outwards correspondence 1878–89, 18 January,1888, ANZ (Wgtn).
20 DAAL/D28/6h Nugget Point Outwards correspondence, 19 May 1881, ANZ (Dn).
21 Ibid. 24 May 1881, ANZ (Dn).
22 ML–Portland Island 3/1 Outwards correspondence 1881–89, 8 March 1882, ANZ (Wgtn).
23 ML–Brothers 3/2 Outwards correspondence, 11 February 1911, p. 3, ANZ (Wgtn). For the reference to Tutt's perceived public opprobium see ibid., 11 February 1911, p. 9. Tutt's final shot is ibid., 2 May 1911.

Chapter 12
1   DAAL/D28/6h Nugget Point Outwards correspondence 1871–81, 26 August, 1880, ANZ (Dn).
2   DAAL/D28/7a Nugget Point Lighthouse Outwards correspondence 1896–1913, 8 March 1912, p. 416, ANZ (Dn).
3   DAAL/D28/4c Dog Island Outwards correspondence 1936–45, 1 November 1938, ANZ (Dn).
4   Robson papers Robson-Rollaston Correspondence MS–Papers–0037–131, Robson to Haast, 13 September 1878, ATL.
5   M. P. K. Sorrenson, 'Walter Baldock Durrant Mantell', Dictionary of New Zealand Biography, Vol. 1, pp. 267–8.

6   Robson papers Robson-Rollaston Correspondence MS–Papers–0037–131, Robson to Haast, 9 October 1878, ATL.

7   Robson papers Robson-Rollaston Correspondence MS–Papers–0037–131, 18[?] October 1878, ATL.

8   Colin Miskelly, 'The identity of the Hakawai', *Nortornis*, Vol 34, 1987, pp. 95-116.

9   Robson papers Correspondence MS–Papers–0048–27, 20 May 1880, ATL

10 Robson-Rollaston Correspondence MS–Papers–0037–131, Robson to Haast, 29 May 1880, ATL. The letter to Buller is Ibid., 19 May 1880.

11 ZAAP 15125 Ia Cuvier Island Outwards letterbook 1889–1914, 23 January 1913, ANZ (Ak).

12 ML–Stephens Isl 3/1 Outwards correspondence 1894–1910, Folder I Section 4, pp. 58–9, 15 July 1897, ANZ (Wgtn).

13 ML–Brothers 3/2 Outwards correspondence 1910–1911, 31 March 1912, p. 45, ANZ (Wgtn).

14 ZAAP 15130 Ia Mokohinau Outwards letterbook 1915–23, 9 November 1922, p. 184, ANZ (Ak).

15 ML–Farewell Spit 3/2 Outwards correspondence 1924–30, 3 April 1928, p. 67, ANZ (Wgtn).

16 ML–Stephens Island Outwards correspondence 3/5 1937–44, 1 August 1939, ANZ (Wgtn).

17 ML–Portland Island 3/8 Outwards correspondence 1947–48, 3 June 1948, ANZ (Wgtn).

18 ML–Portland Island 3/9 Outwards correspondence, 1949–52, 9 October 1950, ANZ (Wgtn).

Chaper 13

1   DAAL/D28/10c Puysegur Point Outwards correspondence 1892–1907, 26 July 1902, ANZ (Dn).

2   ML–Cape Egmont 3/2 Outwards correspondence 1895–[95] 1915, 24 October 1913, ANZ (Wgtn); ibid., August 1915, p. 401.

3   ML–Cape Egmont 3/3 Outwards correspondence 1915–31, 5 August 1915, p. 37, ANZ (Wgtn).

4   ML–Pencarrow 3/1 Outwards correspondence 1898–1926, 29 March, 1917, p. 333, ANZ (Wgtn).

5   ZAAP 15120 Id Cape Brett Outwards letterbook 1941–46, 12 August 1941, ANZ (Ak).

6   ZAAP 15125 2a Cape Brett Outwards letterbook 1946–52, 16 October 1947, ANZ (Ak).

7   ML–Farewell Spit 3/5 Outwards correspondence 1947–51, 16 February 1949, ANZ (Wgtn). Ibid., 9 May 1949

8   ML–East Cape 3/4 Outwards correspondence February–July 1950, 13 June 1950, ANZ (Wgtn).

9   DAAL/D238/4c, Dog Island Outwards correspondence 1936–45, 4 September 1945, ANZ (Dn).

10 ZAAP 15136 2f, Cape Reinga Outwards letterbook 1955–56, 23 May 1956, ANZ (Ak).

Chapter 14

1   ZAAP 15140 Ic Tiritiri Matangi Outwards letterbook 1955–56, 8 June 1955, ANZ (Ak).

2   Ibid.

3   DAAL/D28/10c Puysegur Point Outwards correspondence 1892–1907, 8 April 1896, p. 41, ANZ (Dn).

4   On the basis of observations while at Mokohinau Sandager contributed to the *Transactions of the Royal Society of New Zealand, 1868–1961*, on local species and their spawning and other facts, on the island's birds, and a more general article on sea-trout (or salmon). These, as well as other references to him (which show the extent others drew on his work) can be viewed at http://rsnz.natlib.govt. nz/search/results.html?text=Sandager (last accessed 1 October 2007), while Wikipedia has entries

on Sandager's wrasse, the sea bird named after him. I am indebted to Betty Benjamin for the quoted material.

5   Anders Hansen to T. F. Cheeseman, undated [1906–09], Thomas Frederic Cheeseman Papers, 1867 – 1923, MS 58, Box 8, Folder 2, Auckland War Memorial Museum Library.

6   Robson papers, Correspondence, Letter 358, MS–Papers-0048-27, Robson to Günther [undated] September 1880, ATL.

7   Ibid.

8   ML–Brothers 3/1 Outwards correspondence 1877–1882, 30 November 1878, ANZ (Wgtn).

9   ML–East Cape 3/5 Outwards correspondence July 1950–March 1951, 10 July 1950, ANZ (Wgtn).

10 Robson papers, Correspondence, Letter 358, MS–Papers-0048-27, Robson to Günther [undated] September 1880, ATL.

Bibliography

PUBLISHED MATERIAL

Aplin, Jeanette, *The Lighthouse Keeper's Children*, Cape Catley Ltd, Auckland, 2007

Beaglehole, Helen, *Lighting the Coast A history of New Zealand's coastal lighthouse system*, Canterbury University Press, Christchurch, 2006

Begg, A C and N C, *Port Preservation*, Whitcombe and Tombs, Christchurch, 1973,

Hart, Samuel, 'Lighthouse-keepers' experiences Going for the mail, *The Public Service Journal*, 20 December 1919

Hart, Samuel, 'Lighthouse-keepers' experiences The Flying Scotchman', *Ibid*

Miskelly Colin, 'The identity of the Hakawai', *Nortornis*, Vol 34, 1987

Marine Department *New Zealand lighthouses Equipment for electrification and radio beacons*, Compiled by H. W. T. Eggers under the direction of W. L. Newnham, Marine Engineer, Government Print, Wellington, 1944,

Readers Digest Complete Book of New Zealand Birds, Reed Methuen: Auckland, 1985

Rimmer, Anne, *Tiritiri Matangi A Model of Conservation*, Tandem Press, Auckland, 2004

Sorrensen, M.P.K., 'Walter Baldock Durrant Mantall', *The Dictionary of New Zealand Biography*, Vol. I, Department of Internal Affairs/Allen & Unwin, Wellington, 1990

Taylor Peter, *As Darker Grows the Night*, Hodder & Stoughton, Auckland, 1975

ARCHIVAL AND UNPUBLISHED MATERIAL

Anders Hansen to T. F. Cheeseman, Auckland, Undated [1906–09], Auckland Museum

Creamer, W. E. H., 'The Tall White Tower', unpublished manuscript, 196?, ATL

League of Mothers Lighthouse Board, correspondence book and papers, 1929-45, 77-173-144/1 to 77/-173-144/7; correspondence and papers 1930-38, 77-173-45/1, ATL

Marine Department Records

Auckland lighthouse journals and letterbooks, ZAAP, 15118–15143m Series, and (single item) AQQW , 15130, 2a, ANZ (Ak). Records here relate to Cape Brett, Cuvier Island, Mokohinau, Cape Maria van Diemen, Cape Reinga. These papers were transferred from the Auckland Institute and Museum Library (the War Memorial library) to ANZ

Lighthouse records, Dunedin, DAAL, D28, Series, ANZ (Dn). Records here relate to Cape Saunders, Centre Island, Dog Island, Moeraki, Nugget Point, Taiaroa Point, Puysegur Point, Waipapa Point

Lighthouse stations, outwards letterbooks and correspondence, ML–Series 3, ANZ (Wgtn). Records here relate to Cape Egmont, Cape Palliser, Castlepoint, East Cape, Farewell Spit, French Pass, The Brothers, Manukau Heads, Pencarrow, Portland Island, Stephens Island

Park, A. E. and H. M. Diaries. Private papers, compiled by Mrs Vida Wilden, Alexander Edward Parks' granddaughter. Kind permission of Betty Benjamin

Robson, Charles Hepburn

Correspondence with Sir Walter Buller, 19 & 20 May 1880, Ms–Papers–0048–27, ATL

A selection of the correspondence with Dr Julius von Haast. Robson-Rollaston Correspondence, MS–Papers–0037, folder 31, ATL

Correspondence with Dr. Gunther, FRS, September 1880, Letter 385 micro-MS-coll-20-2600, Australian Joint Copying Project: Miscellaneous services, microfilm, ATL

Robson, Charles Hepburn Orlando
Diary 1872–1903, MS–Papers–6271–1, ATL

Springer, E. J. 'Isolated Graves near New Zealand Lighthouses', MS–Papers–2328, ATL.